Studying Lacan's Seminar VII

Studying Lacan's Seminar VII offers a contemporary, critically informed set of analyses of Lacan's ethics seminar and astute reflections about what Lacan's ethics offer to the field of psychoanalytic thought today.

The volume interrogates the seminar with fresh voices and situated curiosities and perspectives, making for a compellingly exciting range of explorations of the crucial matters related to the ethics of psychoanalysis. The chapters question and tease out the paradoxes Lacan draws attention to in his seminar of 1959–1960, and in addition, they offer radical engagements with the seminar in light of theories of racism, inequality, capitalism, education, and subjectivity. The key elements in Lacan's seminar are explained, debated, and reconsidered with Antigone, *das Ding*, and the inevitable "*ne céder pas sur son désir*" duly unpacked, examined, and ruminated upon.

Studying Lacan's Seminar VII will be of interest to psychoanalytic scholars and students of Lacanian psychoanalysis, as well as psychoanalytic therapists and analysts. It will also be of interest to scholars and students of politics, philosophy, and studies at the intersections of racism, film, feminism, sociology, gender, and queer theory.

Carol Owens is an Irish psychoanalyst, clinical supervisor, and Lacanian scholar. She has lectured and published extensively on Freudian and Lacanian psychoanalysis, and has edited, co-edited, authored, and co-authored several volumes on Lacanian psychoanalysis as applied to the clinic, culture and society. Her most recent book is *Psychoanalysis and the Small Screen – The Year the Cinemas Closed* (with Sarah Meehan O'Callaghan, Routledge, 2024). She is the series editor for Studying Lacan's Seminars, the first dedicated series on Lacan's seminars. She is a member of APPI, APCS, and an affiliate member of CP-UK.

Studying Lacan's Seminars
Series Editor: Carol Owens

Studying Lacan's Seminars brings together leading Lacanian scholars and practitioners from across the globe to participate in a contemporary examination of Lacan's seminars, many of which are newly translated into English. Featuring practical examples from case studies and packed with cultural illustrations from film, literature and beyond, these books will provide vital companions for students and readers of Lacan. The first dedicated series on Lacan's seminars, each book will cover the fundamental concepts while at the same time applying a contemporary perspective informed by the standards considered important by scholars and practising Lacanian psychoanalysts today.

Previous and forthcoming titles in the series:

For more information see https://www.routledge.com/Studying-Lacans-Seminars/book-series/SLS

Studying Lacan's Seminar VII

The Ethics of Psychoanalysis

Edited by Carol Owens

Routledge
Taylor & Francis Group
LONDON AND NEW YORK

For Mari Ruti In memory

Designed cover image: Hellelil and Hildebrand the meeting on the Turret stairs by F. W. Burton

First published 2024
by Routledge
4 Park Square, Milton Park, Abingdon, Oxon OX14 4RN

and by Routledge
605 Third Avenue, New York, NY 10158

Routledge is an imprint of the Taylor & Francis Group, an informa business

British Library Cataloguing-in-Publication Data
A catalogue record for this book is available from the British Library

ISBN: 978-1-032-58603-8 (hbk)
ISBN: 978-0-367-42033-8 (pbk)
ISBN: 978-1-003-45079-5 (ebk)

DOI: 10.4324/9781003450795

Typeset in Times New Roman
by Apex CoVantage, LLC

Contents

Acknowledgements

This volume has taken a while to come together. It was interrupted – like many things – by the COVID-19 pandemic which took its toll variously and sadly on some of the contributors to this volume meaning in at least three cases their ultimate need to drop out of the project. I am grateful to each of those colleagues for their efforts and desire to work with me on this book even though they could not see it to fruition. In other ways, the pandemic affected the pace and sense of urgency that I would normally inflict upon myself and my fellow scholars; we all needed to slow down a bit. I am deeply grateful to each of the contributors to this volume – Lorenzo, Jones, Sheila, Sheldon, Todd, Dany, Sarah and Calum – for their labour and time, and for responding to my invitation with such enthusiasm in the first place. As Derek Hook in his endorsement of the volume points out, it isn't really possible to come up with a more exciting and stellar crew to comment on Lacan's ethics. Their work is remarkable, and in putting their work together here, I feel the honour of the curator who brings a tour of earnest art lovers around one of the Guggenheims, pointing to this painting and the next, showing how the light is managed, how the shadows are suggested. I am humbled and inspired by their fabulous remarks and arguments, by the impeccable explanations and breathtakingly smart articulations with the themes of Lacan's wonderful ethics seminar. I am further honoured with their friendship and with their support for the larger project aimed at with this series of books dedicated to studying Lacan's seminars.

As always, I am blessed with the support, great friendship, and sound advice from Ian Parker, who is the series advisor for *Studying Lacan's Seminars*. Thanks Ian.

The good people at Routledge are inimitably helpful and supportive, and I thank Susannah Frearson, Saloni Singhania, and Kate Hawes for their ongoing enthusiasm for this project.

Thanks to Stephanie Swales for being there for me all the way on almost every project, always interested and kind.

Thanks to my lovely family, Carles, Tomàs, and Oscar, for tolerating the Lacan nerd in their lives, and to sweet Camilla for her interest and encouragement. (One of my sons says I should thank our dog too for his waggling and good nature, so I will. Thanks Toby.)

Finally, I thank the National Gallery of Ireland for permission to reproduce *Hellelil and Hildebrand the meeting on the Turret stairs* by Frederick William Burton on the front cover of this book. I chose this image, wanting in part to steer away from tired images of Antigone and how she has come to epitomise the be-all and end-all of Lacanian ethics, but also because this beautiful painting (voted Ireland's favourite painting in 2012), which seems to belong to the courtly love tradition, a theme Lacan discusses at length in the seminar, turns out in fact to tell the story of another woman who goes beyond the beyond for a brother, and who loses everything as a consequence. The moment in time captured by Burton is inspired by a medieval Danish ballad translated by the artist's friend, Whitley Stokes, in 1855. The ballad tells the story of Hellelil who fell in love with one of her personal guards Hildebrand, Prince of Engelland. Her father disapproved of the relationship and ordered her seven brothers to kill Hildebrand. However, Hildebrand defended himself well, killing Hellelil's father and six of the seven brothers before Hellelil interceded to save her youngest brother. This saved brother had Hellelil tortured and imprisoned where she later died, and poor Hildebrand died of his wounds. A reproduction of the painting hangs in the Registry office in Dublin in front of the desk where couples face the registrar as they are being wed, and the postcard of the painting is the most popular selling postcard in the National Gallery of Ireland's collection – especially among adolescent customers!

Note on the Editor

Carol Owens is an Irish psychoanalyst, clinical supervisor, and Lacanian scholar. She has lectured and published extensively on Freudian and Lacanian psychoanalysis. She has edited *The Letter – Irish Journal for Lacanian Psychoanalysis*, and has edited, co-edited, authored, or co-authored several volumes on Lacanian psychoanalysis as applied to the clinic, culture, and society. Her most recent book is *Psychoanalysis and the Small Screen – The Year the Cinemas Closed* (with Sarah Meehan O'Callaghan, Routledge, 2024). She is the series editor for *Studying Lacan's Seminars*, the first dedicated series on Lacan's seminars, covering Lacan's fundamental concepts while applying a contemporary perspective informed by the standards considered important by scholars and practising Lacanian psychoanalysts today (https://www.routledge.com/Studying-Lacans-Seminars/book-series/SLS). She is a member of APPI, APCS, and an affiliate member of CP-UK. She sits on the editorial board of *Analytic Agora* and *Psychoanalysis, Culture and Society*, and is the corresponding editor at the *PCSReview*.

Notes on Contributors

Sheila L. Cavanagh is a professor at York University, Toronto, and a clinical candidate at the Lacan School of Psychoanalysis in Berkeley, California. She is past coordinator of the Sexuality Studies Program at York and former chair of the Canadian Sexuality Studies Association. Cavanagh co-edited *Somatechnics* journal and now sits on the editorial boards of *Psychoanalysis, Culture & Society; Studies in Gender and Sexuality*; and *Parapraxis* magazine. Her scholarship is in Lacanian psychoanalysis, gender, and sexuality studies. She edited a special double issue of *Transgender Studies Quarterly* on psychoanalysis (2017), and co-edited *Skin, Culture and Psychoanalysis* (2013). Cavanagh's first book, *Sexing the Teacher*, was given honourable mention by the Canadian Women's Studies Association; her second book, *Queering Bathrooms*, is a GLBT Indie Book Award finalist and recipient of the CWSA/ACEF Outstanding Scholarship Prize Honourable Mention (2012). She is completing her third book, titled *Bracha L. Ettinger & Jacques Lacan*.

Lorenzo Chiesa is Senior Lecturer in Philosophy at Newcastle University where he co-convenes the Faculty Research Group in Critical Theory and Practice. He also teaches at the European Graduate School. He was previously Professor of Modern European Thought and Director of the Centre for Critical Thought at the University of Kent. His main books include *Subjectivity and Otherness. A Philosophical Reading of Lacan* (MIT Press, 2007); *The Not-Two. Logic and God in Lacan* (MIT Press, 2016); and *The Virtual Point of Freedom. Essay on Politics, Aesthetics, and Religion* (Northwestern University Press, 2016). His new monograph, *God Is Undead. Atheism and Agnosticism in Psychoanalysis*, co-authored with Adrian Johnston, is forthcoming. Chiesa serves as editor of the book series Insubordinations at MIT Press.

Sheldon George is Chair of the Department of Literature and Writing at Simmons University in Boston, Massachusetts. His scholarship centres on application of cultural and literary theory to analyses of American and African American literature and culture. George serves as Chair of the Executive Committee for the MLA Forum Psychology, Psychoanalysis and Literature. He is an Associate Editor of *Psychoanalysis Culture & Society* and has coedited two special issues of the journal: "Lacanian Psychoanalysis: Interventions Into Culture and Politics" and "African Americans and Inequality." George's book *Trauma and Race* (2016) was the first to offer an extended Lacanian analysis of African American racial identity. He is co-editor, with Jean Wyatt, of *Reading Contemporary Black British and African American Women Writers* (2020), and his recent publications include the pioneering collection of essays, co-edited with Derek Hook, titled *Lacan and Race: Racism, Identity and Psychoanalytic Theory* (2021).

Jones Irwin is Associate Professor in Philosophy and Education at the Institute of Education, Dublin City University. His most recent book is the co-edited collection on *Paulo Freire's Philosophy of Education in a Contemporary Context: From Italy to the World* (Peter Lang 2022). In 2022, he was Visiting Professor to the Education Faculty, University of Catania, Sicily, Italy.

Todd McGowan teaches theory and film at the University of Vermont. He is the author of *Enjoyment Right and Left, The Racist Fantasy, Emancipation After Hegel, Capitalism and Desire, Only a Joke Can Save Us*, and other works. He is also the co-editor (with Slavoj Žižek and Adrian Johnston) of the Diaeresis series at Northwestern University Press and is co-host of the *Why Theory* podcast with Ryan Engley.

Sarah Meehan O'Callaghan is an independent scholar within the fields of Lacanian psychoanalysis, body/disability, drama, and sexuality studies. Her PhD was an interdisciplinary study of the trauma of the body in the drama of Artaud, Beckett, and Genet within a Lacanian psychoanalytic perspective. She has published psychoanalytic articles on disability, sexuality, the phallus, and the intersections of phenomenology and psychoanalysis. She is co-organiser of the Irish Psychoanalytic Film Festival. She is a member of EROSS@DCU (Expressions, Research, Orientations: Sexuality Studies) and was co-organiser of several conferences on the theme of arts, disability, and sexuality.

Calum Neill is Professor of Psychoanalysis and Continental Philosophy at Edinburgh Napier University, Director of Lacan in Scotland, and Editor of the Palgrave Lacan series. He is the author of three books: *Jacques Lacan: The Basics* (Routledge, 2023), the first entry-level introduction to Lacan's ideas; *Without Ground: Lacanian Ethics and the Assumption of Subjectivity* (Palgrave, 2011); and *Ethics and Psychology: Beyond Codes of Practice* (Routledge, 2016). He is the editor of *Lacanian Perspectives on* Blade Runner 2049 (Palgrave, 2020) and co-editor of the four-volume set, *Reading Lacan's* Écrits (Routledge, 2018, 2019, 2022, and 2023).

Dany Nobus is Professor of Psychoanalytic Psychology at Brunel University London, He is a Founding Scholar of the British Psychoanalytic Council, and former Chair and Fellow of the Freud Museum London. He has published numerous books and papers on the history, theory, and practice of psychoanalysis, most recently *Critique of Psychoanalytic Reason: Studies in Lacanian Theory and Practice* (Routledge 2022). In 2017, he was awarded the Sarton Medal of the University of Ghent for his outstanding contributions to the historiography of psychoanalysis.

Editor's Introduction

I first started to read Lacan as a PhD student in England in the early nineties and returned to him just shy of a decade later when I commenced my studies in psychoanalysis at Trinity College Dublin with Ross Skelton, and my clinical training at University College Dublin with Cormac Gallagher. Back in the nineties, however, very few of Lacan's seminars had been translated into English and published. It all began for me with *The Four Fundamental Concepts* and *The Ethics* – those two knocking around with me since then, on my bookshelf, on my desk, irreverently left around cracked open, and occasionally stuffed into a carry-on bag. I first read *The Ethics* on my own, in fits and starts to begin with . . . hung up over Antigone, yes of course, what a gal going beyond the beyond . . . what a textbook example of 'not giving up on your desire'! Next I read it with a small group led by the remarkable Irish Lacanian scholar Helena Texier in preparation for a conference/workshop on the seminar, in Paris 2005 with Colette Soler's forum.[1] In three sweltering summer days on the rue d'Assas, clinicians with many years of experience pored over the fine details of the seminar, questioning the ideas for their utility for the clinic, scrupulous theorists dissected the dense sections on *das Ding*, on Kant, on the death drive. Antigone was not, after all, a foregone conclusion for an ethics of psychoanalysis, or at least not in any straightforward manner! There were debates, arguments, lengthy discussions into the small hours, coffee-fueled reprises the next day. Lacan, it was argued, didn't always check his sources, sometimes was a bit glib, threw statements around incautiously at other times. But when he did get it right, he could be splendid. It was concluded that we needed to read Lacan carefully, not take things for granted, and continue to consider and interrogate the relevance of his ideas and concepts for our times, our clinics, our research. That core idea has stayed with me throughout my engagement with Lacan's work, and is the prevailing theme throughout this series on Lacan's seminars which I have the privilege of editing.[2]

I returned to the seminar a few years later, this time to give a lecture on the ethics of psychoanalysis in Manchester in 2008 to a mixed group of philosophers, social workers, and psychotherapists not very well versed in either Lacan or psychoanalysis. I called my talk 'Psychoanalysis, Ethically Speaking (The Good, the Bad, and the Lacanian)'. That was a fun challenge, to indicate the points of tension that Lacan introduces around the notion of the 'sovereign good', as well as what inadvertently counts for 'bad' in the seminar; and, having located myself in the position of 'the ugly', or perhaps better said, the one who speaks an ugly truth, I laid out Lacan's weird-sounding proposition regarding the betrayal of desire.

A couple of years later on in 2010, I came to the seminar again, as the APPI conference here in Dublin took for its theme "How to Act – Ethics and the Psychoanalytic Clinic in a Culture of Suppression and Demand." This time I returned to Antigone but was less certain of the place I had regarded her (and the play) when I first read the seminar. Aside from my various readings of the seminar, what had also taken place was more than a decade of clinical experience, and this changed how I felt about what I thought Lacan was saying about Antigone (Owens, 2012). My paper at this conference reflected my new feelings about Antigone, and in general my curiosity about Lacan's shifts in tone and focus throughout the ethics seminar; where he stayed, how he strayed. Reading that paper now, more than a decade further into my clinical work, I see how my readings of certain theorists inflected both my understanding of Antigone's role in Lacan's ethics of psychoanalysis and my sense at the time of the injustice of overlooking the supporting characters in the tragedy, that sense itself affected by my own transference to the clinical work.

Describing my own experience of reading this seminar over the years, it seems to me both incredible and simultaneously not at all surprising that I can have had such varied encounters with it. In part, this is, as I have tried to account for it, correlated with the different stages of my own clinical formation and times of my engagement with Lacan's teaching. In part, my various encounters with the seminar have been affected by my transference to my work in the clinic, by my sympathy, let us say, with the other characters in the tragedy – the Ismenes, the Creons, the Haemons – the ones who, just as in the psychoanalytic clinic, are left behind picking up the pieces (or going to pieces).

This volume of chapters that you are about to dive into is written by an exceptional group of scholars, some of whom are clinicians as well as academics. Inviting this special group to contribute here would, I felt certain, scatter several cats among the pigeons; we would have a full range of encounters with the seminar. There would be lively critique, interrogation, and debate. No stones left unturned, as it were. But more than this, we would end up with a collection of chapters reflecting the situated interests and curiosity of each author. In fairness, Antigone doesn't divide the room all that much, but I am so pleased to offer in this volume a variety of takes on Lacan's reading of Antigone. But then also, there is attention given to the excited enthusiasm of Lacan's working of *das Ding* only for him to leave it there rather abandoned later in the seminar, and thereafter, as well as critical recuperations of *das Ding* as related to the *hommosexuelle*, to racism, to capitalism. Finally, considered and critical attention is given to Lacan's proposal in the last moments of his seminar that, from an analytical point of view, the only thing of which one can be guilty is of having given ground relative to one's desire (Lacan, 1992, p. 319).

In what follows I will provide a bit of traditional introductory context through which it is hoped the reader can access the individual chapters and their engagement with the seminar. As the reader will discover, the chapters in this collection each have their own particular focus in the seminar and in various ways, via various arguments, hone in on that theme or sets of themes accordingly. But it is also true that each chapter delves deeply into the seminar extracting a start or finish point overlapping with other chapters. It's a kind of Seminar VII joke for me and the authors here that although it was agreed that only one of them would concentrate on Antigone, most of them ended up writing her into their own chapters. So much for editorial guidelines! But how could it have been otherwise?

Beyond Good and Evil

Early on in the seminar, Lacan emphasizes that moral experience in its customary reference to sanctions places the person in a certain relation to their own action that concerns not only an articulated law but also a direction, a trajectory, a "good" that he appeals to, thereby engendering an ideal of conduct (Lacan, 1992, p. 3). For Aristotle, the ethical person is one whose choices of action are oriented in the direction of the supreme human good and as such concern an activity of the spirit in accordance with excellence. In his seminar, Lacan articulates Aristotle's *Nicomachean Ethics* with the problem of an ethics as such (ibid., p. 36). In Marc De Kesel's view, Lacan attaches such importance to Aristotle in the course of the seminar because the basic principles of psychoanalysis are "brought into sharper focus through a confrontation with his thought" (De Kesel, 2009, p. 65).[3] De Kesel persuasively argues that as Aristotle founds ethics in the relation between desire and reality, and as this relation implies an ethical judgement, a judgement about what is good or not for the desiring subject, Lacan's psychoanalytic reading of this moral judgement acts to decentre the classical foundational premises of ethics, in turn allowing him to establish a new definition of the ethical good and ethics as such (ibid., pp. 65–66). This very notion is at the core of several of the chapters in this collection.

The collection opens with Lorenzo Chiesa's chapter titled 'Supreme Being-in-Evil, Criminal Good, and Criminal Desire: Lacan After Antigone, After Sade, After Kant'. Covering a huge amount of ground from the seminar, Chiesa is concerned to present a new reading of the seminar by way of a close scrutiny of its treatment of evil. Chiesa thereby effects a decentring of good and evil in Lacan's treatment of it in the seminar. We are directed to read the chapter in two halves. In the first half, evil is discussed with respect to Lacan's updating of the Freudian assessment of human nature as related to the Thing, Lacan's own tentative delineation of jouissance, and the key role he assigns to the contradictions of Christianity in order to shed light on the Thing and jouissance as "malignant". In the second half, Chiesa interrogates Lacan's investigation of evil through Sade and Kant, specifically highlighting how he seems to believe that a certain overestimation of Evil (as either absolutized into a first principle or mistaken for the Good) explains Sade's and Kant's comparable and failed modern endeavour to construct human nature as a Thing on the basis of the moral or immoral Law.

Jones Irwin's chapter re-mobilizes an investigation of Lacan's Ethics as an 'Ethics *Contra* Morality' and considers the implications thereof for contemporary education. For Irwin, the iconoclastic thrust of this trope is indicated from the very beginning of the seminar. By referring to the 'attraction of transgression' (1992, p. 1), Lacan indicates that the study of ethics in psychoanalysis is as concerned with so-called wrongdoing as it is with doing good. There are few precedents for this dual focus in the history of ethical thought, Irwin argues, especially as, in this instance, a certain complicity seems to be also claimed with regard to evil or wrongdoing. Moreover, invoking Aristotle's concept of 'ethics' rather than, for example, Plato's concept of 'morality', Lacan is making a suggestion that the ethics of psychoanalysis may have a broader remit than moral judgement. As such, a possibility is opened up that morality and its norms may actually be undone by the study of ethics. Effectively, for Irwin, this would be ethics *contra* morality. In the second part of the chapter Irwin explores some of the potential affinities and disaffinities which such an approach can be said to have with more recent examples of ethical education.

Das Ding, Sublimation, and Other Problems

The trouble with the good, psychoanalytically speaking, is that insofar as it involves the pursuit of happiness, of pleasure, it also involves the unconscious drive in its circulation of what Freud had called *das Ding* and which in this 1959–1960 seminar Lacan will posit as 'beyond the pleasure principle'. Freud's term *das Ding* comes from his *Project for a Scientific Psychology* describing that part of what is perceived but cannot be recognized by the activity of thought but that 'stays together as a thing' (Freud, 1950, p. 331). In the seminar a structural opposition set up by Lacan counterposes the Freudian system of unconscious representations *Vorstellungen* regulated by the pleasure principle with *das Ding* situated beyond the pleasure principle as that which cannot be represented or imagined. Lacan calls *das Ding* the beyond of the signified. As something which is perceived by the activity of thought but not recognized, this thing will be inscribed by Lacan as something fundamentally lacking in a relationship to an individual, but at the same time it is here in this primordial place of lack that Lacan locates the impetus of desire. This place of lack causes desire to be set in motion. Insofar as *das Ding* is place of the lost object, the pleasure principle governs the search for the lost object and imposes the detours which maintain the distance in relation to its obtainment. In this seminar Lacan will posit the place of *das Ding* as occupied by the supreme good, the sovereign good, which for Freud is the mother who is also the object of incest and as such is a forbidden good. This for Lacan, is the foundation of the moral law as turned on its head by Freud. The sovereign good is a forbidden good.

Three chapters in this collection focus in closely on *das Ding*. Sheila L. Cavanagh's chapter critically examines how Lacan uses the example of courtly love to illustrate the centrality of desire to the psychoanalytic project in his seminar on ethics. Cavanagh points out that while much attention has been given to the status of the *Thing* in Lacanian ethics, less has been taken up with the status of the *Thing* in relation to the exalted Lady of courtly love and the mother (as primordial Other). Cavanagh goes on to consider how Lacan narrates the *Thing* of relevance to courtly love through various incantations of the feminine and the mother. She argues that masculine desire for the unattainable Lady is not only *hommosexuelle*, but also, an expression of the hysteric's discourse. Like the female hysterics of the Victorian era whose bodily symptoms defy medical explanation, Cavanagh invites us to think about the male courtier's lovesick claims. In Cavanagh's chapter, both respond to the asexuality foundational to phallic jouissance and the non-existence of the Woman in masculine love.

Coming at *das Ding*, the Lady, and the male courtier from another place entirely, Sheldon George brings his critical investigations of racism to his chapter in this collection (see George, 2016). In his *Ethics* seminar, George points out, Lacan ties the figure of the Lady in courtly love to a cultural process of sublimation that defines societal manners and sensibilities for centuries to come. But, George argues, Lacan ignores that the courtly lover, the knight who pursues the Lady through endless tasks and insurmountable challenges aimed at proving his love, was often a soldier of the Crusades, which pitted Christians against the darker peoples of the Middle East. George's chapter goes on to trace the historical emergence of race as a category of difference developed in the Crusades while also tying the Lady to the culture of manners and gentility that emerged in the antebellum American South. The Lady is read as the key figure facilitating a sublimation of libidinal drives that find their expression through culturally accepted atrocities of racism. Such atrocities, George argues, aim at a recuperation of the derelict white body that is denied access to *das Ding,* or the Lacanian Thing. The last part of his chapter focuses on the practices of lynching black men that plagued especially the postbellum South; the charred body of the black lynching victim is tied to efforts to manifest for white postbellum subjects the Thing of the Real that the courtly lover and the racist lyncher equally pursue through sublimation of the (white) Lady.

In his own terms, Todd McGowan begins his chapter by calling attention to the disappearing act performed by the concept of *das Ding*. As he remarks, it disappears after its introduction in the seminar and, despite the prominence that it has early in the seminar, Lacan does not bring it up when he lays out his conception of the ethics of psychoanalysis. McGowan thereby attempts to rethink the ethics of psychoanalysis by filling this lacuna by taking *das Ding* as the point of departure for theorizing ethics. *Das Ding*, he notes, emerges through the act of sublimation that elevates an ordinary object out of its ordinariness. When this occurs, the subject can enjoy this Thing that transcends the realm of everyday objects. *Das Ding* provides the subject with an orientation for its existence, an orientation that enables it to establish a transcendent value in the form of the sublimated object that becomes the Thing. McGowan argues that given this understanding of sublimation, the ethics of psychoanalysis can be thought of as an ethics that tries to navigate a path beyond capitalist relations of production. Sublimation is the key to the structure of the drive and the key to taking up an ethical position in the midst of enforced commodification. The only path out of the logic of the commodity lies in holding fast to the emancipatory power of sublimation, which Lacan himself abandons when he theorizes the ethical position. Sublimation creates *das Ding*. It is only by confronting the fundamental absence of *das Ding* – including its absence in the conclusion of *Seminar VII* – that as far as McGowan is concerned we can free ourselves from the blandishments of the commodity.

Beyond the Beyond (. . . Fear and Pity, etc.)

In *Civilization and its Discontents* Freud states that the field of ethics deals with the *sorest spot in every civilization*: the fact that there is no ethical rule which governs our co-existence with others – and the commensurate sacrifice of pleasure necessary to this end – without paradox. The imperative – *love thy neighbour as thyself* – Freud notes, is fundamentally *at odds with what is possible* for the subject (Freud, 1930, p. 142). Straight up he tells us that the so-called ethical demands of the superego include issuing commands without troubling itself about the "facts of the mental constitution of human beings" and moreover without asking itself whether it will be possible for people to obey it. Just as directly, in his seminar on the ethics of psychoanalysis Lacan tells us that what the superego demands has nothing to do with that which we would be right in making the universal rule of our actions. In obeying the demands of the superego we betray our desire, our guilt arising not because we have broken *the* law in some way or another but rather because in continuing to obey the superego imperative – keep on enjoying – we have given up on our desiring. This is what Lacan calls the ABC of psychoanalytic truth (Lacan, 1992, p. 310).

It is in order to sketch out this ABC though that Lacan will stage for us the *fascination of an exception*, someone who doesn't give up her desire. A someone who – as he tells us – "is evoked whenever there is a question of a law that causes conflict in us even though it is acknowledged by the community to be a just law" (ibid., p. 243). However, Lacan's fascination with Antigone privileges a very particular interpretation of a psychoanalytic ethics and foregrounds all sorts of commensurate paradoxes. It has also raised a number of questions for psychoanalysts and Lacanian and other scholars. For example, we could ask whether Antigone's act in fact illuminates anything about the ethical duties of psychoanalyst and/or analysand. Or, as Yannis Stavrakakis has rather pointedly suggested, would the truly radical ethical act be to traverse the lure of Antigone altogether? (Stavrakakis, 2007, p. 119).

What is so alluring for Lacan in Antigone? It turns out that one element is Antigone's inhumanity, her going beyond the limits of the human, in fact her uncivility (Lacan, 1992, p. 263). That Antigone is essentially uncivilized is the point around which so much hangs (including, ironically, and ultimately, Antigone herself). In other words, and as Lacan says towards the end of May 1960, *Antigone as text* offers us something other than a lesson in morality. This something "other" underscores his attempt to distinguish between a specifically superegoic transgression of the law on the one hand and a transgressive ethics of pure desire on the other.

On the one hand, as Molly Anne Rothenberg has remarked, the excessive nature of the subject may be interpreted as either the missing piece that will unite the social field or as the obstacle to its coherence, which means that the social field opens and closes at every point as fantasies about the other's desirability or danger mobilize defences to ward off the effects of excess (Rothenberg, 2010, p. 43). Indeed, Chris Dunker suggests that Antigone's "destabilizing excessive act" is representative of the inconsistency of social systems in determining the subject. He suggests that one possible interpretation of Antigone's act is that it indicates the lack in the symbolic order, in so far as she shows us the exact point where different social systems become unable to join together into a harmonious whole, but rather constitute a system of contradictions (Dunker, 2011, p. 38).

On the other hand, what may be mobilized is an ethical stance which involves every subject taking responsibility for their singular excessive dimension and jouissance. (In this vein, the acts of suicide bombers might be justifiably interpreted on the model of Antigone's excessiveness as an "ethics of jouissance", even if, as Francis Restuccia has argued, this interpretation is based upon an insufficiently nuanced reading of "passion" in Lacan [Restuccia, 2006, p. 17].)

Lacan devotes three lessons of his seminar to Sophocles' tragedy *Antigone*. In his chapter in this collection, Dany Nobus provides us with a detailed explanation of these lessons. Alongside the many conceptual considerations, Nobus also re-examines Lacan's interpretative methodology. In this respect, Nobus demonstrates that Lacan did not merely apply established psychoanalytic notions to Sophocles' text, but rather implicitly adopted the 'Zadig-Morelli' method that had been advanced by Freud as indicative of psychoanalytic interpretative technique, and which relies on the identification of minuscule, yet highly charged, details in the composite picture of a textual narrative.

What Nobus refers to as Lacan's revisionist interpretation of *Antigone* is critically analysed in light of historical and contemporary scholarship on the tragedy, whilst his reasons for including the tragedy in a seminar on the ethics of psychoanalysis are also discussed and evaluated. Nobus shows that Lacan regarded Antigone as the undisputed protagonist of the play, who also represents the source from where the catharsis (the purification of the psyche in the audience) is allowed to flow. However, he also argues that, in doing so, he did not promote Sophocles' heroine as the fictional paradigm for the state of mind psychoanalysts are expected to induce in their patients during the process of analysis and which they could therefore hold up as the aim (goal, objective) of the treatment.

Chiesa concludes his own chapter by arguing that Antigone, and what he refers to as her "criminal desire" as opposed to Creon's "criminal good", assumes an ambivalent pre- or proto-ethical function precisely with reference to the traversal of the insidious and resilient fantasy Sade calls "supreme Being-in-evil". Chiesa also insists: Antigone is not an ethical model for psychoanalysis. Instead, he reads Lacan's ethics of psychoanalysis as an ethics of desire that requires our acknowledgement and overcoming of Antigone's own tragic "holocaust", her paradigmatic embodiment of the antinomic status of the human condition as such at its point of in-difference. On the one hand, Chiesa suggests, her desire is a "pure desire" for difference. On the other, such a pure desire is without any mediation a "desire for death" or indifference.

Todd McGowan approaches *Antigone* via his discussion on sublimation. Even though Lacan doesn't mention sublimation in his discussion of *Antigone* or in his formulation of the ethics of psychoanalysis in the final session of the seminar, McGowan insists, sublimation is clearly evident in what Antigone does and in how we respond to her. Given the language that he uses to describe her, Lacan himself undoubtedly considers Antigone a sublime figure, an instance of the beautiful that puts us on the track of the real of our desire. She is a sublime figure because of her own sublimation. She attains a sublime value for us as spectators through her insistence that Polyneices has a sublime value for her.

What stands out for McGowan in Lacan's analysis of Antigone then is the position that she comes to occupy in the play. Her insistence on burying Polyneices regardless of the consequences places her beyond the limit that governs the realm of the good, a realm that Lacan calls the service of goods. This suggests to McGowan the result that inheres in the act of sublimation. Sublimation and the drive that accompanies it place one beyond the pleasure principle and beyond the service of goods. While *Antigone* predates the capitalist socioeconomic system by approximately two thousand years, McGowan suggests that Lacan finds himself drawn to the play and to Antigone because her sublimation places her at odds with the capitalist system, a system that functions by reducing every object to its exchange value. The ethics of psychoanalysis that he identifies as such is an ethics that tries to navigate a path beyond capitalist relations of production.

Beyond Guilt and Betrayal

In his seminar on the ethics of psychoanalysis, Lacan argues that the notion of the good is inherently problematic for psychoanalysts. He asks (of analysts): "Which good are you pursuing precisely as far as your passion is concerned? That question concerning our behaviour [as analysts] is always on the agenda. At every moment we need to know what our effective relation is to the desire to do good, to the desire to cure" (ibid., p. 218). Moreover, he argues that we have to deal with this notion of doing good as if it were something that is likely to lead us astray and in many cases to do so instantly. He condemns therapeutic practices which have as their aim wanting to do one's best for the subject as benevolent fraudulence. To make oneself the guarantor of the possibility that a subject will in some way find happiness in analysis is itself a form of fraud (ibid., p. 303). The ethics of psychoanalysis has nothing whatsoever to do with specifications about prescriptions for, or the regulation of, the service of goods (ibid., p. 313). Which is not to say, by the way, and as Lacan himself remarks, that in the course of the process of the analysis the subject won't encounter much that is good for him, in fact, all the good that he can do for himself, but only if he eliminates from his wishes – false goods (ibid., p. 300). In fact, he will go so far as to say that a radical repudiation of the ideal of the good is necessary (ibid., p. 230).

So, the analyst cannot promise what she cannot deliver and she cannot promise anything that could be construed as having the value of the supreme or sovereign good. As Lacan puts it: "Not only doesn't the analyst have that sovereign good that is asked of him, but he also knows that there isn't any" (ibid., p. 300). In his 1919 paper *Lines of Advance in Psycho-Analytic Therapy*, Freud defines the ethical dimension of the analyst as a renunciation of the directing of the patient's conscience:

> We refused most emphatically to turn a patient who puts himself into our hands in search of help into our private property, to decide his fate for him, to force our own ideals before him, and with the pride of a Creator to form him in our own image and see that it is good.
>   . . . we cannot accept . . . . that psychoanalysis should place itself in the service of a particular philosophical outlook on the world and should urge this upon the patient for the purpose of ennobling his mind. In my opinion, this is after all only to use violence, even though it is overlaid with the most honour-able of motives.
>
> (Freud, 1919, pp. 164–165)

What the analyst has to give, according to Lacan,

> unlike the partner in the act of love, is something that not even the most beautiful bride in the world cannot outmatch, that is to say, what he has. And what the analyst has is nothing other than his desire . . . an experienced desire.
>
> (ibid., p. 300)

And this desire is not of the order of promoting a psychological normalization vis-à-vis sexual practice or orientation, psychological harmony, or the achievement of untroubled happiness. The moral dimension of psychoanalysis progresses by means of a return to the meaning of an action and to the relation between that action and the desire that inhabits it (ibid., p. 313). What the analyst takes seriously is that desire is nothing other than that which supports an unconscious theme, the very articulation of that which roots us in a particular destiny (ibid., p. 319).

What Lacan will say towards the end of this seminar is that the only thing that we can be guilty of – analysts or analysands – is of giving up on our desire. He says: "[I]n the last analysis, what a subject really feels guilty about when he manifests guilt . . . always has to do with . . . the extent to which he has given ground relative to his desire" (ibid.), not to give ground relative to one's desire requires that desire be recognized and taken as such. And this is a position which for most of us gives rise to anxiety. In fact, Lacan will say that the subject hesitates when he or she is on the point of bearing false witness to desire (ibid., pp. 109–110). Desire always aims for an object, as we have seen, but there is a difference between acknowledging the trajectory of desire as that which illusorily substitutes objects for that which is radically missing and the belief in the idea that the object would be attainable if only we could get to it.

By contrast with those scholars who have extracted 'Do not give up on your desire!' as the key ethical precept from Lacan's seminar, in his chapter Dany Nobus argues that Lacan's conclusions were much more subtle: rather than being given the freedom to act upon their desire, patients are brought to the point where they can acknowledge and assume the tragic reality of the human condition, notably that the very 'fact of being' shall always remain insufficient to lead one's life successfully, properly, and happily.

In her chapter Sarah Meehan O'Callaghan interrogates the ethical question of the singular subject's relationship to desire with particular reference to this final section of the seminar: *The Tragic Dimension of Psychoanalysis*. Her chapter considers the ethical implications of desire as both singular (such as within an individual analysis) and as an act contained within a wider social or socioeconomic context. Meehan O'Callaghan asks, what are the difficulties and ambiguities concerning not giving ground relative to desire when human beings exist not simply alone but always in a relationship with the other/Other? Within this relationship to the Other, the social or socioeconomic reality of the singular subject is pervaded by structural inequalities. While desire is fundamental to the being of the Lacanian subject and thus is an essential existential component of a life, Meehan O'Callaghan insists, a phenomenal account of the lived conditions of desire as both social and cultural expands on this being. What is at stake in taking a stand against the Other, she asks. And, how do we as subjects of the unconscious but also as subjects of the state do our 'public good' collectively while remaining ethical in the singular psychoanalytic sense? According to Lacan, Meehan O'Callaghan points out, no matter what path we take toward the 'good', we will pay a price. Her chapter argues that it is important to elaborate further on what we can say of this price, since the price of freedom or desire is not equal across citizens.

And, finally, while not claiming to having the last word, but actually pretty much having the last word, Calum Neill's chapter traces the final session of Lacan's Seminar VII where he draws many of the key strands of the seminar together as close as he can to a conclusion. The insights of the seminar for Neill are, however, such that the very thinking through of ethics that Lacan has performed itself precludes the idea of a conclusion. Accordingly, this non-conclusive conclusion then allows us to grasp the open ethics Lacan is advocating, one which Neill suggests avoids both the Charybdis of a prescriptive morality and the Scylla of an 'anything goes' approach and instead places desire, as a compass, at the heart of ethics.

And that, dear reader, is that.

It is hoped that this fine collection of chapters will illuminate, excite, intrigue, and above all allow the reader to begin to, or continue with, their study of Lacan's seminars in good company.

Carol Owens

Notes

1 For a time, almost a decade, every two years, Colette Soler and her colleagues organized and hosted an English-speaking conference on some of Lacan's seminars: Transference, Ethics, Anxiety, Encore, RSI. This presented analysts and scholars from all over the globe with the fantastic opportunity to hear and participate in contemporary theoretical and clinical engagements with these incredible seminars spanning the 1960s and into the 1970s. The English-speaking conference on the ethics of psychoanalysis took place in June 2005.
2 The Studying Lacan's Seminars series aims at the production of fresh, contemporary, critical scholarly engagement with Lacan's seminars. *Studying Lacan's Seminars IV and V: From Lack to Desire* was published in 2019 (Owens and Almqvist), *Studying Lacan's Seminar VI: Dream, Symptom, and the Collapse of Subjectivity* (Cox Cameron) was published in 2022. Volumes on Seminars VIII, IX, XVII, and XX are in progress. https:// www.routledge.com/Studying-Lacans-Seminars/book-series/SLS
3 Marc de Kesel's book on Lacan's ethics seminar is essential reading for anybody wishing to engage with Lacan's ideas expressed therein. Indeed, de Kesel's text is referred to throughout the current collection (cf. De Kesel, 2009).

References

De Kesel, M. (2009). *Eros and Ethics – Reading Jacques Lacan's Seminar VII*. Trans. S. Jöttkandt. Albany: SUNY Press.
Dunker, C. (2011). *The Constitution of the Psychoanalytic Clinic – A History of its Structure and Power*. London: Karnac.
Freud, S. (1919). Lines of Advance in Psycho-Analytic Theory. In *The Standard Edition of the Complete Psychological Works of Sigmund Freud* (Vol. XVII, pp. 157–168). Ed. James Strachey. London: The Hogarth Press.
Freud, S. (1930). Civilisation and Its Discontents. In *The Standard Edition of the Complete Psychological Works of Sigmund Freud* (Vol. XXI, pp. 57–146). Ed. James Strachey. London: The Hogarth Press.
Freud, S. (1950). Project for a Scientific Psychology. In *The Standard Edition of the Complete Psychological Works of Sigmund Freud* (Vol. I, pp. 281–396). Ed. James Strachey. London: The Hogarth Press.
George, S. (2016). *Trauma and Race – A Lacanian Study of African American Racial Identity*. Texas: Baylor University Press.
Lacan, J. (1992). *The Ethics of Psychoanalysis 1959–1960: The Seminar of Jacques Lacan: Book VII*. In J.-A. Miller (Ed.). Trans. D. Porter. London: Routledge
Owens, C. (2012). Paradoxes of Enjoyment, Paradoxes of Cruelty (on Not Giving Up on Desire . . .). *Lacunae*, 2(1): 50–61.
Restuccia, F. (2006). *Amorous Acts: Lacanian Ethics in Modernism, Film, and Queer Theory*. Stanford, CA: Stanford University Press.
Rothenberg, M. (2010). *The Excessive Subject: A New Theory of Social Change*. Cambridge, MA: Polity Press.
Stavrakakis, Y. (2007). *The Lacanian Left: Psychoanalysis, Theory, Politics*. New York: SUNY Press.

Chapter 1

Supreme Being-in-Evil, Criminal Good, and Criminal Desire

Lacan After Antigone, After Sade, After Kant[1]

Lorenzo Chiesa

Whither Ethics?

In spite of its uncontested popularity, *The Ethics of Psychoanalysis* stands out as one of Lacan's most elusive and inconclusive Seminars,[2] especially when it is isolated from his later works. On the one hand, unsurprisingly, this has given rise to a vast secondary literature. On the other, and in a similarly predictable manner, over-simplistic, if not misleading, and thus often dichotomic interpretations of its main tenets tend to abound. The so-called Thing is merely mythical, or it corresponds to a repressed primal matter. The Lacanian real has nothing to do with reality, or it amounts to the latter's kernel. Jouissance relies on transgression, or it is given within the limits of the Law alone. Sade's libertines provide us with the hidden and definitive truth of Kant's moral law, or Lacan opposes Sade and, via Antigone, relaunches Kantian ethics at its most radical.[3] And also, Lacan remains at bottom an unrepentant Christian, or he aims at a post-Nietzschean transvaluation of values.[4] As applied to the end of the psychoanalytic treatment and the formation of the analyst, his ethical cogitations still sound extraordinarily elitist and Aristotelean,[5] or they thoroughly debunk Aristotle, including thanks to a revamped examination of Bentham's principle of the greatest good for the greatest number.[6] Most importantly, the fundamental message of the ethics of psychoanalysis, embodied by Antigone, coalesces around "Do not cede on your desire!", or it is precisely such a commandment that evidences to what extent "psychoanalysis has been reabsorbed by the superego" (Safouan, 2001, p. 155).[7]

If taken out of context, all these statements are somehow partly correct in their imprecision. The problem is, of course, reading them together in a consistent way. For instance, what is the ultimate status of the Thing? We can no doubt understand it as the retrospective mirage of an absolute satisfaction that never materialised in the first place, and hence as *a fortiori* irretrievable. But how should we specifically conceive of the physiological and psychic processes that enabled the emergence of such a mirage? More bluntly, how does the real some-thing from which the Thing as illusory originates partake of, or at least relate to, what we normally refer to as reality? And, in close connection to this, although jouissance is, in a sense, merely another name for the mirage of absolute satisfaction propelled yet never attained

DOI: 10.4324/9781003450795-1

by transgressive acts, to the point that, strictly speaking, "we don't ever transgress" (Lacan, 2006a, p. 19), why is really existing jouissance – as basically the paradoxical enjoyment of the absence of absolute satisfaction – nonetheless tantamount to a transgression inherent to the very limits of the dialectic between the Law and desire? How is such a dialectic then brought to the extreme of ineffective transgression by the converging poles of the Law of jouissance (Sade) and the jouissance of the Law (Kant)? If we then turn to the historical coordinates Lacan privileges to tackle these issues, in what ways has Christianity – starting with Saint Paul – both solidified the Mosaic dialectic between the Law and desire and profoundly threatened it by means of its "inhuman" (Lacan, 1997, p. 193) imperative "Thou shalt love thy neighbour as thyself"? And while modern ethics, as inextricable from modern science, is founded on an attempt to overcome this religious tension, why does it immediately capitulate through Kant's and Sade's projects? Should we regard Lacan's genealogy of morals as a dialectic of Enlightenment? Last but not least, is there, after all, an ethics of psychoanalysis?

Lacan's orientation is neither Kantian nor Sadean, neither Christian nor superhuman, neither nostalgically tragic nor cynically postmodern, neither pseudo-democratically utilitarian nor devoted to the master's happiness. So, assuming that "the ethics of analysis – for there is one – involves effacement, setting aside, withdrawal" (p. 10), what can it teach us *per via negativa* and in a non-prescriptive fashion?

I do not claim that I can here offer exhaustive answers to these complex questions.[8] As should be clear from my initial remarks, a cautious approach appears necessary if we wish to stay faithful to the letter and spirit of *The Ethics of Psychoanalysis*. The issue concerning the potential (or not) of Lacan's ethical indications in Seminar VII, within and outside of psychoanalysis, is quite different and lies beyond the remit of my present hermeneutical efforts. I have therefore decided to focus on a relatively peripheral and unexplored matter that emerges as tangential to the open problems I posed, yet also as obviously pervasive in the general domain of the ethical and crucial to *The Ethics* itself insofar as it intersects with most of its main themes, namely, Lacan's treatment of *evil*. Leaving aside adverbial and interjectory uses – as in "not bad!" (*pas mal!*) – *le mal* features in thirteen out of twenty-four sessions, even though it is singled out only once in the titles and subtitles of the edited version of the Seminar. When we also take into account conceptually laden comments on what is wicked (*méchant*), bad (*mauvais*), and fucking bad (*mal foutu*), the count raises to fifteen. If we then equally consider theoretically significant occurrences of cognate terms such as *malédiction* (malediction), *maléficieux* (maleficent), not to mention *malheur* (misfortune), *maladresse* (maladroitness), *maladie* (sickness), and *malaise*, all but five sessions address this manifold constellation. Not coincidentally, the Seminar's opening dialogues with Freud's Mal*aise dans la civilisation* (*Civilisation and Its Discontents*). The very last and overlooked sentence of the Seminar, which could also well figure as its epigraph, warns us that what is at stake in ethics is not "whether man is good or bad in the beginning" (p. 325)[9] but rather what would become of him should his linguistic-symbolic nature be fully and implosively realised.

In the first half of this chapter, I shall carry out a discussion of evil with respect to Lacan's updating of the Freudian assessment of human nature and the Thing, his own tentative delineation of jouissance, and the key role he assigns to the contradictions of Christianity in order to shed light on the Thing and jouissance as "malignant" (p. 187). In the second half, I shall pay particular attention to Lacan's scrutiny of evil through Sade and Kant, specifically highlighting how he seems to believe that a certain overestimation of Evil (as either absolutised into a first principle or mistaken for the Good) explains their comparable and failed modern endeavour to *construct* human nature as a Thing by means of the moral or immoral Law. I shall conclude by arguing that Antigone assumes an ambivalent *pre-* or *proto-*ethical function precisely with reference to the traversal of the insidious and resilient fantasy Sade calls "supreme Being-in-evil" (pp. 197, 215). However much her "criminal desire" fights for very good reasons Creon's "criminal good", for Lacan, her tragic "holocaust" should not be misunderstood as an ethical model for psychoanalysis (pp. 283, 240, 282). The ethics of psychoanalysis as only an outlined ethics of desire, which takes a "small step" (p. 19) outside the criminal good, requires our acknowledgement and overcoming of Antigone's paradigmatic embodiment of the antinomic status of the human condition as such at its point of in-difference.

The Symbolic and the Diabolic

As often happens with Lacan's most overarching hypotheses, his central arguments about evil can best be approached through a series of at first sight contradictory onto-anthropological statements:

1 There is neither natural good nor natural evil.
2 The dialectic of good and evil is given to the human animal as speaking being only with respect to the avoidance of what it fabricates as the Sovereign Good.
3 Such Sovereign Good is actually evil.
4 The dialectic of good and evil structurally tends towards the Good as evil.
5 Such evil is on closer inspection neither good nor evil.

But this apparently disheartening itinerary, along with the genealogical rejection of all previous ethical doctrines (from Aristotle to Kant and beyond), does not simply make us come back to the starting point, consigning us to moral indifference. On the contrary, it opens up the field of ethics proper as mediated by psychoanalysis. The latter functions as both a vehement call to arms against the "criminal good" (be it that of Creon or Robert Oppenheimer) and, much more humbly, nothing other than a "prelude to moral action as such" (Lacan, 1997, pp. 240, 22).

With specific regard to the status of human nature, Lacan's considerations on evil claim to be closely following Freud's but they also profoundly challenge them, without recognising it.[10] On the one hand, summoning the experience of the psy-choanalytic clinic, he takes at face value one of the central axioms of *Civilisation and Its Discontents* according to which the human animal has an innate propensity for "evil, aggression, destruction" (p. 185). On the other hand, tacitly departing from Freud, for Lacan, human nature as evil cannot but exclusively be tackled on the level of civilisation, since there is no human state of nature, or better, there is a retroactive human nature only within civilisation and its unsurpassable discontent. The question of ethics therefore does not lie in establishing "whether what we call man . . . is fundamentally good or evil" but in a critical scrutiny of the good or evil will of the linguistic animal that fashions signifiers in the world, in *Homo sapiens* as *Homo faber* (pp. 125, 214). Or also, what should ethically be at stake is not "some natural evil in man" (p. 259). Similarly, presupposing some natural law, some harmony that awaits to be recovered amounts to evading altogether the question of the good (p. 221).

In a sense, we could suggest that Lacan radicalises Freud's twofold antipathy for Rousseauian and Hobbesian moralising paradigms of human nature, while also underestimating how Freud himself in the end remains quite Hobbesian – for Freud, there is still such thing as an evil human state of nature, yet, contra Hobbes, the social pact results into a blatant fiasco. In opposition to Rous-seau, but also and especially Jung and the neo-Freudians, Lacan condemns the dimension of the "pastoral", namely, that of the search for a natural morality, if not a return to Nature, as a supposed remedy to the discontents of civilisation (pp. 88–89, 92, 4). What is more generally indicted here is the long shadow of Aristotelean ethics and its reliance on a "deep connection" between the human microcosm and the natural macrocosm, which would ultimately merge into a universal order qua the Sovereign Good that remains accessible to us thanks to a knowledge of good and bad habits (pp. 92, 22–23, 10). Psychoanalysis in fact shows that every effort in this naturalising direction – of, at bottom, ordered temperance and anti-bestiality – immediately encounters an unsurmountable resistance in our own moral conscience, or superego. In short, the allegedly good habits prescribed by the superego turn against themselves. The more we comply with them, the more the superego becomes demanding and cruel. This inclination for self-hate, as a vain corrective to the hate of the other, constitutes the most empirical and conclusive discovery of psychoanalysis in the ethical domain, a ground zero of "spontaneous" evil that refutes from the outset any possible "natural amelioration" (p. 89).

But in opposition to Hobbes, and for the same reasons, the order of civilisation can no longer be countered to the malevolent disorder of the individual. Civilisa-tion does not stand simply as that which requires the individual to compromise with his instincts and pay the price for his faults (pp. 107, 7, 89). That is to say, the superego's intrinsic exacerbation far exceeds the register of collective social needs and any interrogation on the origins of morality should primarily tackle the "malfunctioning of [the superego's] brakes" (pp. 6, 143). It is history, and not a mythical state of nature, that more and more proves to correspond to the site of a disquieting irregularity (p. 176). More emphatically, "the symbolic complements and completes itself with the diabolic" (p. 92).

In other words, in order to understand why humans are undeniably "egotistical, sordid" (p. 25), Lacan focuses on their very relation to language. Due to a series of contingencies in the natural history of the species – coalescing around a prematurity of birth and an ensuing libidinal prematurity retained as sexual neoteny – the human animal's linguistic and symbolic resourcefulness is coextensive with a "radical inadequation", whereby its vital needs and the living organism as a whole do not take centre stage in psychic development and investment (pp. 28, 104).[11] But if thus, as nicely put in Seminar I, "the symbolic system is not like a piece of clothing which sticks onto things" (Lacan, 1988, p. 265), then, as crucially spelled out in Seminar VII, this system will concomitantly attempt to compensate for such a disparity by projecting a certain resolutory "equalisation" beyond the system itself (Lacan, 1997, p. 119).[12] However dysfunctional and conflictual the system already is in its own functioning, as inseparably individual and social, here we enter into a contiguous field where the precarious life of the system prefers its own death. And here we also find the roots of the problem of "evil as such" (p. 104).

There is perhaps just one overall ethical lesson that clearly transpires in various guises throughout Seminar VII: we should prevent the symbolic difference that we are from entropically indifferentiating itself into nature as the illusion of the Thing. What is definitely evil – from the standpoint of difference and against any confusion of indifference with a supreme Being-in-evil – is losing difference. At its most structurally diabolic, beyond good or bad intentions, the symbolic system aims only at wiping itself out.

This Evil Thing of Ours

In *The Ethics*, Lacan sketches three possible theories of the origins of evil. According to the first, associated with Eastern wisdom, in particular Taoism, but also with some aspects of Lutheranism, evil arises with work. This leads us to a "position of renunciation" (Lacan, 1997, p. 123), a curbing of action and praxis.[13] As for the second, epitomised by Catharism, evil instead stems from matter, or better, the transformation of a primordial matter into another matter, whereby generation becomes synonymous with corruption. We respond to this through a concerted practice of ascetic self-extinction, a purification aimed at preventing the perpetuation of this world as essentially harmful and at the reintegration into an Edenic world (pp. 123–124). The third, distilled by psychoanalysis but already sensed in multiple premodern cultural phenomena as temporally and geographically distant as courtly love and the potlatch, postulates that evil emerges as the Thing together with language (pp. 124, 97).

The Thing has always been there for the human animal (p. 260). As speaking beings, we seek the Thing since we mistake evil for the good (p. 270). And this is the case because we project onto its field "something beyond" (p. 214), something beyond language perceived as the alleged unitary principle of language, while, on the contrary, its attainment would equate not only to the unmasking of the Thing as no-Thing but also to the demise of the species, the disappearance of our linguistic environment into an indifferent some-thing. In short, as Lacan keeps on insisting throughout Seminar VII, by taking seriously the death of God, the most important contribution of psychoanalysis to the ethical field is its disposal of any traditional and lingering ideal of the good, of a Sovereign Good as transcendent and final, including one that would persist beyond good and evil (pp. 3, 11, 70, 95–96, 300).[14] But with this very move and the turning of ethics on its head, the problem of evil, which has always been tackled starting from the assumption of the Sovereign Good, itself changes dramatically (p. 185). On such an immanent level, coterminous with the transcendental illusion of the Thing yet devoid of "the idea of the transcendence of some good that is able to dictate to man what his duties are", the exaltation of evil no longer has any transgressive, not to mention revolutionary, value (p. 70). In the absence of the Good, every particular instance of the good is not really good, it never directs us at an "all-the-best" – also and especially when it openly aspires at the Good – and, conversely, particular evils may prove to be better than the good at containing the Good as evil (pp. 217–218).

Confronting the evil Thing therefore requires a complex operation. On the one hand, it must be kept at a distance, and that is a pervasive theme of *The Ethics*.[15] On the other, and at the same time, its space must nonetheless be occupied in some mitigated/sublimated form as an enduringly evil space. Lacan only hints at this second issue – for instance, when he suggests that sublimation basically consists of circumscribing the place of the Thing with our very own species-specific inadequation (pp. 150, 152). But the fact remains that, for him, the non-relational relation with the "inhuman" Thing is what the human is all about – the Thing "maintains the presence of the human"; "it is defined by the fact that it defines the human" (p. 124) – and repudiating the Thing, as science does, has itself catastrophic consequences.

Lacan arrives at these conclusions by means of two lines of argument: one is more philosophical; the other is more clinical and reformulates Freud's pleasure principle. At bottom, the former revolves around Lacan's understanding of the Thing as "that which of the primordial real suffers from the signifier" (p. 118). In other words, human reality as linguistic has to do only with selected parts of the primordial real (pp. 45, 47). But this equally means that the inextricably psychic and physiological constitution of the human animal into a speaking being relies at its centre on the Thing as that which of the primordial real has been excluded by language (pp. 71, 118). The Thing therefore lies outside of signification while not transcending language (pp. 54–55). The Thing is not nothing while it is distinguished solely in a linguistic way as absent and alien (p. 63).

Another way to express this basic framework is to say that language introduces a hole into the primordial real that by itself knows neither emptiness nor fullness (pp. 120–121). To put it simply, as a piece of clothing, not only does language not stick onto the primordial real (since it is differential) but also, sliding on or drifting in it, it concomitantly does not cover it in its entirety (since it is incomplete). The speaking being emerges here by delimiting the primordial real not covered by language as a void and by projecting onto it a fullness that was never there in the first place. This is the Thing as a "mythical point" (p. 90). The Thing is in fact not an object (p. 158). The Thing is not nothing, yet it is no-Thing. The Thing as a supposed archaic Object retroactively appears to be lost only after we find in its vacant place the objects of linguistic reality, whereby it can only be represented by – and as – "something else", by – and as – things that are never *the* Thing (pp. 106, 118, 129–130).

But, moving quickly, if this is the case, then what is distinctively evil, in the sense of a potential collapse of the human as such, is filling in the gap that negatively gives us the Thing – and, positively, things – by paradoxically acting in the name of the Thing – or, which has the same goal, by ignoring the void altogether. Lacan speaks here of a fashioning of signifiers (in the broadest possible sense of production) in the image of the Thing as a purported totality, or One-All, whereas the Thing can instead be obtained only as that for which we have no image, as a "veiled unity", and at best *ethically* be domesticated by making the structural void *stand out* as a constructed "vacuole", or, if you wish, a "conscious and controlled destruction" (pp. 125, 118, 150, 152, 235).

As for Lacan's psychoanalytic considerations in this context, the crux of the matter is conceiving the dialectic between language and the void, on the one hand, and the Thing, on the other, in terms of the pleasure principle and its beyond (p. 134). The Freudian eradication of the Sovereign Good first and foremost empirically concerns the elimination of the traditional analogy between a supreme yet undefinable pleasure and a full satisfaction, or happiness, in a moral sense (pp. 42, 221). Albeit in contrasting if not opposite ways, devoted to determining at each turn which concrete pleasures outline the Good (p. 185), hedonism remains a constant throughout the history of moral reflection. Its tenacious topicality signals modernity's failure to develop a novel ethics. But, corroborating everyday experience, psychoanalysis refutes hedonism. Clinically, it shows that pleasure as a release of unpleasurable excitation – with the latter fundamentally depending on our species-specific inadequation – amounts to nothing other than a limitation of suffering, that is, the maintenance of a however unstable homeostasis (pp. 185, 25). While there is no doubt an intrinsic tendency towards going beyond this normal functioning, precisely because of our projection of a resolutory appeasement into such a beyond (and hence "the field of the pleasure principle is beyond the pleasure principle"), when we venture in that direction and try to "force the access to the Thing" we soon reach a level of unpleasurable excitation that becomes psychosomatically "unbearable", and we withdraw (pp. 185, 104, 80, 224, 222).

Against any kind of hedonistic morality, which, for Lacan, *mutatis mutandis* spans from Aristotle to Sade, Aquinas to Bataille, this critically means that the pleasure principle's association with the good should be reduced to just keeping us away from the projected Good Thing as a mere "refraction" (pp. 185, 72). So, there are the good and bad objects – of libidinised reality – arranged according to the alternation pleasure/unpleasure of the pleasure principle, which is one with the system of signifiers as thus indistinctly linguistic and affective, and then, elsewhere, there is the Thing, evoked as the Good by the pleasure principle that revolves around it at a distance but actually located "beyond . . . affectivity" tout court (pp. 63, 72–73, 102–103). In my view, the latter is a crucial specification. As Lacan suggests in a couple of underestimated passages, the illusion of the Thing does therefore not only concern a lie about the Good but also and more fundamentally a "lie about *evil*" as a "first lie", a lie about the Thing as an allegedly "hostile" substance (pp. 73, 52).

That is to say, if we were truly to access the Thing nothing could be articulated or felt on its level, not even pain (pp. 73, 32). Pain – and the cry, the curse, the groan – instead amounts to a primal defence (pp. 73, 239), a threshold that shields us from the waning of the no-Thing of the Thing into sheer entropic indifference once we get too close to it. Pleasure as good turns out to be painful. Yet pain as evil is not the Evil of a transcendent affect. In our search for the Good, as we reach the modest limit of the quantity of excitation tolerated by the alternation pleasure/unpleasure, what we witness is not an overcoming of the limit as an enhancement of nefarious affects, but a "scattering" and "diffusion" of that excitation *on* this very limit, the transformation of the very same quantity of unpleasurable excitation into painful "complexity" (pp. 58–59).[16]

In other words, and more psychoanalytically, Evil itself emerges only in a retroactive way, namely, through its delimitation in the pleasure-in-pain of the symptom ("the relationship of the subject to *das Ding* is marked as bad, but the subject can only formulate this fact through the symptom") (p. 74). Or better, the fantasy of Evil ultimately depends on the symptom's jouissance – the here involuntary as ontogenetically unconscious construction of the vacuole Lacan will later call *object a*.

The Paradoxes of Malignant Jouissance

Jouissance is not yet a fully developed and coherent notion in *The Ethics*.[17] Its explicit treatment remains confined to the way in which the speaking being is positioned with respect to the relation between the Law and the Thing. However, we are clearly and repeatedly told that jouissance should be regarded as evil (Lacan, 1997, pp. 184, 187, 189, 197, 237).

In a first sense, and in close connection with Lacan's reconceptualisation of the pleasure principle, jouissance is evil because it amounts to depriving the other of the good (p. 229). Jouissance does not simply correspond to the pleasure-in-pain dictated by the fact that the pleasure of releasing excitation always remains inextricably bound to the unpleasurable failure to obtain complete satisfaction, or the Good. Insofar as the relation to the Thing is always linguistic, that is, intersubjective, my pleasure as (not so) good is also always countered with the mirage of a Good that is accessible only to the other, of which he has to be deprived, and this is plainly evil (pp. 237, 234). More specifically, the physiological aspect of jouissance – the *use* value of the good – cannot be separated from the question of "the birth of power", namely, of jouissance in terms of having – economic – goods at one's disposal, of *jouissance* use (p. 229) as ownership.[18]

Following from this, "to exercise control over one's goods is to have the *right* to deprive the others of them" (ibid.). But if that is the case, then civilisation as such entails a certain structural disorder (ibid.). At bottom, the Law and its inherent transgression always go hand in hand. We should therefore not be surprised that, after all, what keeps civilisation together and sustains the ordinary deployment of the Law is precisely the jouissance of continuously violating it within its own con-tradictory limits, of spending our time conspiring to deprive others of their goods, of envying them to the point of hatred for their supposed possession of a Good we strangely do not even comprehend in any way (pp. 69, 237).

The further paradox Lacan highlights in this context is that the jouissance we might manage to steal from the other becomes more and more detached from its use value. In fact, defending one's acquired goods requires forbidding oneself from enjoying them (qua consuming them) (p. 230). We enjoy depriving others of their enjoyment, but in securing it we only enjoy the power of what we actually do not enjoy.[19] Or also, we delude ourselves into accumulating what we do not really enjoy in view of an absolute enjoyment devoid of privation.

In a second sense, when we instead opt for an immediate fruition of absolute enjoyment and try to overcome the Law along with its inherent transgression, jou-issance is evil since its habitual pleasure-in-pain turns into sheer pain. Rejecting the obscene Law of the good(s) for the sake of a direct entry into the Thing does not promote a strengthening of jouissance not to mention an "uninhibited jouissance" of the Good (p. 177). The diffuse suffering that arises on this level – as the signifier of a limit – suspends the very division between the subject and the other, between the evil I inflict on the other in the name of the Thing and the one I inflict on myself (pp. 80, 184, 261). After just a "first half-serious step", it leads us to cede on our quest for jouissance and retract into our usual pleasurable malaise (p. 185). For Lacan, this scenario illustrates the paradox according to which the Law prohibits the alleged jouissance of the Thing while the latter is already unreachable, for it is no-Thing (p. 159).

Another related paradox ensues here concerning the superego and its evil cru-elty. The death of God, the loss of credibility of the prohibiting "articulated law", has indeed unexpectedly boosted the injunctions of the superego (pp. 176, 3), which can no longer be confined to the complementarity of its normative/pater-nalistic ("You shall not!") and obscene ("Enjoy within the contradictory limits of the Law! Deprive the other with moderation!") dimensions. The more the Law is revealed to always have been structurally inextricable from its inherent transgression, the less the superego becomes tractable. And this applies not only to the "morbidity" of the guilt (p. 2) of the beautiful soul who strictly abides by the explicit rules, sees them multiply exponentially, and is thus silently enjoined to enjoy the transgression that sustains them, but also, conversely, to the defeat of the libertine project, which opens modernity (p. 3). Faced with an insurmount-able barrier that itself creates the illusion of what it bars, whose misjudged and painful transgression can as such in the end only negatively be inscribed as a debt with respect to the Law (pp. 176–177), the libertine will have no other option but to try to breach it by means of a *superegoic regimentation of his very will-to-jouissance.*

In a third and crucial sense, jouissance is therefore evil precisely as the Law's *own* attempted transgression of itself and its inherent transgression, whereby the Law paradoxically seeks to realise itself into the Good Thing. We are here dealing with a sovereign Law that, aspiring to go beyond its contradictory limits, profoundly changes status insofar as it now openly and directly supports the search for absolute jouissance and insofar as the latter in turn reveals its intimate connection with death (pp. 259, 189). While individually transgressing the Law does not unleash any extra jouissance, it is this failure that establishes the defied Law as a "path" to access a "risk" and thus lets us glimpse the lethal goal of jouissance (pp. 195, 177).

More accurately, on this level, which originates from the impasses of the other levels, the cruelty of the superego and the less and less pleasurable pain associated with it gives rise to the Law of jouissance and the jouissance of the Law, and increasingly approximates their implosive equivalence. The end point of such a tendency would amount to the "point of apocalypse" (p. 207) – the self-obliteration of the Law; the final outcome of the symbolic order's confusion of its desire for death with a means to achieve completeness; the reabsorption of the human "pile of garbage" (p. 233) into the no-Thing of the Thing. And it is with reference to this concrete possibility of entropic indifference (Lacan speaks of chromosomic anarchy and repeatedly hints at the atomic holocaust) that it is today ethically mandatory to ask whether we are set to cross "the line", so as to urgently oppose the superego as our only "true duty" (pp. 231–232, 104–105, 7).

To sum up, and bring together this series of paradoxes, Lacan seems to suggest that the Christian commandment "love thy neighbour as thyself" condenses the three ways in which jouissance is evil. First, beneath and thanks to its veneer of altruism, Christianity invigorates egoism. Providing comfort to the other exclusively reflects my imagined comfort; the good of the other is constructed solely in the image of mine; and the "law of equality" amounts to nothing more than a hypocritical camouflage of this state of affairs (pp. 186–187, 195). At bottom, I refrain from frontally assaulting the other, entrust God with the Good Thing, render unto Caesar that which is Caesar's, and even engage in charitable philanthropy only in order to protect my "elementary rights" as already based on depriving the other of the good, or better – as strangely highlighted by the parable of the Unjust Steward – "to embezzle the funds [I am] in charge of", with a view to accrue them (pp. 195, 96).[20]

But, second, all the above is only an alibi not to confront the "fundamental evil which dwells within [the] neighbour", that is, "his harmful, malignant jouissance" (pp. 186–187). Beyond the Ten Commandments and their transgression as inherent to the Law and the functioning of civilisation (the prohibition to covet the other's goods and wife leaves room for coveting them, the banning of lies opens the space for lying, and so on), the love of the neighbour radically demands turning the other cheek. It is not enough for Saint Martin to share his cloak – for it remains a fundamentally egotistic act. He should make himself be raped and killed by the beggar, or rape and kill him, if the latter so wishes (p. 186). Moreover, and most importantly, the neighbour's wickedness is the same as the one that inhabits me (ibid.). Therefore, loving the neighbour entails embracing a form of cruelty, and pain, that cannot simply be distinguished as mine or his (p. 198). This is what aligns the lives of saints with Sadean atrocities (consider "Angela da Foligno who joyfully lapped up the water in which she had just washed the feet of lepers", or "the blessed Marie Allacoque, who, with no less a reward in spiritual uplift, ate the excrement of a sick man") and, conversely, makes of Sade a devoted disciple of the Crucified (pp. 188, 262).[21] In other words, with good reasons, we normally withdraw from the inhuman love of the neighbour just as we withdraw from our quest for a jouissance beyond the Law and its unbearable consequences (p. 194) – because we are not good Christians.

Yet, third, on closer inspection, the love of the neighbour expresses the very fact that the New Law of Christianity clearly proposes itself as a – superegoic – fulfilment of the Law. As already hinted albeit not fully grasped by Paul, the Christian critique of Judaic Law and its inherent transgression also corresponds to a Law that intends to embody the Thing head on and thus unintentionally becomes "inordinately sinful" (Lacan deems the promise of Resurrection to be epiphenomenal to such – bad – Good News) (pp. 189, 193). This is the "paradox of the Law" (p. 193) and of our post-Aristotelean ethical predicament. After all, the commandment to love the neighbour tries to compensate for Christian atheism, its being a religion based on the death of God, that is, on the collapse of an externally secured and thus attenuated Law, which now instead loses any capacity for "mediation" (pp. 178, 193–194).

Sade After Kant: Evil Beyond the Pathological Good

The basic point Lacan makes about Kant's ethics and Sade's contemporary anti-ethics is that they both witness to the implosion of any Aristotelean ethics of temperate hedonism based on the Sovereign Good, and yet, they also both contradictorily end up attempting in vain to rehabilitate the latter as new figures of the Thing (Lacan, 1997, pp. 77, 79–80, 70). By rejecting all *Wohl*, the pathological-evil goods that function according to the pleasure principle and aim at securing the temporary "comfort of the subject" (p. 72), in favour of the delineation of *das Gute des Dings* on the horizon beyond the pleasure principle, Kant still misses the crucial fact that such supposed Good – or better, the jouissance obtained in its failed pursuit – is actually evil for the speaking being. While Sade correctly identifies the presumed access to the Good with evil tout court, he nonetheless reifies it into an Evil first principle, and thus ultimately maintains in a reversed way the same moral and ontological structure he intends to destroy.

Historically, for Lacan, Kant and Sade represent a watershed moment. On the one hand, their only apparently opposite moral law, unfolded by means of a similarly universal and categorical imperative ("Act so that the maxim of your will may always be taken as the principle of laws that are valid for all"; "Let us take as the universal maxim of our conduct the right [of any person] to enjoy any other person whatsoever as the instrument of [their] pleasure") (pp. 77, 79, 202), formally brings the Christian fulfilment of the Law to its most extreme albeit inevitable consequences. On the other hand, the novelty of Kant's and Sade's projects is that they endeavour to literally *real*-ise the Law into the Thing exclusively through and within the limits of the superegoic Law, that is, without any outside providential intervention. The place of the Thing, once occupied by God or the numen, is filled in with a "reality that commands and orders", a universal maxim as a "pure signifying system" (p. 55).[22] Most significantly, the death of God (the end of the delusion of a benevolent Nature, for Sade; the impossibility of a phenomenology of noumena, for Kant), already theologically anticipated but also sublated by Christianity, and the search for a moral compass that can cope with his disappearance is now inscribed against the background of what nature, the real, and reality are for *science* as the hegemonic discourse of modernity. Kant's ethics and Sade's anti-ethics, as equally "extreme, almost insane" and thus predictably unsuccessful, can only be understood in terms of a reaction to the "blind and enigmatic . . . world of modern physics" (pp. 70, 76, 77, 79).

However botched, Kant's and Sade's are embryonic ethics of the real, which psychoanalysis must further interrogate and build on (pp. 11, 76).[23] This means that, following the scientific revolution, the real is for them no longer, in an Aristotelean fashion, presupposed to correspond to an intrinsically ordered Nature, whereby the Sovereign Good could be established on and reached through a substantial synergy between the macro and microcosm (pp. 11, 22). Ethics tout court should take that as its starting point.[24] In other words – and this is a leitmotif throughout Lacan's oeuvre – what the likes of Nicolas of Cuse, Galileo, and Newton accomplish – arguably beyond their original intentions – through, first, astronomical discoveries that refute celestial spheres, and, second, a mathematical algebraisation of science and its tangible technological effectiveness is a separation of the "world of language" from its previous inclusion into a presumed "eternal nature" (p. 121). But in modern science the increasing and exponential enhancement of logical consistency goes together with an equally inexorable augmentation of the contingency of reality, up to the point that, after Einstein and his dismissal of space and time as a priori, "one final day we may find that the whole texture of appearance has been rent apart" and "the whole thing might just disappear" (pp. 122, 77).[25] Kant's and Sade's paradoxical response to this predicament, which they profoundly and courageously sense, would be a somehow desperate endeavour *to rescue phenomenal reality by real-ising the Law as a new, and finally consistent, (human) noumenal Nature.*[26] Seminar VII insists on this point, which is far less prominent in "Kant with Sade", and has been overlooked by commentators. Lacan could not be more adamant: Kant's moral maxim ultimately promotes a "law of nature"; Sade's anti-morality paves the way for a "natural society" (pp. 77, 79).[27]

Lacan's line of argument is here sketchy, convoluted, yet fascinating and overall persuasive. First, in an Aristotelean context, phenomenal reality is guaranteed for humankind by that which always returns to the same place, as epitomised by the supposed eternity of celestial bodies (pp. 74–75). The assumption of a fundamental correspondence between the micro and macrocosm as well as the possibility of creating an ethics out of it relies on this. Second, modern physics demonstrates that celestial bodies are themselves corruptible and function according to laws that are the same as those on Earth (p. 75). There is thus no longer anything that ultimately answers the demand for the security of the return. Yet ethics remains related to the search for what always returns to the same place (ibid.). Third, Kantian ethics – and, more implicitly, Sadean anti-ethics – tries to overcome this impasse. The pathology of every good action that does not comply with the categorical imperative is strictly connected with the pathological, as ontologically unsecured, status of the reality opened by modern science (pp. 76–77). More to the point, Kant's proposed way out would be a "moral law articulated with the aim of the real as such" (p. 76) – where the real as such arises as the blind and enigmatic remainder of phenomenal reality as soon as the latter is no longer secured to eternity – that is to say, a moral law that, again, thanks to the real-isation of the Law could provide us with a renewed Thing. In other words, and from a slightly different perspective, with Kant, "the moral law . . . insofar as it is structured by the symbolic, is that through which the real is *actualized* [*se présentifie*] – the real as such" (p. 20).[28]

It should be noticed that, in *The Ethics*, Lacan's notion of the real is still patchy. The real cannot simply be reduced to phenomenal reality, although such a distinction is often presented in a terminologically confusing way. It clearly partakes of the void that emerges concomitantly with the differential structure of language, yet it is also at times misleadingly equated with the Thing, which, strictly speaking, should rather be understood as an imaginary projection of an unreal fullness onto the void.[29] Moreover, its specificity as the margin of incompleteness that necessarily accompanies the consistency of scientific symbolisations remains only hinted at. What is instead beyond doubt is that Lacan *rejects* Kant's ethics of the real. In short, the latter presents us with a right diagnosis – about the incompatibility of Aristotle's hedonistic Sovereign Good with the age of modern science – and a wrong prognosis – about the (at least asymptotic) possibility of relaunching the Thing via the real-isation of the Law and thus of recuperating the Sovereign Good in an alternative version. Bluntly put, while, ethically, there is a "good side" of the Thing – when we both keep it at a distance and mitigate/sublimate it by making stand out the void from which its illusion derives – Kant's formula of duty as a "universally applicable rule of conduct" directed at the *Gut* occupies the opposite position – that is, it tries to fill in the void (p. 108).

More specifically and practically, in relation to this abstract schema, the main and dangerous limit of Kantian ethics lies, for Lacan, in its ignorance of the "problem of jouissance" (pp. 188, 189) and the evil that goes with it. This is where Sade, who knowingly adopts the bad side of the Thing and deliberately takes it for the good one, not only is "consistent" with Kant's *Critique of Practical Reason* but also "completes" it and "yields its truth" (Lacan, 2006b, p. 646). As both disdainful of the moderation afforded by the pleasure principle and its ontologically unwarranted and ethically dubious goods, in their quest to force entrance into the Thing as the Sovereign Good, Sade's and Kant's moral laws equally "eliminate from morality every element of sentiment" (Lacan, 1997, p. 79). Or, better, they equally submit the path towards ultimate satisfaction to just one feeling, *pain* (pp. 80, 108) – whether in the guise of a universal and hence reciprocal right to enjoy others without their consent or of the inflexibility of a cruel injunction that nullifies every "good" action which is not valid for all.

Lacan stresses that Kant acknowledges the centrality of pain (*Schmerz*) to his ethics (p. 108). However, what Kant fails to recognise is the *pleasure*-in-pain, or jouissance (from which one normally soon retracts, for it heads to entropic self-extinction) awarded by the "moral masochism" (p. 20) he himself evokes. More precisely, Kant omits the fact that the pain he presumes to subsume under the Law in the name of the Good cannot actually be controlled by the Law and that, on the contrary, an unbounded Law like his is actually more inseparable from jouissance than a bounded one. To be even more accurate, while disposing of the dialectic between the bounded Law and its inherent transgression, which, like for Sade, duly amounts for him to the pathological "good", what Kant severely disregards is the reversibility, and final indistinction, between the pure jouissance of *the Law* – the impersonal cruelty of the superegoic imperative – and the pure Law of *jouissance* – the pleasure-in-pain of embodied moral masochism. On the other hand, for Sade, it is adamant that the two coincide. As Lacan convincingly spells out by analysing the most political parts of *The Philosophy in the Bedroom*, Sade's individual will-to-enjoy without constraints as a "Law of *jouissance*" also constitutes, without solution of continuity, a fundamental social *Law* pointing at the "foundation of some ideally utopian social system", in turn conceived as a truly republican *natural society* (p. 202).[30]

Sade's wicked world therefore stands for one, if not the only, possible logical outcome of the Kantian project, which Kant does not see (p. 79).[31] Given that this project tacitly entails the free circulation of sado-masochistic (pleasure-in-) pain between the subject and the other, as already tested by superegoic Christianity, Eichmann could thus unfortunately yet coherently argue that he was a good Kantian.[32]

Lacan After Sade: Beyond Evil as Good

Lacan's confrontation with Sade is undoubtedly complex. Although the Marquis should not at all be regarded as a "precursor" of Freud, in the sense that his sexual aberrations would be functional to soliciting extremes on which to found a transgressive ethics of psychoanalysis, he should be singled out as a "very solid" ethical thinker – much more solid than Kant (Lacan, 1997, pp. 191, 188). Still, Sade's anti-ethical system remains after all "ridiculous" and "derisory" (pp. 212, 260, 316). And yet, this same failed system implicitly indicates a "will to create from zero, a will to begin again" (p. 212), which the ethics of psychoanalysis needs to embrace in an alternative manner.

Lacan primarily focuses on a series of productive tensions in some of the leit-motifs of Sade's libertine novels. First, they correctly exemplify how as soon as we get closer to the "central void" of the Thing (p. 202) erroneously taken to be an access to unlimited jouissance and instead materialised into a soon unbearable pain, the body of the neighbour becomes fragmented – in the direction of entropic indifferentiation. To the extent that the Sadean will-to-enjoy without constraints is taken to be a universal Law, and my appropriation of the part of the body of the other supposed to award me a moment of satisfaction will be reciprocated by my lending to the other a part of my body, this also applies to the sadist's own body (ibid.).[33] But, second, Lacan insightfully observes how such a fragmentation is contradicted by Sade's insistence on an "indestructible" other (ibid.), that is to say, the fact that the victim always survives the worst ordeals and even remains attractive. In other words, the image of the other as our fellow self that can be maintained only within the narcissistic-altruistic libidinal economy of the pleasure principle remains intact even though we are clearly located in the context of the pursuit of a jouissance beyond the pleasure principle. Third, all this is further entangled by Sade's ultimate scenario of a suffering brought to the level of "eternal" torture (ibid.). Unpacking Lacan's far from linear arguments, we may suggest that in order to contain its inevitable deadlock – namely, entropic indifferentiation – Sade's painful Law of jouissance – and jouissance of the Law – as aiming at the Thing is forced to withdraw into the imaginary territory of the petty jouissance granted by the Law's inherent transgression, and that these two incompatible junctures are then in turn conflictingly sublated into a *fantasy* of eternal suffering as the absolute jouissance of a supreme *Being*-in-evil. Last but not least, this very sublation is strangely undermined, with respect to Sade's own life, by his vocal wanting "nothing of himself to survive", that his tomb be made inaccessible and covered with bracken (pp. 202–203).

Lacan's dissection of Sade's fantasy – with the latter going as far as proving "the imaginary structure of the limit" of the Thing and confronting "the subject with the most radical kind of interrogation" (pp. 197, 220) – as well as its wider ontological and ethical repercussions represents in my opinion one of the peaks of Seminar VII. It is best approached if we consider this fantasy as threefold and increasingly daring. On a first level, Sade would simply demonstrate he is an "inferior eroti-cist", or, we may add, a vulgar sadist, whose very modest jouissance is boringly "depressing" (pp. 188, 197). This does not simply mean that, as Lacan remarks, "the path of jouissance with a woman is not necessarily to subject her to all the acts practiced on poor Justine" (ibid.). It more comprehensively, and abstractly, entails that, although Sade resolutely breaches the pleasure principle – by rejecting the service of goods along with the Law's inherent transgression – and intuits the problem of jouissance as pain, he nonetheless here conceives the pain of jouis-sance as a *means* to pleasure, an ultimate subjectivised bliss, whereby the sadist inevitably ends up merely highlighting his own *impotence* in this respect (pp. 282, 80), and returns to the less uncomfortable field of the pleasure principle and the imaginary other.

On a second level, and trying to obviate this impasse, Sade's fantasy, whose content now corresponds to eternal suffering, would endorse a sheer "jouissance of destruction", in which crime becomes virtue tout court and evil exists for the sake of evil alone – *not* pleasure (p. 197). Evil as a virtue is carried out in the name of an ontological first principle, "the Supreme-Being-in-Evil", and ultimately amounts to it (pp. 197, 215). More to the point, what Sade postulates at this stage through the so-called System of Pope Pius VI is, unsurprisingly, *Nature* as a system of Evil. His anti-ethics thus at bottom consists of "realising to the most extreme point [our] assimilation to absolute evil" (p. 197), precisely by real-ising the Law as the indistinct Law of jouissance and jouissance of the Law. With specific regard to the working of Nature as an Evil system, Sade assumes on this level of his fantasy that the pure thrust of Nature is obstructed by its own (symbolic) forms – which themselves turn out to be chaotic and actually evil, in spite of their seeming goods – and that it is therefore up to humankind's crimes – including and especially the refusal of reproduction – to collaborate with *Nature's* thrust to new creations. To sum up, the outcome of Sade's anti-ethics is here the advancement of a cyclic series of creations/destructions orchestrated by Nature as Destruction thanks to our mischievous and self-effacing support.

Lacan has no hesitation in defining the fantasy according to which human crimes might contribute to the maintenance of a cosmic concord of things through discord as "poor" and "worthless" (p. 212).[34] Against Bataille's view that Sade would thus promote an idea of being as unruliness and malfunction (*dérèglement*),[35] what is on the contrary at stake from an ontological standpoint is a resumption of the religious tradition of the "fundamental wickedness" of *God* as supreme life (pp. 201, 215). This is after all a comforting metaphysical anchor on which to secure the human predicament. In the end, Sade's proposed integration into evil Nature, surreptitiously taken for a psychic and unified Ego, would put forward nothing other than an inverted kind of harmony as a most profound cure (pp. 197, 210). On close inspection, his libertine blasphemies preserve a very solid reference to the divine term, up to the point that Nature as its own creator is now even requested to account for the most extreme anomalies – which Aristotle would have instead relegated to the irrelevant sphere of bestiality (pp. 4–5). Phenomenologically, this is also how we should read the centrality of pain in Sade's universe. Faced with the contingency of scientific reality, on the one hand, and the concrete inaccessibility of the jouissance of the Thing, on the other, Sade phantasmatically retaliates by reifying and eternalising suffering as the threshold of the no-Thing. We are here dealing with the "apotheosis of sadism": "Suffering is conceived of as a *stasis* which affirms that . . . which is" and we witness to a "*divinisation* of everything that remains of [the Thing], namely, of the limit in which being subsists in a state of suffering" (pp. 261–262).

But, on a third level closely linked to the second, Sade's fantasy also paves the way for a realist and materialist ontology Lacan subscribes to, as well as a related ethics yet to be developed. Lacan's argument is subtle and can easily be missed. However, it seems to me that without this passage the role he later assigns to Antigone remains incomprehensible or prone to misinterpretations. The key point has to do with what he calls the "second death", namely, "death insofar as it is regarded as the point at which the very cycles of the transformations of nature are annihilated" (p. 248).[36] He emphasises how, in Sade's fantasy and the way in which he treats his own death, the jouissance of destruction is not simply confined to wiping the slate clean in view of new creations *within* an endless series of creations/ destructions supervised by Nature. Sade equally, and contradictorily, mentions "more total destructions", such as preventing the regeneration of corpses into other forms of life (p. 211).[37] In other words, Nature would ultimately want annihilation, or better, self-annihilation. We can certainly understand this in terms of yet another totalising fantasy: Nature is a self-annihilating *principle; Nature* is a crime against Nature (p. 260); self-annihilating Nature is nothing but a variant of the supreme *Being*-in-evil, now more consonantly conceived as eternal death. However, on this level, Sade's fantasy also *undoes* itself to the extent that the "direct will to destruction" (or death drive) it expresses, which should as such be distinguished from a mere tendency towards entropy, cannot but paradoxically summon at the same time a "will to make a fresh start" and "for something Other" (p. 212). The latter should in turn not be confused with the eternal cycle of natural metamorphoses since it instead indicates an "initial intention" pertaining to the domain of *linguistic* nature from which the will to destruction itself originates (p. 211).

We could reformulate this from a slightly different perspective by adopting the terminology I have used on other occasions to illustrate a crucial and more extensive issue in Lacan's para-ontology.[38] While, when sustained, the pursuit of the Thing as *One* – to which we all succumb in various degrees – would unintentionally lead the Sadean libertine (or the Kantian prude) to entropic *indifference*, by eventually associating the Thing with the second death, Sade also shows us that if the very same pursuit is intentionally aimed at the nihil what is concomitantly albeit fleetingly obtained is the point of in-*difference* – as the ethical possibility of creating again *from zero*. This is the case because the nihil, or void, is not indifference but rather the other side of language. We can therefore make sense of why Lacan counterintuitively speaks of the second death as a real "position of being" (p. 248), opposed to the phantasmatic supreme-Being-in-evil.

Antigone's Holocaust, the Ethical Value of the Being of Language, and the Criminal Good

For Lacan, Antigone is not at all a model for the ethics of psychoanalysis. In a nutshell, her actions instead paradigmatically encapsulate the antinomic status of the human condition. Ethics should subsequently be developed on the basis of such an antinomy. Or also, psychoanalytical ethics is not a tragic ethics but one that starts off from the assumption of the tragic dimension of the life of the animal that happens to speak (Lacan, 1997, p. 313).

Much more clearly than Sade's traversal of his own self-annihilating fantasy, which in spite of hinting at a new creation from zero remains after all subdued to the supreme Being-in-Evil, Antigone epitomises "pure desire", on the one hand, and the "desire for death", on the other, by structurally and hence heroically embodying both of them *without any mediation* (pp. 282–283).[39]

According to Lacan, what is crucial in Sophocles' tragedy is, first, Antigone's relentless insistence on wanting to bury Polynices and, second, her being buried alive because of that. The attempt to avoid his second death, here better understood than in Sade as the complete elimination of any symbolic inscription of his previous existence,[40] not only makes her face her second death prior to the first – she is reabsorbed into the undifferentiated undead whilst still alive – but also and especially, within the same process, on the threshold of her tomb,[41] turns her into the "pure and simple relationship of the human being to . . . the signifying cut that confers on him the indomitable power of being what he is" (p. 282). Lacan fiercely claims that here the value of language as the value of being paves the way for thinking ethical value (p. 279).

More to the point – and presenting as a threefold sequence what Lacan instead reads as a synchronic continuum – Antigone starts off by defending Polynices' "absolute individuality" (p. 278). Her brother is, of course, an enemy and traitor, yet he needs to be buried; he is what he is and as such he is "something unique" (p. 279) beyond the good and evil dictated by the Law. But it is precisely and incongruously this very defence of Polynices as a being of language, of his difference, that leads Antigone to embrace a stubbornly uncompromising stance for which "That's how it is because that's how it is", that is, a reification of difference, whereby her not ceding on her (as her brother's) pure desire is swiftly transformed into a tremendous impasse, a "criminal desire", a desire for indifference – which, in addition to having her buried alive, more generally unleashes a veritable "holocaust" in Thebes (pp. 278, 283, 282). However, finally and most importantly, for Lacan, this same indistinction between a pure desire for the maintenance of individual difference and its falling back into an indifferentiating desire for death – which is nonetheless clearly not a mere suicide (p. 286) – gives rise to a distinct, albeit necessarily vanishing, point of in-difference. When entering her tomb alive, Antigone "sacrifice[s] her own being in order to maintain that essential being which is [the limit]" (p. 283).

Again, like in Sade, it is the second death that gives Antigone, and us, "a relationship to being", in spite of natural metamorphoses and even history, on an extreme level that displays the cut, the being of language as such (p. 285). In the tragedy, Lacan says, she immortalises the limit – as, I would add, now universalised, belonging to the *Homo sapiens* species in toto. But unlike in Sade, this is not accompanied by the metaphysical subterfuge of eternalising pain. We could suggest that, in the wake of Oedipus, her father, the price Antigone has to pay for fleetingly incarnating the cut is becoming "the scum of the earth, the refuse, the residue, a thing empty of any plausible appearance", that is, her own entropic indifferentiation. More accurately, being entombed alive, she "makes actual the conjunction of life and death. [She] lives a life which is dead, which is that death which is precisely" – always already! – "there under life" (Lacan, 1991, p. 232).

Antigone's complete overcoming of the pleasure principle, including the pain-in-pleasure of jouissance, also enables us to briefly clarify the relation between desire, jouissance, and the drive (the latter notion figures rather prominently in Seminar VII, but Lacan will systematise it only in Seminar XI). In short, desire is the drive as unsatisfied by the partial satisfaction of jouissance obtained through the drive. In this sense, *pure* desire becomes indistinguishable from a desire for death, whereas the drive, which is itself at bottom a death drive, normally *sustains* the symbolic order (Lacan, 1997, pp. 211, 209) – that is, the "pathological" dialectic between the Law and jouissance. On the one hand, the drive orients the pleasure principle with respect to the Thing as a mythical point by circling around it and thus obtaining the partial and paradoxical satisfaction of jouissance (p. 90). The circuit of the drive deviates from the Thing as a goal and should therefore better be understood as the continuous repetition of a drift (pp. 90, 110). On the other hand, desire as uncoupled from the drive aims directly at the real void of the no-Thing, the nihil that goes together with the symbolic order and functions as a basic differentiating threshold beyond which the void is nothing but entropic indifference.[42]

Lacan insists on the fact that here we enter into the field of a "radical desire" as "absolute destruction . . . beyond putrefaction" (p. 216). While psychoanalysis should be devoted to liberating the subject from the illusion of the goods and the Good that hinders desire, the most impellent ethical question it should nonetheless ask is "how far can we go in this direction?" (pp. 219, 221, 230). For Lacan, Antigone certainly goes too far. Her desire aims at the beyond of the limit, where human life cannot subsist (pp. 262–263). And yet again, it is precisely the moment she crosses the limit that makes desire as such visible (pp. 248–249, 268). But, still, the visibility of such differentiating threshold also concomitantly prevents us from seeing the "true nature" of what happens on the other side, namely, an indifference for which "there is no longer any object" (pp. 249, 281).

With specific regard to Antigone's vicissitudes, the dialectic of such a point of in-difference also sheds light on Lacan's apparently contradictory take on how she positions herself vis-à-vis the Thing. In a first sense, Antigone's desire is not a desire for the Thing. It is on the contrary a desire for desire – for the maintenance of her brother's inscription into the symbolic order and the symbolic order at large. In this way, it opposes the *Law*'s desire for the Thing, namely Creon's attempted fulfilment of the Law. *As such* Antigone's desire is also antinomically a desire for death as an inflexible rejection of the Law outside of which she cannot survive – in this sense, she is "separated . . . from structure" and already dead as alive (p. 271). *But*, crucially, she is aware of this; she does not confuse the outside with the Thing. *Yet* in a second sense, her desire for death does get confused with the Thing. In her own way, she too "mistakes evil" (symbolic death and indifferentiation) "for the Good", even though her Good is different from everyone else's (p. 270). That is to say, reading in between the lines of Lacan's arguments, there is eventually a short circuit between her choosing to be "the guardian of the being of the criminal" (p. 283), Polynices, which she pays with her own second death, and the lingering mirage that the latter may grant her access to an ultimate incestuous satisfaction.

"My brother *is* my brother", and you cannot not bury him, deprive him of the value of being a being of language, also stands for "my brother is *my* brother", namely, a totalising fantasy whereby, as Sophocles puts it, "I will lie down, my loving friend, my almost lover, here with you" (pp. 278, 265).[43]

What Lacan instead clearly spells out is that, notwithstanding this short circuit, Antigone's "criminal desire" offers us a potent critique of the "criminal good" epitomised by Creon, its inadvertent tendency towards indifferentiation whilst aiming at the Thing. Lacan claims that Creon is a Kantian *ante litteram*. I would specify that, as interpreted by Lacan, he is rather a sadistic Kantian who, moreover, applies the formalism of Kant's and Sade's universal moral law to the service of the *pathological* goods rejected by Kant and Sade.[44] Or also, against Aristotle's elitism, Creon pursues a democratic optimisation of the Aristotelian pleasure principle as directed at everyone by means of a Law without limits that cannot but be located beyond the pleasure principle. More precisely, Creon seeks the good as the good of all but his "error of judgment", of which he is unaware, is "to want to turn everyone's good into . . . the Law that overflows and crosses the limit" (pp. 258–259). Obviously, the alleged Law of the good as the Law without limits crosses the limit (of the Law itself) as soon as Creon decides to inflict the second death on Polynices, his enemy, the evil traitor of the good, which – as the attempted elimination of any symbolic inscription of the dead Polynices – is followed in short succession by Antigone's defiance of such Law, her own second death, and the obliteration of Thebes (the end of the Law tout court). According to Lacan, Creon's criminal good thus shows us that "the good cannot reign over all without an excess emerging [with] fatal consequences" (p. 259). Expanding on Lacan's remarks, it is also important to stress that although Creon's criminal good aims at the fulfilment of the *Law* as the Thing, unlike Kant and Sade, he ignores the fact that this would correspond to the realisation of the Law – which Kant and Sade in turn misread as a new human nature instead of identifying it with the self-extinction of the *Homo sapiens* species.

I think this final passage is mandatory in order to understand the otherwise perplexing association Lacan makes between Creon's criminal good and the current hegemony of the discourse of science – as entwined with hedonistic capitalism. Today, the "politics of the good" as the discourse of the "general good, of the good of the community" amounts to that of science (pp. 236, 233).[45] The latter fully unveils for the first time the self-destructive power of the symbolic order and in this way puts life as such into question (p. 236). Although all ages somehow felt they were confronting something terminal, and the imagination has always toyed with it, we are now in possession of an "absolute weapon", the atomic bomb (p. 104). This does not mean that the end of the world will necessarily happen tomorrow or the day after tomorrow, but the prospect for which the scientific "world of the good" will drag us all to the second death is not only possible but also the possible par excellence (pp. 104, 232). In comparison to this scenario – "the real unchaining that threatens us" – Sade's petty horrors, as ultimately sublated into a supreme Being-in-evil, can at most only engender some fleeting disgust in us (pp. 232–233). Insofar as science by now functions by itself, and forgets nothing, here the discourse of the general good even lies outside the sphere of good and bad intentions: neither misguided kings nor sadistic perverts will unleash the holocaust, but anonymous bureaucrats, whose motivations no longer include any calculation of pleasure and pain (pp. 236, 233). Or better – as explained in one of the most politically prophetic moments of *The Ethics*, delivered in 1959–1960 – this impersonal "move toward the slaughter house" still clings to and is facilitated by the imposition of a "prescribed good" by means of information as a "hubbub of voices", yet, the superegoic good of today's "frightening discourses of power" goes well beyond the goods of the pleasure principle that traditionally used to mask our desire for death: having crossed the line, it thus becomes meaningless to ask "whether [these discourses] are sincere or hypocritical, whether they want peace, whether they are assessing risks" (p. 231).

Unsurprisingly, Lacan refers to the increasing involution of such an acephalous setting, the contemporary radicalisation of the criminal good, as the "project of evil as such" (p. 104) and thinks it fundamentally has to do with science's relation to the Thing. The historical, and potentially catastrophic, failure of science is that it repudiates or forecloses the Thing (p. 131). The Thing should be kept at a distance, but it cannot be bypassed altogether – because, in the end, it is the Thing that maintains the human as a mediating function between the real and the signifier (p. 129). More precisely, while art symbolically organises the void of the no-Thing (since there is after all no such thing as the Thing) and religion symbolically avoids this void by thereby respecting it as the fantasised locus of the plenitude of God, science assumes a position of unbelief with respect to it, which, Lacan adds, is itself a form of belief and a position of discourse with regard to the Thing.[46] But if, on the one hand, the presence of the Thing as no-Thing is repudiated in the name of the ideal of absolute knowledge – which already contradicts the fact that science actually draws the effectiveness of its mathematical algebraizations from the void of the no-Thing – on the other, it is this very ideal that ends up "posit[ing] the Thing while it pays no attention to it" (p. 131). Foreclosed in the symbolic, the no-Thing returns in the real: in the disappearance of phenomenal reality caused by physics; in the possibility of the nuclear holocaust.

In Seminar VII, the arguments Lacan puts forward to substantiate this pivotal set of issues are still rudimentary and sporadic.[47] But the related point he makes here about the deadlock of ethics in modernity, his own version of the dialectic of Enlightenment, is potent. In short, at the dawn of modernity, Kant and Sade explicitly aim at the Thing by means of a real-isation of the Law. They are both obviously unsuccessful, for their proposals are practically unviable – in fact they had "no social consequences at all" (p. 79) – and, should that not suffice, ontologically misleading. Today, instead, science disregards the Thing and, precisely by disregarding it, it equally albeit unintentionally promotes a real-isation of the Law (via the ideal of absolute knowledge), which might prove apocalyptically successful and materialise in the self-extinction of the species. As Lacan quips, Kant's categorical imperative has today been upgraded to "Never act except in such a way that your action may be programmed" (p. 77), while, it should be added, against

Kant, we still keep on abiding by the empty shell of the pathological service of the goods – the Ten Commandments in the guise of human rights secured through humanitarian wars and despotic political correctness; Aristotelean hedonism in the guise of an allegedly liberating injunction to enjoy that only leads to frustration and further aggressiveness.

A Small Step Outside the Criminal Good

So, whither ethics? Seminar VII has many concentric overtures in this regard, but none of them is actually developed. Let me briefly sketch how they open increasingly broader horizons whose vistas will have to be detailed beyond Lacan:

1   The ethics of psychoanalysis revolves around the question of *desire* (Lacan, 1997, pp. 3, 41–42), as equally and contradictorily a desire for desire, or difference, and a desire for death, or indifference. Antigone embodies such a contradiction but does not solve it.
2   The ethics of psychoanalysis as an ethics of desire opposes the *superego* (pp. 7, 302–303, 310), or better any attempt at real-ising the Law, which structurally follows from the dialectic between desire and the Law and unintentionally tends towards indifference in the name of the One – whether openly pursuing the Thing (Christianity, Kant, Sade) or positing it while repudiating it (Creon, science).
3   The ethics of psychoanalysis tries to reinvent the *dialectic* between desire and the Law (pp. 83–84) in a way that prevents, or at least curbs, its tendency towards indifference. Or, which is the same, it envisages an ethical inhabiting the order (ἔθος) of language in which habit (ἦθος) no longer shapes signifiers in the image of the Thing.[48]
4   The ethics of psychoanalysis corresponds to an ethics of the *real* precisely in the sense that such a treatment of signifiers as coterminous with the no-Thing of the Thing introduces something new in its place, in a fashion whereby "*not everything* is caught up . . . in the struggle for goods", the Good, and "the necessary catastrophe that it gives rise to" (pp. 29, 203, 207, 235). Renouncing the search for the Good amounts to equating the good with the elimination of "false goods" (p. 300).
5   The ethics of psychoanalysis thus amounts to an ethics of *sublimation* (p. 87), where what matters is not so much raising an object to the dignity of the Thing – as a surrogate reconciliation – but rather, through the same anamorphic movement, the *active* creation of a void, or vacuole, at the centre of the system of signifiers – as a primitive symbolisation (pp. 112, 94, 142, 150).[49]
6   The ethics of psychoanalysis as an ethics of sublimation therefore also delineates a new *erotics* yet to be configured. As demonstrated by courtly love, eroticism itself has an ethical function when it makes the vacuole appear – for instance, through concrete sexual techniques such as amor interruptus or foreplay that, contrary to the pleasure principle, materialise the "pleasure of desiring" (p. 152).

7 The ethics of psychoanalysis as a potential erotics that, by refusing the service of goods and the illusion of the Good also promotes an "acknowledgement of the Other", cannot in turn be separated from the *political* meaning of the ethical and the question of ideology (pp. 152, 230). A progressive is a fool who tells the truth – ultimately about the no-Thing of the Thing. A reactionary is a knave, a "Mr. Every-man with more determination" (p. 183) – unashamedly supportive of the real-isation of the Law into the Thing. But individual foolery soon turns into collective knavery. That is to say, telling the truth about the no-Thing against the Law easily becomes ideologised into a telling the truth about truth, namely into a Truth, as yet another instantiation of the real-isation of the Law (pp. 183–184). The political import of the ethics of psychoanalysis lies in abiding by the "truth of the first stage", obviating the passage from truth to the truth about truth, and the transformation of progressive foolery into "metaphysical knavery" (p. 184).[50]

8 The ethics of psychoanalysis as a critique of the thin line dividing progressive political foolery from reactionary metaphysical knavery has at the same time a clear ontological dimension. Surprisingly at first sight, the ethics of psychoanalysis is a *creationist* ethics. But what Lacan repeatedly and provocatively refers to as creation *ex* nihilo should better be understood as creation, or symbolic effectiveness, *cum* nihilo. Once again, we are dealing here with the inextricability between language and the void as well as the retroactive, yet structural, illusion of the Thing they promote. On the one hand, through the ages, the Thing as the central problem of ethics has been posed in terms of the question: "If a reasonable power created the world, if God created the world, how is it that whatever we do or don't do the world is going so *badly*?" (pp. 121–122). The central dilemma traditionally linking ethics, ontology, and theology is thus already more centred on "Why did He do such a botched job?" and "Why is there something (symbolic) only *with*, or alongside, nothing?" than on "Why is there something rather than nothing?" On the other hand, after the death of God, we can certainly try to reflect upon *being*, as opposed to any transcendent *Being* or Creator, *and* the concomitant nihil on the basis of nothing more than the contingent and always-already reversible "break that the very presence of language inaugurates in the life of man" (p. 279) – or, in my jargon, the threshold of in-difference. *Yet*, in modernity we cannot but also continue to think, however paradoxically, in an old-fashioned creationist manner: "The idea of creation is consubstantial with your thought" (p. 126). Now that God is dead the question about creation and a first principle is at best only displaced onto the question concerning a God that guarantees there is no God – and this question, which has to do with science and its approach to the Thing, Lacan says, "is the goal of our inquiry this year" (p. 127).[51] More specifically, "even if you don't give a damn about the Creator, it is nevertheless the case that you think the notion of evil in creationist terms" (p. 124), whereby the superego's main function is transformed into and reinforced as sheer "hatred for God" (p. 308). In other words, as long as we are in a world of signifiers, we necessarily albeit

involuntarily posit something *beyond* signifiers – and nature as in-differently symbolised – that is, some kind of variation on the Thing on which signifiers would ultimately depend (p. 212). Not only Sade's supreme Being-in-Evil as a final arche but also, similarly and unexpectedly, Freud's own death instinct as a "suspect" and "ridiculous" (disaggregating) first *principle* beyond the pleasure principle – which in the end mistakes nature with the human subject – are testament to such a regression (pp. 212–213).[52] Lacan's proposed solution (ingeniously counterintuitive but finally unconvincing in my view because, as we just saw, he himself already demolishes it with his critique of modernity's alleged atheism) is to insist on "an absolute beginning, which marks the origin of the signifying chain as a distinct order", does not presuppose the Being-of-being, and eliminates "creative intention as supported by a person" (pp. 213–214).[53]

While the discovery of the unconscious might have lasting, and positive, general ethical consequences, psychoanalysis does not assume that a much-needed innovation of ethics, and therefore *hope* tout court, is necessarily possible (pp. 291, 14, 234). According to Lacan, perhaps we have indeed already crossed the line.

Notes

1 This chapter was written in the winter of 2020–2021, under Covid lockdown. I would like to thank Moritz Herrmann and Frank Ruda for their comments on an advanced draft. Translations have been modified and emphases added where necessary.
2 Contri perspicuously speaks of a "problematic Seminar, a sort of permanent and unfinished survey" (Contri, 1994, p. viii).
3 For an inventive reading that manages to synthetise both positions, see Žižek, 1998.
4 For rather unconvincing and opposite takes on this, see, for example, Reed, 2013, and Themi, 2014.
5 See Kirschner, 2012.
6 Jacques-Alain Miller himself seems to adopt a very favourable stance on Bentham in some passages of his unpublished 1996–97 course "L'Autre qui n'existe pas et ses Comités d'éthique".
7 Moustapha Safouan was long the champion of a critical resistance to the reduction of the ethics of psychoanalysis to the injunction "Do not cede on your desire!" See also Miller, 1984–85.
8 I have analysed different aspects of Seminar VII in Chiesa and Toscano, 2005; Chiesa, 2007, 2015a, 2015b.
9 In a way, this is Lacan's *anti*-Nietzschean starting point *beyond* good and evil.
10 *The Ethics* nominally remains a Freudian Seminar. But there are also several crucial points where Lacan disagrees with Freud, for instance, with respect to the socially useful value of sublimation as a reconciliation (ibid., p. 94), the aesthetical dimension of sublimation (ibid., p. 238), the way in which love has historically changed (ibid., p. 99), Freud's personal abiding by an ethical ideal of temperance and "patriarchal civility" (ibid., p. 177), his limited (Aristotelean) understanding of the Christian commandment "Love your neighbour as yourself" (ibid., pp. 186, 193), and, more seriously, his conceiving of the death instinct in terms of energy and ultimately of a first principle (ibid., pp. 204, 212).
11 As the choir in *Antigone* has it – in Lacan's quite free translation of verse 370 of Sophocles' tragedy – "he advances and he is 'artful', but he is always 'screwed'" (ibid., p. 275).

12 See also Chiesa, 2021.

13 Or, in more current jargon, a glorification of inoperativity.

14 "It is interesting to write a . . . genealogy of morals [but] not in Nietzsche's sense" (Lacan, 1997, p. 35).

15 Marc De Kesel has rightly insisted on this; see De Kesel, 2009.

16 Diana Rabinovitch and De Kesel tackle this issue but it seems to me they both miss the second, and most important, level of Lacan's argument. Again, the "lie about evil" does not only mask the evil Thing in the guise of a Sovereign Good but, more deeply, it associates the very evil of the Thing with an alleged transcendent field of Evil affects. See Rabinovitch, 2001, pp. 19–33; De Kesel, 2009, pp. 116–120.

17 In "The First Gram of Jouissance" (Chiesa, 2015b), I have stressed this. Following a recent and detailed rereading of Seminar VII (and having closely consulted also alternative unofficial versions of the Seminar, which tend to be more precise, or at least more inclusive), I here present a far more sympathetic reading. Needless to say, what is gained in terms of coherence with regard to Lacan's arguments is perhaps paid with a certain forcing of his text, however exegetically sustainable this forcing might be.

18 This argument – which Lacan only sketches – could originally be developed in terms of a psychosomatic genesis of *surplus* value – which he hints at in Seminar I: "The symbolic world of the prices on the stock market and the multiplication table is entirely invested in pain" (Lacan, 1988, p. 130).

19 As Frank Ruda puts it (private communication), this is, of course, quite reminiscent of Hegel's master and slave dialectic. I would add that it also confirms Lacan's insistence on the fact that the crux of this dialectic is not the "struggle for pure prestige" but its being located on the level of the pleasure principle and the psycho-*pathology* – in a Freudo-Kantian sense – of everyday impotent power.

20 This specific aspect of Lacan's critique of Christianity strongly resonates with Nietzsche's critique of Paul: "'Salvation of the soul' – in plain language: 'the world revolves around *me*'. . . . The poisonous doctrine '*equal* rights for everyone'" (Nietzsche, 2007, p. 40).

21 See also Lacan, 2006b, p. 666.

22 To be more specific, for Lacan, in the case of Kant, the moral law becomes the pure and simple application of the universal maxim as a *form*. Sade would be more consequential and honest than Kant in that he openly identifies the moral law with a pure and simple *object* (Lacan, 1997, p. 70): or better, the *universal maxim* is itself the empirical object of the law – the right to enjoy and ultimately the brutality of Nature (Nobus, 2017, p. 17). But what first and foremost matters here is that Sade himself promotes a universal maxim, like Kant. Interestingly, Virno comes very close to treating Kant in the way Lacan treats Sade: "The productivity of practical reason, organized by a law that prescribes only the necessary construction of laws, on the one hand abstracts from every ethical content proposed by experience, while on the other it constitutes its objects in full autonomy, which will, however, have no determination outside the simple universal form" (Virno, 2021, p. 122).

23 Zupančič's *Ethics of the Real* (2000) remains compulsory reading on this general point.

24 At one point, Lacan seems to go as far as suggesting that, historically, we cannot strictly speak of ethics before this (Lacan, 1997, pp. 75–76). In other words, Aristotelean morality is *not* ethics.

25 See also Agamben's surprisingly similar point: "The hypothesis I intend to put forward is that, if quantum mechanics relies on the convention that reality must be eclipsed by probability, then disappearance is the only way in which the real can peremptorily be affirmed as such" (Agamben, 2018, pp. 42–43).

26 Quickly reading between the lines of Lacan's arguments, in the case of Kant, the Second Critique would therefore be an *ontological* completion of the First. Developing this fascinating point would require a book of its own. As Moritz Herrmann reminds us (private communication), in the preface to the Second Critique, Kant himself already posits

that practical reason realises what pure theoretical reason can only hint at or presuppose without being able to prove it, namely, freedom as causality (see Kant, 1997, esp. pp. 5–6). But Lacan goes further than this: the Second Critique would aim at ontologically completing the incompleteness of phenomenal reality by means of the real-isation of the Law as itself both human nature and the noumenal Thing.

27 More to the point, in Kant, the moral maxim is presented as "the law of a nature in which we are called upon to live", and not simply as "the law of a society". Nature is thus organised as an object that is relative to our rule of conduct (Lacan, 1997, pp. 77–78). See also Chiesa, 2007, pp. 171–172.

28 If the real-isation of the Law is conflated with the Thing, then, conversely, such Law can also be conceived of as the Law of the Real.

29 See also Chiesa, 2007, pp. 131–136.

30 Of course, "republican" should also be read here in the Latin etymological sense of a res publica, a public Thing.

31 One could further complicate this point by also bringing in Kant's own notion of "radical evil" (Kant, 2018). In short, from a Lacanian perspective, Kant's radical evil as the human propensity to act against the universal moral law is actually far better than the supreme Good of what Kant identifies as das Gute des Dings, which ultimately coincides with a Sadean universe.

32 On Eichmann's claim that he always complied with Kant's categorical imperative, see Arendt, 2006, p. 136.

33 See also Marquis de Sade, 1988, p. 273.

34 See also Lacan 2006b, p. 667.

35 The English translation renders this as "immorality", which misses the point.

36 See also Lacan, 2006b, p. 655.

37 See also Marquis de Sade, 1966–67, p. 212.

38 See for instance, Chiesa, 2016, pp. 60–75.

39 The English translation is here misleading. We are dealing with a "pure desire" that, from another angle, is a "desire for death", yet this cannot simply be conflated into a "pure and simple desire of death as such".

40 Sade's fantasy of eliminating the cycle of natural creations/destructions is in fact already an eminently symbolic operation – for there is no cycle whatsoever in nature in-itself and for-itself, just sheer indifference.

41 This happens via Antigone's "splendour" (Lacan, 1997, pp. 247–249). I cannot here dwell on the aesthetical dimension of Lacan's argument. Suffice it to mention that, for Lacan, there is no Freudian ethics without a preliminary Freudian aesthetics (ibid., p. 159).

42 But, again, antinomically, it is only from the perspective of such a second death that we can speak of a "realisation of desire" (ibid., pp. 294–295).

43 Thus, Antigone's apparently anti-superegoic desire for the void can no longer simply be opposed to Kant's and Sade's superegoic desire to be One, which sustains their aim to real-ise the Law. This is not only the case in the sense that the outcome of both would amount to indifference (as the end result of the 0 without the 1, for the former, and of the 1 without the 0, for the latter), but also because Antigone's desire for the void as an incestuous desire to be One is dialectically matched by Kant's and Sade's desire to be One as itself a desire for the void (which is evident in the most advanced stage of Sade's fantasy). From a slightly different perspective, we witness here to the distinction and complementarity between neurosis, or at least hysteria (Antigone), and perversion (Kant and Sade) as equally dependent on the symbolic order's own undecidability between annihilation and totalisation.

44 In this sense, we can understand Lacan's otherwise unintelligible claim that Creon is not only Kantian but also and at the same Aristotelian (ibid., p. 314).

45 On how this is currently manifested by the "imperative to 'trust science'", see Nedoh, 2020, p. 316.
46 In this more specific sense, science differs from Creon. The latter in fact *confuses* the laws of the earth with those of the gods, the Thing, which, however, he does not repudiate (Lacan, 1997, pp. 276–277).
47 On Lacan's later treatment of science's conflictual relation with the real, see Chiesa, 2016, pp. 34–39, 62–64, 87–90 and Chiesa and Johnston (forthcoming).
48 I am here trying to synthesise a series of quick points Lacan derives from Aristotle's *Nicomachean Ethics* on the complex etymology of "ethics" in Seminar VII (Lacan, 1997, pp. 10, 22) and *Television* (Lacan, 1990, p. 39).
49 However vague Lacan remains on this point, it should now at least be clear that such a desire for the active creation of a void, for a return to the threshold of in-difference that *reinstates* the 0/1 (primitive symbolisation) and starts all over again, should not be misunderstood with Antigone's desire to *plunge* into the void.
50 For a different and inspiring reading of the fool and the knave in Lacan, see Johnston, 2021.
51 The reference to science, which is quite crucial here, has been expunged from the official version of Seminar VII.
52 On Freud's eventual reliance on the One, Lacan will become much harsher in later Seminars (see, for instance, Lacan, 2018, p. 108). Note also how, already for the Lacan of Seminar VII, Sade *and* Freud are not even on the level of the *implicit* God that guarantees there is no God – as, for instance, a science based on the notion of the chaosmos is. For both Sade and Freud there still *explicitly* is an ultimate first principle, however paradoxical.
53 Jean-Luc Nancy comes very close to this stance when he states that "*ex nihilo* means: undoing any premise, including that of nothing", and that only through a thus conceived *ex nihilo* "atheism [is] clearly freed from the schema of an inverted theism" (Nancy, 2008, pp. 24–26). I think we can and should do *better* than what Lacan and Nancy similarly propose. For a tentative way out of this predicament, see what I have been elaborating as materialist agnosticism, agnostic atheism, and para-ontology in Chiesa, 2016, and Chiesa and Johnston, forthcoming.

References

Agamben, A. (2018). *What Is Real?* Stanford: Stanford University Press.
Arendt, H. (2006). *Eichmann in Jerusalem: A Report on the Banality of Evil*. London: Penguin Books.
Chiesa, L. (2007). *Subjectivity and Otherness*. Cambridge, MA: MIT Press.
Chiesa, L. (2015a). Psychoanalysis, Religion, Love. *Crisis and Critique*, 2(1).
Chiesa, L. (2015b). The First Gram of Jouissance. *The Comparatist*, 39.
Chiesa, L. (2016). *The Not-Two: Logic and God in Lacan*. Cambridge, MA: MIT Press.
Chiesa, L. (2021). Anthropie: Beside the Pleasure Principle. *Continental Thought & Theory*, 3(2).
Chiesa, L. and Johnston, A. (forthcoming). *God Is Undead: Psychoanalysis Between Agnosticism and Atheism*. Evanston, IL: Northwestern University Press.
Chiesa, L. and Toscano, A. (2005). Ethics and Capital: Ex Nihilo. *Umbr(a): A Journal of the Unconscious*.
Contri, G. (1994). Avvertenza del curatore. In J. Lacan (Ed.), *Il seminario: Libro VII: L'etica della psicoanalisi*. Turin: Einaudi.
De Kesel, M. (2009). *Eros and Ethics*. Albany: SUNY Press.

Johnston, A. (2021). A Mass of Fools and Knaves. In C. Zeiher (Ed.), *Stupidity and Psychoanalysis*. Lanham, MD: Rowman & Littlefield.

Kant, I. (1997). *Critique of Practical Reason*. Cambridge: Cambridge University Press.

Kant, I. (2018). *Religion within the Boundaries of Mere Reason*. Cambridge: Cambridge University Press.

Kirschner, L. A. (2012). Toward an Ethics of Psychoanalysis: A Critical Reading of Lacan's Ethics. *Journal of the American Psychoanalytic Association*, 60.

Lacan, J. (1988). *Freud's Papers on Technique: The Seminar of Jacques Lacan: Book I*. New York: W. W. Norton & Company.

Lacan, J. (1990). *Television*. New York: W. W. Norton & Company.

Lacan, J. (1991). *The Ego in Freud's Theory and in the Technique of Psychoanalysis: The Seminar of Jacques Lacan: Book II*. New York: W. W. Norton & Company.

Lacan, J. (1997). *The Ethics of Psychoanalysis: The Seminar of Jacques Lacan: Book VII*. New York: W. W. Norton & Company.

Lacan, J. (2006a). *The Other Side of Psychoanalysis: The Seminar of Jacques Lacan: Book XVII*. New York: W. W. Norton & Company.

Lacan, J. (2006b). Kant with Sade. In *Écrits*. New York: W. W. Norton & Company.

Lacan, J. (2018). *. . . or Worse: The Seminar of Jacques Lacan: Book XIX*. Cambridge: Polity Press.

Marquis de Sade, D. A. F. (1966–67). *Nouvelle Justine, Oeuvres Completes* (Vol. 7). Paris: Cercle du Livre Précieux.

Marquis de Sade, D. A. F. (1988). *Juliette*. New York: Grove Press.

Miller, J.-A. (1984–85). 1, 2, 3, 4. Unpublished Transcript.

Miller, J.-A. (1996–97). L'Autre qui n'existe pas et ses Comités d'éthique. Unpublished Transcript.

Nancy, J.-L. (2008). *Dis-Enclosure*. New York: Fordham University Press.

Nedoh, B. (2020). "Now I Become Death, Destroyer of Worlds": Science, Perversion, Psychoanalysis. *Journal for Cultural Research*, 24: 4.

Nietzsche, F. (2007). *The Anti-Christ, Ecce Homo, Twilight of the Idols*. Cambridge: Cambridge University Press.

Nobus, D. (2017). *The Law of Desire*. London: Palgrave Macmillan.

Rabinovitch, D. (2001). Le mensonge sur le mal. *Psychanalyse*, 5.

Reed, R. C. (2013). A Lacanian Ethics of Non-Responsibility. *Pastoral Psychology*, 62.

Safouan, M. (2001). *Lacaniana: 1953–1963*. Paris: Fayard.

Themi, T. (2014). *Lacan's Ethics and Nietzsche's Critique of Platonism*. Albany: SUNY Press.

Virno, P. (2021). *Convention and Materialism*. Cambridge, MA: MIT Press.

Žižek, S. (1998). Kant and Sade: The Ideal Couple. *lacanian ink*, 13.

Zupančič, A. (2000). *Ethics of the Real*. London: Verso.

Chapter 2

Ethics *Contra* Morality in Lacan's Seminar VII

(and Implications for Contemporary Education)

Jones Irwin

Introduction

Lacan's own schematic 'Outline of the Seminar' (Lacan, 1992, p. 1) allows us to develop our understanding of the specific context of Seminar VII on *The Ethics of Psychoanalysis* (1959–1960). Lacan indicates that the particular lens of 'ethics' allows to open up what is 'new' in Freud's thought to be highlighted (Lacan, ibid.). Although Lacan's thought is strikingly original and idiosyncratic, he always described his thought system as a 'return to Freud'. Lacan signals the importance of employing the term 'ethics' in his seminar, in distinction to the word 'morality'. "If I say ethics, you will soon see why" (Lacan, 1992, p. 2). The subtitles of this initial outline are also significant. The sub-theme of 'From Aristotle to Freud' indicates the genealogical and historical dimension of this study.

The iconoclastic thrust of this analysis is indicated from the very beginning of the text. By referring to the 'attraction of transgression' (*'la faute'*; Lacan, 1992, p. 1), Lacan indicates that the study of ethics in psychoanalysis is as concerned with so-called wrongdoing as it is with doing good. There are few precedents for this dual focus in the history of ethical thought, especially as, in this instance, a certain complicity seems to be also claimed with regard to evil or wrongdoing. Moreover, in invoking Aristotle's concept of 'ethics', rather than for example Plato's concept of 'morality', Lacan is making a suggestion that the ethics of psychoanalysis may have a broader remit than moral judgement. Instead, as we will see, in exploring the original Aristotelian topic (from the latter's own *Ethics*, also originally an oral seminar written down subsequently by Aristotle's students) a possibility is opened up that morality and its norms may actually be undone by the study of ethics. Effectively, this would be ethics *contra* morality. Of course, in a slightly different but related sense, this aspect of a subversion of morals is also a paradigmatic Freudian theme.

Despite Lacan's oft purported allegiance to Freud, I will argue nonetheless that the ethics of psychoanalysis in Lacan's own thought brings a strong originality to the debate. This is most striking in the connections which Lacan makes between the topic of ethics and the topic of love or 'jouissance' which he engages in his twentieth Seminar titled *On Feminine Sexuality, The Limits of Love and Knowledge*

DOI: 10.4324/9781003450795-2

(Lacan, 1998), often referred to as 'Encore'. In a famous reference, Lacan name-checks the seminar on ethics in the first sentence of his later seminar, citing a certain problematicity but also indicating an indispensable connection between the themes of ethics and 'love' or 'jouissance' in psychoanalysis (Lacan, 1998, p. 1). In looking also at how Lacan's thought relates to our contemporary situation in 2023 (both philosophically and existentially), I will also look to the very particular relation between this specific understanding of the ethical and the emergence of a relatively new discourse and practice of 'ethical education' (Irwin and Badurova, 2023) both in Ireland and internationally. Here, I will focus on both the comple-mentarity and the dissonance between Lacan's ethics of psychoanalysis, on the one side, and the relevant discourses and practices of contemporary education on the other (especially as these discourses are specifically influenced by the philosophies of Paulo Freire and John Dewey [Freire, 1996; Dewey, 1973; Irwin, 2012]). First, however let us look at some of the specifics of Seminar VII, perhaps one of Lacan's most extraordinary discussions.

The Attraction of Transgression in the Context of Seminar VII

'The Attraction of Transgression' is given as one of the first sub-themes of Seminar VII (Lacan, 1992, p. 1). As Porter notes as translator, the word *la faute* is slippery in translation, and as well as 'transgression' other equivalents might be "wrong, error, mistake to blame, misconduct and offense" (Porter, 1992, p. 1). It is perhaps surprising that Lacan should choose this as his first topic, if we were expecting a treatise on morality, but this is precisely Lacan's point when he says that we are treating of 'ethics'. Nonetheless, Lacan is also keen to clarify that his investigation of ethical and moral issues is nothing new to psychoanalysis; "it is impossible not to acknowledge that we are submerged in what are strictly speaking moral prob-lems" (Lacan, 1998, p. 2).

It is at this point that the argument takes a very specific swerve:

> our experience has led us to explore further than has been attempted before the universe of transgression. That is the expression with an extra adjective my col-league Hesnard uses; he refers to the morbid universe of transgression, and it is doubtless from this morbid point of view that we approach it at its highest point.
>
> (Lacan, 1992, p. 3)

Thus, we have 'transgression' as our key theme related somehow crucially to the domain of ethics per se. Moreover, there is a paradoxical connection here between a specific 'morbidity' but also a notion of a 'highest point' of trans-gression, as if this latter was capable of some kind of elevation. This seems on initial inspection quite confusing, to link morbidity and a high valuation of trans-gression, and moreover to make this unusual association of concepts in the very domain of ethics.

Lacan immediately goes further in his argument: "in fact what we are dealing with is nothing less than the attraction of transgression" (Lacan, 1992, p. 2). Talking to the attractiveness of transgression already indicates a certain undoing of traditional forms of moralising, and here it is clear (although unacknowledged) that the influence of Georges Bataille's thought is important on Lacan's argument. Bataille's thought is part of a Surrealist milieu which includes other dissident and radical thinkers such as Antonin Artaud (Irwin, 2010), also existing in complex relations to Lacan's practice and thought. Lacan goes on to develop an argument which seeks to distance itself from not simply traditional moralism (or 'obligation') but also from libertinism or more Enlightenment conceptions of pure individual freedom. Instead, Lacan wishes to simultaneously maintain both the sense of ethical breadth beyond moralistic obligation but also the "omnipresence of a sense of guilt" (Lacan, 1992, p. 3). We might note here that Bataille titled one of his most important texts (from 1943) *Le Coupable* (*Guilty*) (Bataille, 2011). It is this 'conflictual character' of the ethical experience which Lacan also wishes to explore and foreground. This passage also sees Lacan introduce his key concept of 'jouissance' or 'enjoyment' which will play a very significant role in his later thinking, especially in Seminar XX (Lacan, 1998).

Lacan castigates the moralistic approach to ethics, as well as the egoistic tendency in psychoanalysis, for seeking to "calm . . . the guilt . . . . the taming of perverse jouissance" (Lacan, 1992, p. 4ff). Aristotle's *Nicomachean Ethics* (Aristotle, 2009) is also cited here as a key index of a different way of thinking about the ethical. Rather than transgression being seen as an unequivocal negative aspect of human life, Lacan rather (invoking Freud's *Totem and Taboo*) indicates it as a kind of 'felix culpa' ("or happy sin") where somehow transgression becomes essential to human development and progress, even in an ethical sense (Lacan, 1992, p. 6ff.); "something to which the realm of civilisation owes its development". If this seems surprising or even shocking, we might refer to De Kesel's related pronouncement in his close book-length analysis of this same Seminar, "a psychoanalytic cure is a strange business" (De Kesel, 2009, p. 1). We might also refer to Lacan's own meta-level reading of his neo-Freudian vision: "the truth is always new" (Lacan, 2008, p. 8).

Thus, we can already see how Lacan's ethics of psychoanalysis, far from instigating some kind of new moralism, will in fact destabilise the whole edifice of traditional morality. Lacan's ethics of psychoanalysis is also an ethico-politics, of significant impact and transformatory potential. As De Kesel notes, Lacan's thought "completely shakes up all the accepted ways of thinking about good and evil and forces an entire revision of traditional ethical thought" (De Kesel, 2009, p. 5). But rather than signalling some kind of nihilism, this is rather a wellspring of ethical possibility; the idea that there is no inherent natural goodness in human beings is the only possible starting point for any (post)modern ethics, debunking both transcendent-religious moralities and, equally, secular rationalist ones.

Feeding into this new reading of the ethical is Lacan's immediately preceding seminar 'Desire and Its Interpretation' (1958–1959), which Lacan regarded as unfinished. We can also see connections further ahead to Seminar XX, on 'Love, Knowledge and Feminine Sexuality' (Lacan, 1998). De Kesel sees the connecting themes of desire, ethics and Eros (or 'love') as crucial. Lacan puts it thus: "In the irreducible margin as well as the limit of his own good, the subject reveals himself to the never entirely resolved mystery of the nature of his desire" (quoted in De Kesel, 2009, p. 4). This leads De Kesel to title his book on this Seminar, *Eros and Ethics*; "our relation to morality is fundamentally libidinal" (De Kesel, 2009, p. 6). What emerges in this reading of the seminar is that Lacan's engagement with the historical tradition of moral philosophy, whilst critiquing substantive notions of the Good, nonetheless retains a link to specific ethical theories (such as those of Kant and Aristotle). Both the latter thinkers on ethics revolutionise our understanding of the moral universe of humanity, with Aristotle's move away from Plato's Good to a concept of *eudaimonia* ('flourishing' or 'happiness'), while Kant's philosophy enacts a 'Copernican revolution' in foregrounding a universal subjectivity which structures our very understanding of the moral life.

Nonetheless, in both instances, something further is required. Key to this something further will be the Lacanian notion of 'jouissance': "He will discover that that basic difference between the 'ethics of psychoanalysis' and Kant's moral obligation is to be located in the notion of enjoyment (jouissance)" (De Kesel, 2009, p. 9). How might we understand the implications for ethics per se? What develops as the seminar evolves is an 'ethics of the singular', that is an ethics that is not centred on general or universalisable rules, but on a 'singular enjoyment' that can be said to withdraw from all forms of generality or universality. As Lacan develops the argument here, the concept of the 'aesthetic' (also so crucial for Kant and of course for Nietzsche) and the concept of 'sublimation', linked more directly to a 'return to Freud', will become fundamental.

Lacan's development of his thinking on the ethical in this context is nuanced and complex. It is also not without significant ambiguity and difficulty of interpretation. Dennis Porter's 'Translator's Note' (Porter, 1992) to Lacan's seminar (Lacan, 1992) foregrounds some of the specific aspects of importance in the way Lacan addressed such topics in his seminars. In the first case, the audience of the seminars was very familiar with Lacan's thought which allows the discussion to be both allusive and to use a complex pedagogy, making extra demands on the listener. Second, as an oral presentation (not written down or published by Lacan himself but edited later by key students) there is a certain kind of process at work. Porter refers to it as the "excitement . . . of encounter with a thought in the making" (Porter, 1992, p. viii). Third, as the seventh seminar in the series, Lacan often refers back to previous themes and discussions and this inter-textual dimension is both a key aspect and also part of the difficulty and complexity of interpretation.

Nonetheless, despite these layers of hermeneutic and pedagogic subtlety, the broad conceptual contours are fairly clear. In focusing in Seminar VI on the question of 'desire', what emerges in Seminar VII is in the first instance an attempt to critique the reading of psychoanalysis (and of Freud) which would see the function of the latter as a becalming or therapy for desire. This is precisely the paradox of

Seminar VII. In invoking a concept of 'ethics' which he had previously excluded from his reading of Freud, Lacan might give the initial impression that he is seeking to develop a moralisation of desire. Nothing could be further from the truth. Instead, this new foregrounding of ethics is also a re-reading of 'ethics with desire' which can be seen (*contra* attempts to domesticate both categories) as actually freeing up these categories from their previous understanding. "From a Freudian point of view, the reality principle is presented as functioning in a way that is essentially precarious" (Lacan, 1992, p. 30). Lacan contrasts the Freudian reading of 'reality' or the human world with both realism and idealism. "Idealism consists in affirming that we are the ones who give shape to reality, and that there is no point in looking any further. It is a comfortable position. Freud's position . . . . is something very different" (Lacan, 1992, p. 30).

Instead of the ethics of psychoanalysis representing some kind of reunification with the world or reality, it rather constitutes a reawakening to the precarity of existential life. "Reality is precarious. And it is precisely to the extent that access to it is so precarious that the commandments which trace its path are so tyrannical. As guides to the real, feelings are deceptive" (Lacan, ibid.). When Lacan thus tells us that the kernel of the *psyche* is 'ethical through and through', this is a rather more destabilising tenet than it may first appear to be. In connecting desire to ethics, both are radicalised beyond previous identifications – this in effect is what Lacan means by the 'scandal' of psychoanalysis (De Kesel, 2009, p. 48). This is an ethics which is vehemently *contra* morality and morals, at least when the latter are understood conventionally. Additionally, Lacan is clear that the discussion which follows cannot lead to any practical or applied ethics on the basis of psychoanalysis. It is wholly unclear how Lacan's work in this context might give us any insights with regard how to act or how to live our lives in a better or a different way. The therapeutic dimension of Freudianism (significantly popular at the time of the Seminar, late 1950s onwards) is being thoroughly disavowed by Lacan at this juncture. Instead, this enigmatic juxtaposition of ethics and desire sees something different emergent: "To lend an ear to the unruly, impossible desire we are" (De Kesel, 2009, p. 52). Instead of therapy, we appear to have an accumulation of *paradox, aporia* and, finally, *impasse*. In the next section, I will explore some of the implications of this radical reinterpretation of psychoanalysis.

The Implications of Lacan's Reading of Transgression in the Seminar

The implications, as developed by Lacan further into Seminar VII, are stark: "The step taken by Freud is to show that there is no Sovereign Good" (Lacan, 1992, p. 70). This is brought to a head in chapter VII, 'Drives and Lures', where Lacan traces the critique of 'moral conscience in Freudian thought:

> The moral conscience . . . shows itself to be the more demanding the more refined it becomes, crueler and crueler even as we offend it less and less . . . . In

short, the insatiable character of this moral conscience, its paradoxical cruelty, transforms it within the individual into a parasite that is fed by the satisfactions accorded it.

(Lacan, 1992, p. 89)

Freud had spoken in *Civilisation and Its Discontents* overtly of a "very special quality of malice, of bad influence – that is the meaning of the French word *méchant*" (Lacan, 1992, p. 89). This argument is very reminiscent of Nietzsche's internalist critique of morality in his *On the Genealogy of Morals*, the upshot of which is that morality is not in fact what it says it is (i.e., the good) but actually the opposite; morality is a kind of evil perpetrated by the human being against itself. Lacan uses the paradigmatic example of the classical play by Terence, translated as either 'He Who Punishes Himself' or 'The Self Tormentor' (Lacan, 1992, p. 89).

One may wonder where this discussion on the 'ethics of psychoanalysis' is going to lead. We might refer here to Lacan's later Seminar XX where the positions are slightly revised but the psychoanalytical message remains continuous. In the first section of that Seminar, titled 'On Jouissance' (and very much developing the thematics from Seminar VII), "jouissance is what serves no purpose" (Lacan, 1998, p. 3). A further relevant point is made such that "analysis does not allow us to remain at the level of what I began with, respectfully of course – namely, Aristotle's ethics" (Lacan, 1998, p. 3). This lack of purpose, guided by Lacan's key concept of 'jouissance', also already in Seminar VII is therefore unlikely to lead to any definitive conclusions. In Miller's edition of the seminar, he brings the last three sections together into what is termed 'The Tragic Dimension of Psychoanalytic Experience' (Lacan, 1992, p. 291ff.). Lacan indicates at the outset that what will follow, short of definitive conclusions, will rather be 'inconclusive observations' or 'paradoxes' (Lacan, 1992, p. 321ff.). Central to this final discussion of the ethics of psychoanalysis will be the reintroduction of the concept of 'desire' which had already been the main topic of the previous seminar. Here, the concepts of desire and ethics are intrinsically connected by Lacan, such that

it is because we know better than those who went before how to recognize the nature of desire . . . that a reconsideration of ethics is possible . . . that a form of ethical judgement is possible . . . . Have you acted in conformity with the desire that is in you?

(Lacan, 1992, p. 314)

In an important discussion of this paradigmatic moment in Seminar VII, De Kesel points out how this discussion on desire by Lacan is often turned into a kind of "categorical imperative, such that Lacan would be replacing the Kantian Categorical Imperative with a Categorical Imperative of 'Freud's Copernican Revolution'" (De Kesel is citing Critchley's reading here; De Kesel, 2009, p. 262ff.). This passage is therefore often misquoted as an actual imperative such that '*ne pas céder sur son désir*' ('don't give ground relative to your desire') becomes the ethical ground. For De Kesel, however, Lacanian psychoanalysis can furnish no such pre-scriptions. Rather the ethics of psychoanalysis as delineated here in the final pages of Seminar VII is far more recalcitrant and paradoxical. "An ethics that decenters the existing moral measure through reference to the other 'immeasurable measure' can only leave a mass of paradoxes in its wake" (De Kesel, 2009, p. 263). This of course is also the 'tragic' dimension of Lacanian ethics. These last pages seek to give us an image of ourselves, but nonetheless this image rather points to how our very fundamental 'desire' eludes us or escapes us at the very same moment. This is also the paradoxical quality of Lacanian ethics, that we are given the possibility of confronting ourselves in the sphere where we usually disappear or are hidden to ourselves. And at the same time, the paradox is that such a confrontation is effec-tively impossible. "It offers a paralyzing image that forbids us from taking it as an example, and through the anamorphic structure confronts us with the impossibility of being present at that which we see" (De Kesel, 2009, p. 268).

It is striking that as Lacan brings his Seminar to an 'inconclusive' conclusion under the sub-title of 'the paradoxes of ethics', that he should invoke as an ana-logue to the process he is describing as an ethical psychoanalysis that of the ancient Greek 'catharsis' (Lacan, 1992, p. 322). This kind of catharsis in psychoanalysis of the Lacanian variety, just as in the case of Greek tragedy, will not be 'pacificatory' (Lacan, 1992, p. 333).

> It is in this respect that the great religious work is distinguished from what goes on in an ethical form of catharsis . . . . Purification cannot be accomplished unless one has at least established the crossing of its limits . . . that the subject learns a little more about the deepest level of himself than he knew before.
>
> (ibid.)

Ethics is thus a 'crossing of limits' but one which must be distinguished from, for example religious logic, in that the latter seeks a 'recuperation' (Lacan, 1992, p. 332), whereas the ethical catharsis involves a necessary kind of incompletion or dispossession. If you are seeking some kind of science of desire or of ethics, Lacan warns, there can only be dissatisfaction at the end of Seminar VII: "Science, which occupies the place of desire, can only be a science of desire in the form of an enormous question mark" (Lacan, 1992, p. 325). In this, we might say that Lacan and psychoanalysis have succeeded in being more authentically philosophical than the history of philosophers and philosophy itself. In the next section, I will explore some of the potential affinities and disaffinities which such an approach can be said to have with more recent examples of ethical education.

Applying Lacan's Ethics to a Critique of Contemporary Ethical Education

As discussed above, the genealogy of the ethical which Lacan outlines in the semi-nar seeks to complexify the reading of Freud (effectively against the contemporary

Freudianism) and to dissociate it from a simple therapeutic solution or appeasement. Similarly, in connecting this reading of Freud back to Aristotle's ethical thought (Aristotle, 2009), there is a redeployment of the Aristotelian concept of 'katharsis' or catharsis. In this reading, catharsis signifies incompletion and a questioning of scientific closure or conclusiveness. On first inspection, this can seem to be quite a negative interpretation of the ethical, and one can wonder at how it might make any sense for contemporary ethicists or moral thinkers or activists. However, there are (perhaps surprisingly) some very strong affinities between this thinking of the ethics of psychoanalysis in Lacan and some emergent conceptions of ethical education in contemporary pedagogy.

Terence McLaughlin, the values and religious education theorist, refers to contemporary schooling as being "engaged in a practical enterprise of great complexity which calls for many forms of practical knowledge" (McLaughlin, 2008, p. 204). Ethos in schools is a multi-layered concept and reality which, as McLaughlin suggests, calls for subtle educational understanding and practice. We might further speak of there being multiplied layers of ethos in schools, which can extend from issues of curriculum and teaching to issues of organisation and administration to the complex of what Norman calls the 'expressive culture' of a school, its various interpersonal levels and relationalities (Norman, 2003). In such a variegated context of education, Lacan's ethics of psychoanalysis begins to have more pertinence than what we might have imagined at first.

It is certainly true that more traditional forms of education and of moral education have sought to instantiate universal and unequivocal norms for educational practice. In the twentieth century, philosophers of education such as John Dewey and Paulo Freire sought to deconstruct such normativity in the name of student and educational freedoms. In seminal works such as Dewey's *Experience and Education* (Dewey, 1973) and Freire's *Pedagogy of the Oppressed* (Freire, 1996), these thinkers pointed to the inherent tensions and contradictions at the heart of the educational project. Significantly for our purposes, both Dewey and Freire, while critical of traditional education (what Dewey called 'traditionalism' and what Freire called 'banking education') were simultaneously critical of what became known as 'progressivism' or modernist, progressive forms of education. For both Freire and Dewey, progressivism simply inverted the values of the tradition and ran into equally intractable problems when it sought to address the complexity and nuance of authentic educational processes and actors. In this, Dewey and Freire have a significant amount in common with Lacan's own trajectory away from both traditional morality but also equally as seeking a distance from modernist or liberatory new moralities (De Kesel, 2009, p. 5).

While the style of argument is somewhat different, and the emphasis on intractability more vehement, in Lacan, nonetheless there is an analogous emphasis on paradox, contradiction and aporia in education by both Dewey and Freire. When it comes to questions of the ethical or of ethical education, this ambiguity becomes all the more relevant to the discussion. As Aristotle noted in his *Ethics*, the study of humanity "is not an exact science" (Aristotle, 2009). In the study of education, this critique emerges in the central discussion of the relation between the respective concepts of 'authority' on the one side and 'freedom' on the other.

The misuse of authority in education and wider society is described by Freire in *Pedagogy of the Oppressed* under the example of what he refers to famously as 'banking education'. In looking at banking education, Freire pays particular attention to what he calls the 'Teacher-Student contradiction' and the 'A-J of Banking Education' (Freire, 1996; Irwin, 2012). Thus, traditional forms of education set up an opposition or 'contradiction' between the omnipotent power of the teacher as authority and the passivity and powerlessness of the student. This represents the value of authority as *authoritarian* – authority is only itself when it is one-way; "the teacher presents him or herself to the students as their necessary opposite; by considering their ignorance absolute, he or she justifies his/her own existence" (Freire, 1996, p. 53). We can all recognise this aspect of Freire's critique of traditional methods of education and his poignant portrait of the psychology of such oppression in his own society in Brazil is extremely powerful and moving (sadly repeated today in Brazil through the former regime of Bolsanaro).

And yet we can say that perhaps this is also the least philosophically interesting of Freire's points in the book for, to the extent that Freire is critiquing traditional forms of authority, he is saying little that is relatively new. This critique of traditional forms of authoritarianism in education and the socio-political sphere is a mainstay of radical traditions in education and philosophy (it also constitutes one aspect of Lacan's own critique of traditional forms of moral philosophy and psychology described above).

But there is another dimension to this critique of authority which is more original in Freire, and which draws his thinking on education closer to Lacan's understanding of the paradoxical nature of the ethics of psychoanalysis. We can already discern this aspect in Freire's 'A-J' of banking education. In the first principles of this conception, we can see the traditional authoritarianism clearly evident.

A. the teacher knows everything and the students know nothing
B. the teacher talks and the students listen – meekly
C. the teacher disciplines and the students are disciplined.

(Freire, 1996)

Here, the authority is all-encompassing and unquestioned, students reduced to powerlessness and meekness, and the suggestion of force or even violence is present in the descriptions of discipline (one thinks of the usage of corporal punishment in traditional education and of the use of violence in colonial society, the latter described vividly by Freire here). But in the developing principles of banking education, one also sees a different emphasis, on what might be considered a more hidden or ideological form of authoritarianism.

D. the teacher acts and the students have the illusion of acting through the action of the teacher
E. the teacher confuses the authority of knowledge with his or her professional authority, which she and he sets in opposition to the freedom of the students.

(Freire, 1996)

Here, the concept of 'illusion' is used for the first time, and we see Freire's fore-grounding of a certain kind of deception or 'ideology' which can be at work in the use of authority. In the case of principle D, Freire is suggesting that nonauthoritar-ian or progressive forms of teaching, ones where the students are supposedly given freedom to 'act', can sometimes mask a more hidden authoritarian aspect; there is just the 'illusion' of freedom, of the possibility of action. Freire seems intent on focusing on residual aspects of the banking mindset in education and politics which can continue to determine even attempts to move beyond and transform traditional approaches. In his later work, for example in *Pedagogy of Hope: Reliving Peda-gogy of the Oppressed* (Freire, 1992), this critical analysis of progressivism turns into an unsparing self-critique, but here his critical analysis is more at the concep-tual level. Freire makes an important distinction between what he refers to as 'sec-tarianism' on the one side and 'radicalisation' on the other. The 'rightist sectarian' attempts to domesticate the present and hopes that the future will simply reproduce this domesticated present. The 'leftist sectarian', in contrast, considers the future pre-established. Both are caught within a fatalistic position or a 'circle of certainty' and both 'negate freedom' (Freire, 1996, p. 19). Thus, such 'sectarian' approaches are not sufficient to go beyond traditional forms of education and politics but rather simply reinforce and repeat them.

Certainly, the critique of the more obvious forms of banking education and poli-tics must be made, where a clear binarism exists between teacher authority and student passivity – thus, A, the teacher knows everything and the students know nothing (Freire, 1996). However, such an objectifying and authoritarian mindset and politics can also be present when we seem to have gone beyond such authority completely. The banking mentality and ideology may also be a hidden component of a progressive education and politics. In this context, we see Freire connect-ing with Dewey's critique of progressivism in *Experience and Education* (Dewey, 1973), where Dewey argues against the 'either/or' option of traditionalism and pro-gressivism as binary alternatives in education and in philosophy. Instead, Dewey argues for a 'both/and'.

But if we critique the traditional authority of education while simultaneously critiquing the emphasis on a supposed freedom in progressivism, what is our third alternative and what happens to the value of authority per se? We can see Freire's dilemma here as analogous to Lacan's dilemma in eschewing both traditional forms of morality on the one side but also anti-moral libertinage on the other. Here, the last principle cited above of Freire's analysis of banking education becomes important: E, "the teacher confuses the authority of knowledge with his or her professional authority, which she and he sets in opposition to the freedom of the students" (Freire, 1996). This statement from Freire is significant because, as with Dewey, Freire is seeking to defend a conception of 'authority' in education and politics – 'the authority of knowledge' – while eschewing the simple identification of this authority with professional authority. It is this latter which must be far more suspiciously critiqued. But the danger of this professionalisation of authority ('the circle of certainty') applies not simply to traditional forms of banking education but also to forms of supposedly emancipatory education, where its repressiveness may be hidden.

For Freire, this tendency to a hidden authoritarianism can thus be fatal for the progressive educator, or at least the one who wishes to be radical rather than sectarian:

the radical, committed to human liberation, does not become the prisoner of a "circle of certainty" within which he also imprisons reality. On the contrary, the more radical he is, the more fully he enters into reality so that, knowing it better, he can better transform it. He is not afraid to confront, to listen, to see the world unveiled. He is not afraid to meet the people or to enter into dialogue with them.

(Freire, 1996, p. 21)

Freire adds here a reference to Rosa Luxemburg: "as long as theoretic knowledge remains the privilege of a handful of academicians in the party, the latter will face the danger of going astray" (quoted in Freire, 1996, p. 21).

Crucial to this notion of radical education, then, is the notion of authentic communication and a critique of the paternalism which destroys all authentic communication. Of course, this sets up a major dilemma for radical education or education and politics which seeks to go beyond banking education and beyond oppression. Too often, the previously oppressed can become the future oppressors, where there is simply a role reversal rather than any authentic transformation of the oppression into real freedom and hope. The question thus becomes: *how can a more authentic practice of authority emerge in radical education which does not simply return us to a newer form of oppression, a more subtle version of authoritarianism and misuse of power?* This is the dilemma which Freire's later work seeks to resolve. It also has a clear connection to Lacan's critique of the therapeutic interpretation of Freudianism and psychoanalysis, and his attempt in the seminar to explore a less obvious path.

Concluding Thoughts

When Lacan tells us in his seminar that, in distinction to the word 'morality', "If I say ethics, you will soon see why" (Lacan, 1992, p. 2), we are introduced to the radicality of his renewal of this problem. Nonetheless, those seeking through a reading of the *Ethics of Psychoanalysis* some kind of resolution or set of answers to the problematicity of existence are to be wholly disappointed. In this chapter, I have explored the complexity of Lacan's analyses in the seminar, especially as they relate to his theme of the 'attraction of transgression' but also in the way in which this analysis speaks to a more meta-level understanding of the project of psychoanalysis itself. By referring to the 'attraction of transgression' (*'la faute'*; Lacan, 1992, p. 1), Lacan indicates that the study of ethics in psychoanalysis is as concerned with so-called wrongdoing as it is with doing good. A possibility is opened up that morality and its norms may actually be undone by the study of ethics.

In exploring a new discourse of education (through a reading of Freire's thought particularly), I have foregrounded how a similar deconstruction of traditional conceptions of morality and authority emerges. In *Pedagogy of Hope: Reliving Pedagogy of the Oppressed* (Freire, 1992), Freire addresses this problem head-on. The subtitle gives us his methodology here – we must 'relive' the task of emancipation, it must remain a process and must never become objectified or turn into a formula. When Freire was asked to consider whether he continued to adhere to the framework of *Pedagogy of the Oppressed* in his later work, into the 1990s (the interview is from 1994): "If you were to ask me, "are you attempting to put into practice the concepts you described in your book [*Pedagogy of the Oppressed*]?", *of course I am*, but in a manner in keeping with the times" (Freire and Torres, 1994, p. 106).

The iconoclastic thrust of Lacan's analysis of ethics also speaks to this contemporaneity. Lacanian ethics *contra* morality, as it is paradoxically formulated in the seminar, can seem forbidding and somewhat difficult to imagine as a practice in the real world. But in exploring a specific example from contemporary education, this chapter has sought to draw an analogy between Freire's simultaneous critique of authority and of (pure) freedom and Lacan's critique. In both, there is continuity and discontinuity. In *Pedagogy of Hope* (Freire, 1992), the subtitle of 're-living' certainly suggests the need to reflect again on one's previous presuppositions from a different time, but in the 're-' there is also the sense of continuity, of return and a certain need to go back to the source. In a related way, Lacan's ethics *contra* morality, this aspect of a subversion of morals, is also a paradigmatic Freudian theme (a 'return to Freud'). Both seek a kind of 'catharsis' through radical critique of both the status quo (or 'tradition') and of its purported supposed alternative resolution. In this, both Lacan and Freire seek new understandings of our human condition which will nonetheless not be 'pacificatory' (Lacan, 1992, p. 333).

Bibliography

Aristotle (2009). *Ethics*. Oxford: Oxford University Press.

Badiou, A. (2006). Lacan and the Presocratics. In S. Žižek (Ed.), *Lacan: The Silent Partners* (pp. 1–15). London: Verso.

Barnard, S. (2002). Introduction. In S. Bernard and B. Fink (Eds.), *Reading Seminar XX: Lacan's Major Work on Love, Knowledge and Feminine Sexuality*. New York: SUNY Press.

Barnard, S. and Fink, B. (2002). *Reading Seminar XX: Lacan's Major Work on Love, Knowledge and Feminine Sexuality*. New York: SUNY Press.

Bataille, G. (2011). *Guilty*. New York: SUNY Press.

Bowie, M. (1991). *Lacan*. London: Fontana.

De Kesel, M. (2009). *Eros and Ethics: Reading Lacan's Seminar VII*. New York: SUNY Press.

Derrida, J. (1972). *Writing and Difference*. Trans. A. Bass. Chicago: Chicago University Press.

Dewey, J. (1973). *Experience and Education*. New York: Collier Books.

Dolar, M. (1989). The Unconscious is Structured as Yugoslavia. *Mladina*, Ljubljana, 15–30.

Dolar, M. (1998). Cogito as the Subject of the Unconscious. In *Cogito and the Unconscious* (pp. 11–40). Durham and London: Duke University Press.

Freire, P. (1992). *Pedagogy of Hope: Reliving Pedagogy of the Oppressed*. Trans. R. Barr. London: Continuum.

Freire, P. (1996). *Pedagogy of the Oppressed*. London: Continuum.

Freire, P. and Torres, C. A. (1994). Twenty Years After Pedagogy of the Oppressed: Paulo Freire in Conversation with Carlos Alberto Torres. In M. P. Laren and C. Lankshear (Eds.), *Politics of Liberation: Paths from Freire*. London: Routledge.

Freud, S. (2002). Civilisation and Its Discontents. In *The Standard Edition of the Complete Psychological Works of Sigmund Freud* (Vol. XXI). London: Vintage.

Ganter, P. (1993). Discussions on Civil Society in Slovenia. In G. Graziano and A. Bilic (Eds.), *Civil Society, Political Society, Democracy* (pp. 350–365). Ljubljana: Slovenian Political Science Association.

Irwin, J. (2010). *Derrida and the Writing of the Body*. Surrey: Ashgate. (New Paperback edition 2016, London: Routledge).

Irwin, J. (2012). *Paulo Freire's Philosophy of Education: Origins, Developments, Impacts and Legacies*. London and New York: Continuum and Bloomsbury.

Irwin, J. and Badurova, B. (2023). *Ethical Education Across European Systems: Concepts, Practices, Dilemmas*. Berlin and Geneva: Peter Lang.

Irwin, J. and Motoh, H. (2014). *Žižek And His Contemporaries: On the Emergence of the Slovenian Lacan*. London: Bloomsbury.

Irwin, J., Žižek, S., and Motoh, H. (2014). From Lacan to Hegel – Interview with Slavoj Žižek. In J. Irwin and H. Motoh (Eds.), *Žižek and His Contemporaries: The Emergence of the Slovenian Lacan*. London and New York: Bloomsbury.

Irwin, J., Zupančič, A., and Motoh, H. (2014). Encountering Lacan in the Next Generation – Interview with Alenka Zupančič. In J. Irwin and H. Motoh (Eds.), *Žižek and His Contemporaries: The Emergence of the Slovenian Lacan*. London and New York: Bloomsbury.

Lacan, J. (1992). *The Ethics of Psychoanalysis: 1959–1960: The Seminar of Jacques Lacan Book VII*. London: W. W. Norton & Company.

Lacan, J. (1994). *The Four Fundamental Concepts of Psychoanalysis*. London: Penguin Books.

Lacan, J. (1998). On Feminine Sexuality: The Limits of Love and Knowledge, 1972–1973. In J.-A. Miller (Ed.), *ENCORE: The Seminar of Jacques Lacan Book XX*. Trans. with notes by B. Fink. London: W. W. Norton & Company.

Lacan, J. (2008). *My Teaching*. London: Verso.

Laclau, E. (1989). Preface. In *The Sublime Object of Ideology* (pp. ix–xv). London: Verso.

Macey, D. (1988). *Lacan in Contexts*. London: Verso.

McLaughlin, T. H. (2008). The Ethics of Separate Schools. In D. Carr, M. Halstead, and R. Pring (Eds.), *Liberalism, Education and Schooling, Essays by T. H. McLaughlin* (pp. 175–198). Exeter: Imprint.

Norman, J. (2003). *Ethos and Education in Ireland*. New York: Peter Lang.

Porter, D. (1992). Translator's Note. In J. Lacan (Ed.), *The Ethics of Psychoanalysis: 1959–1960: The Seminar of Jacques Lacan Book VII*. London: W. W. Norton & Company.

Žižek, S. (1989). *The Sublime Object of Ideology*. London: Verso.

Žižek, S. (1992). *Enjoy Your Symptom: Jacques Lacan in Hollywood and Out* (First edition). London: Routledge.

Žižek, S. (1994). Introduction: The Spectre of Ideology. In S. Žižek (Ed.), *Mapping Ideology* (pp. 1–33). London: Verso.

Žižek, S. (2006a). *Lacan*. London: Granta.

Žižek, S. (2006b). *Lacan: The Silent Partners*. London: Verso.

Žižek, S. and Daly, G. (2003). *Conversations with Žižek*. Cambridge: Polity Press.

Zupančič, A. (2000). *Ethics of the Real: Kant, Lacan*. London: Verso.

Zupančič, A. (2008). *Why Psychoanalysis? Three Interventions*. Uppsala: NSU Press.

Chapter 3

Courtly Love, the *Hommosexuelle*, and the Hysteric in *The Ethics* of Lacan

Sheila L. Cavanagh

In the *Ethics of Psychoanalysis* (1959–1960) Lacan uses the example of courtly love to illustrate the centrality of desire to the psychoanalytic project. It is para-doxical that Lacan would choose a model of love based on unrequited love to illustrate the operation of desire. But desire, for Lacan, circles an enigmatic *Thing* (*das Ding*) that later, in his seminar *Encore* of 1972–1973, he will equate with the idea of *la Femme n'existe pas* (The Woman does not exist). What becomes clear in Lacan's teachings is that desire is fated to miss its object. The Woman, like the exalted Lady of courtly love, is missed in a ritualized fashion. She does not exist but has a function. As I will illustrate in what follows, courtly love, which Lacan describes as an elegant way to deal with the sexual impasse, is modelled upon phal-lic jouissance. But this phallic jouissance has what Lacan calls a *hommosexuelle* and hysterical component (1998, p. 85). The idealized Lady is a support for the masculine position (defined not by gender, but by unconscious sexuality), but the courtly tradition elevates the Woman to the status of the phallus which has under-studied implications for women. Although all sexuated subjects experience phallic jouissance (relating to the 'a') (Lacan, 1998), the Lady (object of courtly love) camouflages the sexual non-rapport for the male-masculine subject in ways that render heterosexuality perverse (as opposed to natural).[1] Courtly love is explicated from the masculine side of love that Lacan will more fully elaborate upon in his seminars on *Feminine Sexuality, The Limits of Love and Knowledge, Seminar XX* (1972–1973) and in *Les Non-dupes Errant, Seminar XXI* (1973–1974), but in what ways does it make sense from the feminine side?

The first iteration of Lacan's musings on courtly love were presented in a lecture he gave at the *Société Française de Psychanalyse* in 1960 titled "Courtly Love as Anamorphosis" (Lacan, 2013). There are a few brief references to courtly love in his lectures on the Freudian case of the homosexual woman which he gives in 1957. These references concern not only what Freud called a *männliche* (a Ger-man word meaning masculine or virile) object choice, but the way the homosexual woman's love is both sacred and structured by lack. While Lacan will not give his lectures on feminine sexuality until the early 1970s (and does not return to the case of the homosexual woman in the now famous lecture of 1960 on courtly love), there are important antecedents in the *Ethics* seminar that I foreground in

DOI: 10.4324/9781003450795-3

my discussion. In *Encore* Lacan writes that courtly love is the only way for the man to "withdraw himself with elegance from the absence of the sexual rapport" (Lacan, 1998, p. 65). Although courtly love is a masculine solution to the sexual non-rapport, questions relating to the Woman, and to feminine desire, begin and underlay Lacan's exposition. In the *Ethics* seminar Lacan asks, following Freud, "What does woman want?" Or more precisely, "What does she desire?" (Lacan, 2013, p. 9). Lacan says that "analytic experience has if anything stifled, silenced, and evaded those areas of the problem of sexuality which related to the point of view of feminine demand" (2013, p. 9). Despite the centrality of the masculine courtier in Lacan's musings on courtly love, the Woman and the feminine are not absent. He puts the Woman in the place of the *Thing* as the origin of desire. He says that "to place in this beyond a creature such as woman [as the artisans of courtly love have done] is a truly incredible idea" (p. 214).

Scholars have laboured over the question of Antigone and how the *Ethics* seminar ends with attention to her radical act, her unwavering desire in the face of a tyrannical King (Butler, 2000, Söderbäck, 2010, Cavanagh, 2017), but less attention has been devoted to the status of the feminine (object) in relation to the *Thing* (*das Ding*) at stake in courtly love. Lacan defines the *Thing* as a Real lack. He also says that "*das Ding*. . . is the mother, [and] also the object of incest . . . a forbidden good, and that there is no other good" (Lacan, 2013, p. 70). In this chapter, I elaborate upon the feminine *Thing* of concern to Lacan's analysis of courtly love. In so doing, I discuss the Lady of courtly love, anamorphosis, and sublimation to foreground my discussion of the *hommosexuelle* and hysterical components of courtly love.

Courtly Love

In 1883 Gaston Paris, a French medievalist, coined the term courtly love (*amour courtois*) (Lewis, 1936). But courtly love is older than its name. It was a mode of courtship developed by the troubadours[2] that shaped ideas, fantasies, and practices of love in Languedoc toward the end of the eleventh century (Denomy, 1965). Much of what we know about courtly love comes from Andreas who between 1186 and 1190 wrote *De Amore*, the three books on courtly love. This style of courtship is said to have been perfected in the castles of Ducal Burgundy, Provence, Aquitaine, and Champagne (Ali, 2013, p. 11) and practiced throughout Europe in the eleventh and twelfth centuries. Courtly love, as understood by Paris, involved an

> illicit, furtive, and extra conjugal liaison that placed the lover in the service of and at the mercy of a haughty and capricious lady, a state that inspired courageous feats and refined behavior, an art governed by highly codified rules of proper conduct, analogous to the tenets regulating chivalry.
>
> (Burns, 2001, p. 29)

Jane Burns contends that what is now called romantic love emerged during the medieval period where "unsuccessful love trysts" (Burns, 2001, p. 24) were analysed by love courts.

Although some medievalists cast doubt upon the legitimacy of the institution, whether courtly love existed as a practice (Benton, 1961, 1968; Donaldson, 1970; Robertson, 1968), it captures the imagination of historians and psychoanalysts alike.[3] In her discussion of desire and language in medieval studies and the controversies surrounding courtly love, Toril Moi (1986) suggests that the archive of courtly love may not document historical reality but that like the Lacanian Real, it has an asymptotic relationship to history. As such, courtly love produces a reality of its own and demands to be read and interpreted as a metonym of desire.

Lacanian psychoanalysis is not unlike courtly love. Both engage something Real and unrepresentable of relevance to sexuality. Like the troubadour who waxes poetic about the Lady until she dismisses him (Moi, 1986, p. 24), the analysand in the Lacanian clinic talks until a scansion (a cut) is made. Both analysand and courtesan suffer in and through the language of the Other. They do not seek sex (exactly), but some*thing* to be resolved at the level of the Other's discourse. Just like the courtly lover analyses the Lady, knowing full well that his fate depends upon her word of approval or reproach, the analyst knows that desire revolves around an enigmatic *Thing* that must be approached via language and interpreted.

Courtly love has been a subject not only of Lacanian exposition, but feminist historical inquire and debate. Medieval courtships involved unauthorized heterosexual liaisons between aristocratic couples, but it was the man's sexual prowess and reputation that was at stake. Little is said and known about the woman as subject (as opposed to idol) in the courtships. Feminist historians take issue with the treatment of women in the medieval period, and feminist psychoanalysts have taken issue with Lacan's formalization of the Woman as the *Thing* (*das Ding*) (see for example Ettinger, 1993). From a feminist perspective, the reduction of the exalted Lady to a homogenous and idealized object, as opposed to a living, breathing, heterogeneous subject, smacks of sexism and misogynist fantasy. But Lacan did not idealize the Woman or reduce her to an object-*Thing* so much as he interpreted the process through which this reduction occurs at the level of masculine fantasy. Without dismissing important feminist criticism relating to the way Lacan theorizes the Woman from the masculine perspective, as opposed to the feminine perspective, we must be clear about the fact that he means to offer an analysis of phallocentrism, which is different from endorsing it.

Lacanian feminists believe that Lacanian ethics tell us something not only about masculine sexuality (which is not exclusive to men), but about the asymmetry of love and the artistry of making do with the impasse. Although non-Lacanian feminists do not typically cast courtly love in a favourable light, feminists influenced by Lacanian psychoanalytic theory are more likely to conclude that the demise of courtly love does not serve women well. In modern culture we lose an ideal of love to palliate the sexual non-rapport. In Colette Soler's view, "Contemporary love has been orphaned by its myths and reduced to the mere contingency of encounters" (2016, p. 151). Likewise, Julia Kristeva (1987) suggests that what is at stake in courtly love is not the woman (as object of adoration) but the maintenance of an idealizing space, a space for love and jouissance enabled by the sexual non-rapport. What Kristeva calls the amatory space of passion is foreclosed upon by scientific reason, secularization, and the march of progress. As she explains, the "main theme of the [courtly love] text appears to be not the psychological initiative of a free individual nor his obstacles but the very space of passion – amatory space" (Kristeva, 1987, p. 293).

The amatory space theorized by Kristeva is what Lacan insists upon when he argues that desire is central to the ethics of psychoanalysis. As he says, "[F] rom an analytic point of view, the only thing one can be guilty of is having given ground relative to one's desire" (Lacan, 2013, p. 319). In the contemporary state of (modern) affairs (interpersonal and otherwise), we have, in Lacanian terms, ceded ground relevant to desire. What is unique about Lacan's approach to ethics, and why I insist upon a reading of his ethics in relation to the feminine, is that there is something about the Woman in his oeuvre that can tell us much about unconscious sexuality. What compels psychoanalytic theorists Bracha L. Ettinger, Julia Kristeva, Geneviève Morel, Ellie Ragland, Collette Soler, and others to engage with his work is that he admits to the complexities of the feminine sexual position and does not shy away from the realities of the sexual impasse in the heterosexual courting ritual that involves, among other things, the making of actual women into object-*Things* at the level of fantasy.

Lacan on Courtly Love

Lacan refers to courtly love as a Christian style of love involving the exaltation of woman (Lacan, 2013, p. 99). While the "cult of the idealized object" (p. 99) has existed since antiquity, Lacan is concerned with the way the courtier pursues the Woman as unattainable object. It must be stressed that Lacan is not castigating male courtiers for pursuing unattainable women in the way a psychologist committed to the setting of 'realistic goals' in their patients' love relationships may do. Lacan is, rather, identifying a historically unprecedented way of negotiating the sexual impasse that concerns us all regardless of whether we are in so-called healthy, monogamous, and marital relationships or not.

What amazes Lacan about courtly love, what he regards as entirely new about the artifice surrounding it, is that it delineates the truth of the sexual non-relation. He describes courtly love as formidable and unprecedented, comparing its dalliances and performative inconsistencies to a "meteor in history" (Lacan, 1998, p. 86). It is no secret that contradictions puncture the discourse of courtly love and that the troubadours give form to something Real (unrepresentable). As Julia Kristeva explains in her discussion of the troubadours and their reverence for the Lady, they go "beyond meaning and bear witness to the unrepresented, the unrepresentable" (1987, p. 283).

Lacan is interested in ambiguities and paradoxes in the musings of the trou-badours. This is because their discourse pivots around, but does not address, the Lady-object per se. He argues that the discourse of the courtiers involves a revo-lution at the level of the signifier. As Marc De Kesel (2009) explains, the "poetic revolution of courtly love reworked, rearranged, remodelled, and refurbished the set of signifiers that regulated sexual difference at that time" (p. 179). The revolu-tion pivots around the Lady-object who does not exist. Courtly love thus turns a spotlight upon the inconsequential status of the actual woman (who assumes an elevated position as Lady) and upon the artifice used to conceal the sexual impasse. Much like an eclipse, Lacan explains that the order of chivalrous appearance cam-ouflages the lack of complementarity, the Real of the sexual non-relation.

The medieval practice of courtly love gave rise to a particular form of culture predicated upon a knowledge of the sexual impasse. It plays in wholly original ways with the universal masculine, a structural logic of the whole (the One), and the particular feminine, as not-all subject to the phallic premise (universal signi-fier). The culture of courtly love is dependent upon the idealization of the Lady as a fantasy-object which is not equivalent to the woman as subject who may iden-tify with the idealising interpolation. In Lacan's interpretation, the Lady (feminine object) is not a subject (in particular) but an ideal (universalizable): "In this poetic field the feminine object is emptied of all real substance" (Lacan, 2013, p. 149). Lacan also explains that the Lady of concern to the troubadourian poet is "never characterized for any of her real, concrete virtues, for her wisdom, her prudence, or even her competence" (p. 150). The particularity of the female subject is of no con-sequence to the lover.[4] Indeed, this is borne out in historical studies of courtly love. Jan Montefiore (1987), for example, confirms that the male-courtier was, despite his proclamations to the contrary, indifferent to the actual woman he refers to in his ballads and, also, indifferent to the fact that the relationship he allegedly seeks does not develop into anything resembling an actual relationship. Toril Moi (1986) con-cludes that the "lover is not interested in the woman; his narcissistic self-display centers on his own desire, his own discursive performance" (p. 25). While the cour-tier proclaims to love, desire, and need the Lady, he is, like the clever hysteric (who I will return to in a later section), harping on about something Real and significant beyond representation.[5]

The troubadours brought news from afar to nobles, they were philosophers con-cerned with beautiful objects, love, betrayal, politics, religion, and chivalry. The messages conveyed in their ballads were given widespread attention and study by royals. What Lacan attends to is the way the troubadours did not stop narrating, in their artful ways, the inevitabilities of the sexual impasse. They used the impasse almost intentionally to enable desire in their prose. Sex (with the Lady) was not their aim. What fascinates Lacan is the way the troubadours and knights[6] of the medieval castles seemed to know that it was not the other sex but jouissance, the drives, and the Real that ultimately matter. Why else would someone commit them-selves so passionately to the pursuit of something they could not have? Although the love was on occasion consummated, as historians of courtly love can attest, this was the exception as opposed to the rule. It was most often the case that the Lady was married to a Lord or someone of higher noble birth and thus out of the admirer's reach. Equally, many a courtly lover had his own wife, children, and real-life mistress(es). Infidelity and adultery were also punishable by death in this historical period. One had to carefully navigate and play with the prohibitions to keep desire alive.

While sexuality studies scholars may legitimately turn to the role of the feudal Lords, the Empire, Christianity, manorialism, patriarchy and so forth to explain the repressive forces operating in the Middle Ages to regulate sexual acts, Lacan focuses on unconscious sexuality which is bound by laws structured by the desire and demand of the Other. From a Lacanian perspective sexuality is not (only) subject to prohibition by an external force like, for example, a Lady's husband, the love courts, or the legal customs of the day prohibiting marriage across differing ranks and social status. Sexuality is bound by jouissance and the cut of language (the mother tongue). Suffice here to say that the structure of desire is enabled by prohibitions in the field of the Other. In Lacanian terms, we can never have *the* object we desire because it does not exist in the way we think it does. When the object is raised to the dignity of the *Thing* it is unattainable, not because of the prohibitions surrounding it but because it does not exist *as* the *Thing*. What we pursue from the masculine side of love more closely approximates a hologram, a semblance appearing for the troubadours in the form of the Lady. But there is a contradiction because, as Lacan will later say, the courtly lover projects the forbidden primary objects relating to the mother's body onto the fantasy-Lady object. As Bracha L. Ettinger (2006) argues in her critique of Lacan, the incest prohibition does not operate in relation to the mother because contact with the maternal body is necessary not only for birth but survival (p. 42). The question of how to understand the sexual non-rapport in relation to the mother is thus a question in need of Lacanian inquiry and exploration. Let us consider who the Lady of courtly love is in relation to both the feminine object (of masculine fantasy) and the mother.

The Lady of Courtly Love

Historical questions abound about the status of the Lady in the courtly love tradition. Is she a substitute for the pagan mother celebrated by the Celts and later disparaged by the Catholic Church? Is she reminiscent of the Virgin Mary, an untouchable, God-like mother of Jesus? Was she a real woman trapped in an unhappy marriage by a tyrannical Lord-husband? Did the courtly knight professing his love want to save her from a loveless, abusive, or passionless marriage? Was the Lady a mere object of exchange between men in a time when women lacked civil rights and entitlements? Did courtly love emerge when women were gaining economic power? (Bloch, 1991). When the rule of the Church was being challenged by the Cathars[7] and others branded heretics? Was courtly love a response to the Church's attempt to gain control of the institution of marriage in the twelfth century, thereby curtailing women's choice to wed and divorce? (Gaunt, 1990, 1995).

These are all important historical questions, but Lacan's ethics, focused on the structure of desire, prompts us to consider the institution of courtly love from another angle. For Lacan, courtly love caused a revolution at the level of the signifier that says less about the changing status of women (as a social group) and more about the creation of a new way to deal with the Woman (who does not exist) and the sexual impasse. To be precise, courtly love concerns what Lacan calls the "enigmatic problem of the feminine object" (Lacan, 2013, p. 125). The feminine object is not the woman in her particularity, but a fantasy-projection irreducible to the beloved (the *agalma*). The object desired is missed in a ritualised fashion because it "presents itself in a form that is completely sealed, blind and enigmatic" (ibid., p. 70). In his discussion of *ex nihilo*, Lacan says that the object is a human creation. In fact, he writes, somewhat enigmatically, that to the extent that the object is created it "may fill the function that enables it not to avoid the *Thing* as signifier, but to represent it" (ibid., p. 119).

The object or substance of courtly love, like the *object a* (object cause of desire) of relevance to phallic jouissance, involves the immaterial *Thing*. What Lacan's reading of courtly love establishes is that this is a feminine *Thing*. Another way to say this is that the Lady is a semblance (a false appearance). She stands in for but is not the *Thing* animating the desire of the courtiers. To illustrate his point, Lacan refers to the work of André Morin, a French romance scholar, who notices that the descriptions of idealized ladies, given by male courtiers, are remarkably similar. This is to say that it is as if all the courtiers were describing one, as opposed to many, women (p. 126). This suggests that the woman (as subject) represents something more than herself at the level of fantasy. As Ragland remarks: "Fantasies seek to fill up lack, cycling rapidly through an interior void, causing a quickening of feeling we call affect" (1995, p. 11). The artisans of courtly love were excited about the fantasy-ideal they found in the unattainable Lady.

In her analysis of Lacan's seminar on the ethics of psychoanalysis, Ellie Ragland (1995) confirms that the "phenomenon of courtly love is all the more astounding . . . insofar as it pinpointed Woman as the cause around which a system of thought circles" (p. 4). She is the elusive *Thing*. The male-courtier knows that the object of his adoration eludes him and that he is destined to experience what Lacan calls "unhappy love" (2013, p. 146). Lacan puts it thus: the "Man asks to be deprived of something real" (p. 179). Like the woman (sexuated on the right-hand side of the graph of sexuation), the courtier may not (only) be interested in the Lady-object but (also) in being deprived of the object. The courtier's interest in the Lady is, like the Other jouissance (relevant to the feminine side), not (only) about the object, but about something unsymbolizable (Real) that cannot be had. The courtier may also be interested in the Woman as symbol emptied of substance. This is to say that it is not sex that the man is after but rather a way to enhance desire by erecting or creating an obstacle to the obtainment of love. We may also ask if this obstacle is sought to introduce a gap between the male-courtier and the Lady (occupying the place of the primary Other) when there was no such obstacle separating the boy-son from the m/Other in the early years of life (before language and the paternal function comes into effect). In his later seminar *Encore*, Lacan stresses the way love is made as opposed to found, fabricated out of nothing as opposed to something one finds (or consummates). But again, there is a lack of attention paid to the way the fantasy of the m/Other (as first object) operates in love and the sexual non-rapport for the courtier.

It seems that the m/Other, like the Lady courted, cannot be approached directly at the level of fantasy in Lacan's theorization. Indeed, he contends that objects of fantasy cannot be apprehended in straightforward ways. He illustrates the problem in relation to anamorphosis (a distorted projection) and says that there must be a dalliance or detour (2013, p. 152). This is to say that the Lady must be pursued through circular and elliptical means. Lacan refers to this curvature as a psychic detour. In his discussion of courtly love, Slavoj Žižek explains it thus: "The space of desire is curved as in the theory of relativity; the only way to reach the Object-Lady is indirectly, in a devious, meandering way – the moment we proceed straight ahead, we miss our target" (1993, pp. 100–101). The psychic detour involves the imaginary which, as Lacan explains in relation to the mirror stage, involves (una-voidable) narcissism and aggression. There is something destructive operating at the level of fantasy and in the Imaginary relation more generally of relevance not only to courtly love, but to what feminists call the objectification of women and to heterosexuality more generally.

Lacan locates the problem of identification in the imaginary object relation, in the way the subject is beholden to an ideal as "forced image of itself" (2013, p. 98). The non-object is introduced in this mirage. Lacan explains how culture "colonize[s] the field of *das Ding* with imaginary schemas" (p. 99) and the culture of courtly love is a case in point. The archive of courtly love is full of poems, let-ters, speeches, and songs about the beauty and cruelty of the beloved, about the unbearable pain to which she subjects the courtier, and about the insurmountable obstacles in the way to consummating that love. Lacan says that what gives the Lady her consistency is not only the way she is put on a pedestal but in the way she is "cruel as the tigers of Ircania" (p. 151). Unfortunately, he does not elaborate upon the reference to Ircania in the *Ethics* seminar, but his assessment of the object relation is clear. The art of courtly love not only enacts a limit by making the Lady unattainable, but it conceals aggression relating to the object (*Thing*). Given that the Woman occupies the place of the *Thing* and is metonymically associated with the feminine and the mother (as primary Other), the object relation is fraught and not without aggression.[8]

Contra those who read the poems of courtly love as involving idealization with-out obscenity, Lacan insists that we acknowledge that the "crudest of sexual games can be the object of a poem without for that reason losing its sublimating goal" (2013, p. 161). Lacan knew that courtly love involved misogyny. His insistence upon the sexual and aggressive character of sublimation (courtly love being Lacan's paramount example of sublimation), is enough to suggest that he did not equate the idealization of the object-Lady with the emancipation of women. Lacan's discus-sion of the way the Countess of Comminges was treated by her husband, Lord

Peter of Aragon, illustrates his awareness of the sadism embedded in courtly love. De Kesel also notes how the troubadours were unfaithful and manipulated women.

> Guilhem IX of Aquitanine (count of Poitiers, 1071–1126), for instance, the first-known troubadour in history, was in fact a Don Juan–like womanizer, while his poetry literally makes a great song and dance about fidelity to the one and only inaccessible Lady.
>
> (De Kesel, 2009, pp. 177–178)

Consider also the brutalities depicted in poems written by the Occitan troubadour Arnaut Daniel (1180–1200) who, as Lacan (2013) says, "breaches the boundaries of pornography to the point of scatology" (p. 161). Daniel pushes his desire for the unattainable Lady to an unlivable extreme, an extreme that "involves his own anni-hilation" (p. 163). After quoting a poem by Daniel at length, Lacan shows us how the Lady called *Domna Ena* occupies a brutal positioning in the void and becomes an object: a "terrifying, and inhuman partner" (p. 150).

Lacan also refers to the "frightening core of the *destrudo*" (p. 194) in jouissance and devotes considerable analytic attention to the sadism of the Marquis de Sade in the *Ethics* seminar. But he does not make a feminist argument about the abuse of women in the rituals of courtly love (or, indeed, in Sadean literature). Rather, Lacan is making a psychoanalytic argument about the void and, by implication, how the Woman figures in relation to it. Like a black hole from which no light can escape, the void can only be approached from a distance or from an arc. The void is a non-place of the primordial impasse where the subject disappears under the weight of the signifier. Lacan is trying to understand the "approach to a center of incandescence or an absolute zero that is physically unbearable" (2013, p. 201). The unbearable is what gets enacted in courtly love. The courtly jouissance is about the plus of a minus, the something (excessive) where there is, in fact, nothing (*das Ding*). *Das Ding* confers an "invisible law" (p. 58). The law of *das Ding* operates in accordance with the pleasure principle. "It is the pleasure principle which, when all is said and done, subjects the search to encounter nothing but the satisfaction of the *Not des Lebens*" (p. 58).[9]

As Ragland (1995) keenly observes, the void will always be inseparable from the question of the feminine, its in-existence because it concerns primary jouis-sance (p. 5) bound to the mother's body. In courtly love, the void is sexualized and given a feminine essence. Primary jouissance is linked to the drives: the voice, scent, look, and touch of the mother's body.[10] While the significance of the m/Other is not always obvious in the Lacanian exposition of courtly love, her centrality is, perhaps, more obvious in his discussion of the Freudian case study of the homo-sexual woman. The role of the m/Other as primordial object is evident in Lacan's discussion of the homosexual woman who loves in a courtly way "for no other satisfaction but to serve the lady" (2020, p. 101). Specifically, Lacan outlines the way lack undergirds the courtly exaltation of the Lady for the homosexual woman and that what is lacking "in this instance is the primordial object" (2020, p. 102).

For the homosexual woman, the lack concerns not only the phallus but an eclipse of the primordial object (m/Other) in what Lacan calls her "staunch paternal fixation" (2020, p. 101). The obstacles to consummating a courtly passion are congruous with the alienating effects of language and, also, the cultural prohibitions on incest limiting access to the mother's body in the later stages of life. The courtly lover projects the forbidden primary objects relating to the mother's body and to the partial drives onto the unattainable Lady-object.

While the Lady-object may seem to hold the promise of plenty, to assuage a void or lack in being, she will ultimately disappoint. What the male-courtier demonstrates is that what heterosexual men seek is not a particular woman elevated to the status of the *Thing* (*das Ding*), but a "repetition of the particular details of jouissance already constitutive of the drives where every person was first fed, bathed, touched, seen, heard" (Ragland, 1995, p. 113). But the loss, tethered as it is to the mother's body, is intractable. The alleged cruelty of the withholding Lady discussed in the poetry of the troubadours is not really about the actions (or sayings) of a particular woman but about a painful (*jouissant*) repetition. The mirage of the Lady-object in the man's eye changes into something catastrophic when he learns that the significatory cuts wrought by his alienating induction into language cannot be undone.

The trick of the courtly lover is to keep the idealized Lady at a permanent distance so as not to prick the fantasy. Lacan compares the *Thing* to a syringe which draws blood and says that the "blood of the Grail is precisely what is lacking" (2013, p. 142). While Lacan comments upon how the *Thing* draws blood from the man, he does not comment upon the toll taken upon actual woman reduced (in fantasy) to a syringe. In Ragland's estimate, the

> burden placed on women is nothing less than the implicit demand that Woman replace the inexistence of a feminine essence, supplying a guarantee of a consistency and continuity insofar as she is imagined as a unified being – is the semblance of such – form within a disparate set of partial functions.
>
> (1995, p. 12)

The feminine essence, like the Woman who does not exist, involves a fantasy whereby there is (or was in the early years of life) no separation between the subject and the primary Other (no syringe-like prick to introduce a gap). This lack of separation between the infant and the m/Other involves what Bracha L. Ettinger calls the non-prohibited incest between the becoming-subject (infant) and the m/Other in the early years of life (2006, p. 186).

From a contemporary feminist perspective, it is surprising that Lacan does not say more about the primary Other in the *Ethics* seminar. Certainly, he refers to her briefly and in passing, but the m/Other is not brought into his discussion of courtly love as fully as she needs to be to round out his discussion of the sexual non-rapport. Nor does he expand upon what he refers to as the (Real) almightiness of the mother (2020, pp. 185–186) or the "unfulfilled and unsatisfied mother . . .

[who] is in search of what she can devour, *quaerens quem devoret*" (2020, p. 187) that he foregrounds in his earlier discussion of the object relation. In *Seminar IV* Lacan insists that his students understand the power of the mother, the way imaginary objects are bound to the maternal body, and the way the "mother constitutes a virtual field of symbolic annihilation, from which each of the objects to come will in turn draw their symbolic value" (2020, p. 178). Contra Melanie Klein, Lacan focuses on the part-objects of the mother's body as "annulled objects" (2020, p. 179) with symbolic value appearing as, or under signifiers of, nothingness. This is not to say that the mother's body is insignificant or nothing, but that her grandiosity, and the infant-toddler's vulnerability and dependence upon her, is managed by introducing a gap, in the form of nothingness, from which the m/Other may become answerable to the child's desire (2020, p. 179). What the child grapples with, in Lacan's discussion of the object relation in the case of the boy-child, is the fantasy of the phallic mother whereby she possesses something appearing in the place of lack.

If we link Lacan's discussion of the phallic mother and the veiled phallus (2020, p. 186) to the courtier's pursuit of the unattainable Lady, the idealized object for whom the troubadour's reputation and ego is contingent upon (she may cast a smile or refuse his declaration of love), we may better understand the way the mother figures into the sexual non-rapport. At the time of the *Ethics* seminar (1959–1960), Lacan had not completed his formulation of the Law of the Mother (Morel, 2018) and does not elaborate upon feminine sexuality until the 1970s. The Law of the Mother involves the way the child is subject to the discourse and jouissance of the mother; her desire is felt by the child to be without limits. In Morel's Lacanian exposition, the child is subjugated to the mother's desire, to her law, her discourse (*lalangue*), and is imprinted by this early object relation in symptomatic ways (2018, p. 306). While Lacan does not bring the mother into the *Ethics* seminar as fully as he might have done, the law and desire of the m/Other underlays his explication of courtly love. The mother is foundational to the structure of desire, the primordial *Thing* around which desire orbits, and should not be sidelined in Lacanian studies of courtly love and the sexual impasse.

Although the mother is potent in structural terms, actual mothers, and woman (even when raised to the status of idealized objects) had little actual power in the Middle Ages (Burns, 2001, p. 24). But as Ragland explains, the "feminism at issue [in Lacanian psychoanalysis] concerns each woman's grappling with the problem of finding a signifier to valorize her (in)existence as Woman because she enters the field of signification for both sexes as mother" (1995, p. 10). The signifier-mother is insufficient to ratify women's being (because she is not-all). In other words, the idealization of the Lady is a way to signify not only the Woman who does not exist but to introduce a difference between the woman (as Lady) and the mother (as primary Other).[11] This is not about the vilification of the mother (as subject), but about the significatory anchoring of the woman's being in the socio-Symbolic.

One may counter that the Lady-signifier comes at a high cost when we consider that the women idealized were subject to thinly veiled threats (should they reject the courtier's advances), beaten and raped by jealous husbands, and had little agency in the negotiation of the courtly script. For example, Walter, the protagonist in Andreas' treaty on courtly love, utters a threat in his allegorical speech. He states that "women who refuse to take lovers suffer horrible torments after death" (Moi, 1986, p. 25). He tried to intimidate and scare noble women into having sex they may not want. We may conclude that the signifier Lady, however important to the articulation of a feminine essence, functioned to camouflage and excuse the brutalities, strategies of intimidation, and manipulation of love on the ground.

This is one of the reasons Lacan turns to the writings of the Marquis de Sade in the *Ethics* seminar. While the troubadours may seem to be more genteel and benign than the male protagonist in Sade's fictional portrait of Justine (who is subject to torture) in *Justine, or The Misfortunes of Virtue*, Lacan's (1998) argument is that the difference is negligible. In his estimate courtly love and the Sadean universe of unbridled jouissance are not altogether different. Both Sade and the troubadours work creatively with the unnaturalness of desire and the "imaginary structure of the limit" (Lacan, 2013, p. 197). Like Sadean fiction, the virtues of abstinence in courtly love ballads do not conceal contempt for the Lady-object. The ascetism and commitment to abstinence in courtly love demand a confrontation with an intolerable limit. The "techniques involved in courtly love . . . are techniques of holding back, of suspension, of *amor interruptus*" (2013, p. 152). Not only does courtly love introduce what Lacan calls a "detour in the psychic economy" (p. 152), but it makes visible a structural limit relating to his love of the Lady. The courtier thus comes face-to-face with something terrifying, not the woman (as living subject) or the Lady (as *object a*) exactly, but the brutality of the sexual impasse, the void along with the ineffectivity of the fantasy he choreographs to conceal his impotence (castration).

Despite the resonance between the fictive world of Sade and the proclamations of love heard in the medieval castles of France, Lacan believes the troubadour to be more adept than the sadistic libertine. The troubadours know about the sexual non-rapport and play with it in artful ways while the sadist does not want to know about it and will not admit to failure without a struggle. Lacan argues that Sade merely fails where the troubadours fail elegantly (as noted above).[12] Courtly love works with the sexual impasse and does not seek to deny or camouflage it. Sade, by contrast, tries to beat the Lady-Object to (near) death. He reveals the aggressivity of desire and mocks the pretense of love (which pleases Lacan), but Sade does not seem to know that the Other cannot be annihilated (while individual women, of course, can be). No matter how cruel and sadistic Sade's male protagonists may be, they cannot integrate or destroy the object of their desire (the Woman). She is unassimilable and thus, counterintuitively, persists.

Unlike Sade, the troubadours know how to keep the Lady (as signifier) in play. In Sade, everything is laid bare and, as Lacan says, sex becomes tedious. Nothing is left to the imagination. Lacan even refers to Sade as an "inferior eroticist" (2013, p. 188), as boring, and "not strictly speaking much fun" (2013, p. 78). In courtly love, as in the enactments of Sade, there is a deliberate use of the signifier. But unlike the courtly lover, Sade cannot accept what he cannot have. The troubadour, by contrast, accepts what he cannot have by making the Lady-*Thing* he does not have into something he can desire. Through his submission to what we might call the law of the Lady he experiences something akin to an Other jouissance (as I will discuss in a later section). But suffice here to say that unlike Sade, the troubadour makes himself subservient to the exalted Lady (regardless of how brutal or objectifying his approach to the actual woman may be) and reveals his lack (castration) before her.

Bruce Fink notes that the "knights often construed their Ladies as sadistic slave drivers, as demanding almost impossible services as homage to them, and as providing only the most meager compensations in the form of signs of esteem and love" (2016, p. 138). Much like the sexual submissives and foot-fetishists of today, the courtiers know that the inaccessible Lady is not only the Domina but a dominatrix. She appears to run the show. But what courtly lovers (and, perhaps, contemporary masochists) know is that the Lady-at-safe-remove is a stand-in for the lost object (the primary Other). We could say the exalted Lady is inhumane in the masculine imaginary structure and not be wrong, but Lacan's point is that she becomes the hallmark of the signifying structure enabling desire.

Anamorphosis

For Lacan, the Other remains with the subject at the level of the image. He thus attends to the history of art, and anamorphosis, in his analysis of courtly love. An anamorphosis is a way of perceiving the object-*Thing* askance, in a partial or distorted form when, in a direct line of vision, it would be imperceptible. Lacan equates anamorphosis with a "polished cylinder that has the function of a mirror" (2013, p. 135). It is, in other words, an optical illusion. An anamorphosis makes something inside the subject appear to be outside the subject (and thus at a distance from the subject). It makes that which is invisible (the Real) not visible exactly, but apprehensible. Žižek describes anamorphosis as an "absent point-of-reference" (1993, p. 101). The troubadour, for instance, catches the object-Lady (as ideal-image) by talking, writing, singing, etc., about and around her. He encases her through his discourse to bring about what Lacan calls, in relation to Antigone, her radiant splendour. "The Object is therefore literally something that is created – whose place is encircled – through a network of detours, approximations and near-misses" (Žižek, 1993, p. 101).

But like all fantasy-objects, the Lady changes. "The anamorphotic aspect is – You think she's this (your greatest Blessing), but she's really that – she's something Else" (Ragland, 1995, p. 16). Much like art is not about representation for Lacan (and more about what cannot be seen at the level of the object), courtly love is not about actual women. The courtly lover, like the artist, is not focused on individual women, but upon the way she demarcates a void in fantasy. Both artisans are concerned with an "optical transposition" that makes a non-visible form into a "readable image" (2013, p. 135). Lacan uses the example of Hans Holbein's 1533 painting *The Ambassadors* (which he mistakenly places at the Louvre when, in fact, it hangs in the National Gallery in London) to illustrate how from a specific spectral angle a skull appears that, from another angle, cannot be seen.

The enigmatic site that cannot be seen is tethered to the *Thing*. The *Thing* is an "intimate exteriority" (2013, p. 139) that Lacan compares to the etchings on the caves of Altamira referred to in Ella Sharpe's (1875–1947) writing on sublimation. Lacan does not endorse Sharpe's work so much as note the way images on dark caverns are not only painted over but difficult to see. What is of interest to Lacan is not what is inscribed on the cave walls but in the various ways the invisible is conjured up in artistic endeavours, including the poetry of the troubadours. Lacan insists that we do not get caught in the quagmire of thinking that art depicts objects seen because the real object of relevance to artists, like psychoanalysts, is the non-visible object. Every good painting conjures up a "reality that is not that of the object represented" (2013, p. 141). As such, it involves a sublimatory gesture.

Courtly Love and Sublimation

Courtly love was an "art," not a feeling.

(De Kesel, 2009, p. 177)

The art of courtly love is, for Lacan, the example of sublimation par excellence. In his estimate, the artisans of courtly love perfected the art of sublimation by elevating the object-cause of their desire, the Lady, to the status of the *Thing* and did so without depleting jouissance. In essence, Lacan modifies the original Freudian understanding of sublimation by demonstrating how it does not involve desexualization. Sublimation is not a simple matter of substitution for Lacan. It is not bound by the reality principle as it is for Freud but, rather, about desire, the signifier, and *das Ding*. There is a difference between *object a* and what the instinct aims for. The object may change, but in the Lacanian interpretation the aim is unchanged. "Between the object as it is structured by the narcissistic relation and *das Ding*, there is a difference, and it is precisely on the slope of that difference that the problem of sublimation is situated for us" (2013, p. 98). What becomes increasingly apparent is that the desire of the Other occupies a central place in the sublimatory art of courtly love. In courtly love there is a shift "from the real (the satisfaction of the sexual drives) to the symbolic, where desire is the Other's desire, where one desires to be desired by the Other, or wants to be loved" (Fink, 2016, p. 137).

The Lady is not only inaccessible; rather she is subject and/or object of privation. Lacan contends that the object of courtly love is not the woman (as subject) but the signifier or, more precisely, the way the Lady is positioned in the domain of the signifying chain circling the *Thing*. As Ragland explains, "love bears the burden of joining the real of the drives to the lack-in-being from which desire first arises" (1995, p. 9). This lack is given form by courting the Lady who is raised to the status of the *Thing* (*das Ding*), a significatory-ideal. As De Kesel explains, sublimation is about the formation of an "autonomous operating signifier" likening it to the monotheistic creation myth whereby everything comes from nothing (2009, p. 180). Lacan's major innovation is that sublimation introduces something extimate (irreducible to the signifier) into the system of symbols. He also refers to the vacuole as the centre of signifiers. Those who question the significance of the signifier in the artifice of courtly love, might consider the hero of *Roman de la Rose ou de Guilaume de Dole*, a thirteenth-century chivalric poem (written in oil and) attributed to Jean Renart, who falls in love with the name of the Lady (as opposed to her body). She is an absent-referent or, as Kristeva says, an "imaginary addressee, the pretext for the [male-masculine poet's] incantation" (1987, p. 287).

Through the pursuit of an impossible love the troubadour approaches the exalted *Thing* in the form of the Lady. But the woman (as subject) is not there. This is what Lacan means when he says that courtly love is about the pursuit of nothing. His central point is that this nothing is something (in the form of *object a*) and not immaterial. The object-lady occupies an emptiness. Referring to another poem by Arnaud Daniel, Lacan relays the words of a shepherdess to her shepherd. "I am, she tells him, nothing more than the emptiness to be found in my own internal cesspit." Lacan tells his audience to "blow in that for a while and see if your sublimation holds up" (2013, p. 215).

Lacan contends that there is an inhuman character to courtly love, an inhuman character "addressed at living beings, people with names, but who were not present in their fleshly and historical reality . . . [but they] were there in any case in their being as reason, as signifier" (2013, pp. 214–215). The Lady of courtly love is a signifier although, as Lacan explains, the signification is addressed to real human subjects and follows the path of desire. The path of the signifier leads to an impassable site or, as Lacan also says, takes the subject to the "site of the *Thing*" (p. 213). The non-object of concern to courtly love conjures up a fantasy that there is something beyond the desiring subject, a sacred place. This sacred place is otherworldly, reminiscent of a religious fantasy and involves the almighty mother.[13]

This is where questions must be asked about masculine sexuality, involving *object a*, and its relation to the mother and *hommosexual* love. In Lacan's graph of sexuation, *object a* is on the feminine side and is the object of phallic jouissance. Lacan explains that the 'a' has the elements of a phantasm which deludes the subject (2013, p. 99). The object of courtly love is thus not an individual subject (a woman) but, rather, the *object a* of primary jouissance that remains after the subject is alienated by language. *Object a* is thus Real (non-material). The 'a' is like a fantasmatic lure tying what is lost at the level of the drives and primary jouissance, associated with the mother's body, to an image or idealised Other. "When the lover is deprived of the sexual 'real,' he finds himself, Lacan says, back at the point of pure desire where he first encountered these gifts in a paradox – at the site of the mother's body which he is quickly required to renounce" (Ragland, 1995, p. 16). As Ragland further explains, phallic jouissance involves a substitution "away from the real of *das Ding*, away from the real of the drives associated with woman *qua* mother" (1995, p. 7). *Object a* is about what has been lost in the early object relation with the mother. Although Lacan does not elaborate upon *object a* in relation to the mother in the *Ethics* seminar, his theorization of *object a* allows for it. He says that the idealised object concerns a "certain lost cord, a crisis, in relation to the object" (Lacan, 2013, p. 99) who is, in the first instance, the m/Other. It follows that the courtier is looking for a repetition of a scene constitutive of his original jouissance, involving the drives, which involved the primary Other (mother). What the man desires is not only to be deprived of something Real (as stated above), but an a-sexual solution to the sexual impasse.[14] This is, in part, what Lacan means when he says in his seminar on the transference which immediately follows the *Ethics* seminar, "It takes three to love, not just two" (2011, p. 132). Lacan is suggesting that the 'a' is required not to join two partners, but to enable each partner to love "oneself in the Other" (Ragland, 1995, p. 106).

It is unfortunate that Lacan does not say more here about the mother given that she "structures [the] man's unconscious," is the "terminal point, the abolition of the whole world of demand" (2013, p. 68) for the man and is the unconscious focal point of courtly love. Lacan's analysis of courtly love reveals that the *Thing* of relevance to desire is the feminine *Thing* metonymically linked to the mother (or primary Other). What acts as a catalyst for desire is the loss of a primary jouissance, involving the mother's body, imposed by language (the cut of the signifier). For Lacan, the mother's body concerns the drives and the Real. "And paradoxically, it is on the basis of this experience of loss that woman *qua* mother – site of the primordial drives – is taken as a guarantee of wholeness, goodness, truth, solidity, trust, continuity, a principle of the 'natural'" (Ragland, 1995, p. 7). But the wholeness one seeks in the Other (as Lady) is unattainable. When one loves it is not about the beloved (as subject), but about a desire to assuage a void in the heart of being. Later, in his seminar *Encore* Lacan is more precise. He says that love is addressed to the semblance. "And if it is true that the Other is only reached if it attaches itself (*qu'à s'accoler*) . . . to *a*, the cause of desire, then love is also addressed to the semblance of being" (Lacan, 1998, p. 92).

As Bruce Fink explains, the "Otherness of the other again drops out of the picture, and we wind up dealing with the One (an idea, ideal, or signifier), not the Other" (2016, p. 150). This is to say that courtly love is masculine and refers, ultimately, to itself but, as I will suggest in what follows, with a *hommosexuelle* element and a hysterical component. The Lady is immaterial as noted above but she exists at the level of fantasy (and as ideal). Apropos of the man's side, the lover is enamoured with *object a*, a phallic and a-sexual form of love. He is engaged in an imaginary structure whereby he looks for something specific in the mirror of the Other relating, not to the Lady, but to his own idealised traits. Lacan writes:

> The idealized woman, the Lady, who is in the position of the Other and of the object, finds herself suddenly and brutally positing, in a place knowingly constructed out of the most refined signifiers, the emptiness of a thing in all its

cruelty, a thing that reveals itself in its nudity to be the thing, her thing, the one that is to be found at her very heart in its cruel emptiness.

(2013, p. 163)

Where we expect to find love we, ultimately, find a hole in the imaginary artifice, the emptiness of the *Thing* (*das Ding*).

In the *Transference* seminar Lacan refers to love, somewhat enigmatically, as comic. Following a brief discussion of courtly love in *Encore*, Lacan jokes: "How do neurotics make love?" (Lacan, 1998, p. 86). No one knows! But when neurotics do make love, they do it in a way that correlates with perversion not as a psychic structure, but as a neurotic act involving what we may, in Lacanian parlance, call *hommosexuellity*. The heterosexual man can only desire women "as the *object a* of his particular perversion" (Ragland, 1995, p. 106). In other words, men are excited by *object a* which has nothing to do with women (as heterosexual objects). What attracts the man is "more or less his image, his reflection" (2013, p. 112) as distinct from the woman (as subject). The image must be understood from the perspective of the Imaginary register. "At this level the object introduces itself only insofar as it is perpetually interchangeable with the love that the subject has for its own image" (p. 98). That is to say that the subject relates to the other through the "mirage of the ego and the formation of an ideal" (p. 98). This, for Lacan, reveals the *hommosexuellity* of the heterosexual man.

Hommosexuelle Love

While Lacan's discussion of courtly love may appear to be one-sided because he focuses upon the male courtier, as opposed to the female courtier, his earlier writing on the female homosexual should be kept in mind. Specifically, Lacan considers how the female homosexual's love is courtly and that the "lady [subject to her love] is loved precisely in so far as she does not have the symbolic penis, though she has all it takes to get it because she is the chosen object of the subject's every adoration" (2020, p. 120). Like the male courtier, the female homosexual adores the Lady-object for what she lacks. In Lacan's view, both suitors love something beyond the Lady-object that "aims at something else besides her" (2020, p. 102). In his discussion of the female homosexual Lacan notes that Freud "seems to restrict, and not without reason, [devotional love] to the register of male experience" (2020, p. 102). It is unclear if Lacan is, in this note about Freud, wanting to consider female sexuality in the courtly equation, suggesting that when females love in a courtly way they are masculine (in sexuated terms), or if he is hinting at the way devotional love may involve, at least for the female homosexual, something relating to the feminine side. Is Lacan suggesting that feminine sexuality cannot be courtly (because it does not concern *object a* in the form of the Lady)? Or is he suggesting that when female homosexuals love in a masculine way they are masculine and virile in precisely the way the male courtly lover is?

It is difficult to know for sure, but Lacan does say that the homosexual woman in the Freudian case occupies a "virile position" and has "taken on the male position" (2020, p. 120).

While Lacan may be faulted for a lack of clarity in his exposition of the male/masculine courtier (in the *Ethics* seminar) and the homosexual woman he referred to in "The Object Relation" seminar, it is important to remember that the way one loves is structural as opposed to biological in Lacanian theory. Moreover, he denaturalises the object relation and cathexis central to the configuration of normative heterosexuality in his exposition on courtly love. This is to say that what looks like heterosexuality conceals gender variance and homoerotic undercurrents. Consider first that Lacan proposes a historical correlation between courtly love and homosexuality. In *Encore* he says that courtly love "appeared at a time at which homosexual amusement had fallen into supreme decadence, in that sort of impossible bad dream known as feudalism" (1998, p. 86). He maintains that there is something *hommosexuelle* about phallic jouissance (p. 84) and refers to the man's love of the Woman as *hommosexuelle* (which puts male-heterosexuality in the realm of perversion).[15] Lacan's *hommosexuelles* believe in the Woman's existence (at the level of fantasy) and in a supreme love. Ragland explains that the "heterosexual man does not manifest a pure love for Woman as does the *hommosexuelle*" (Ragland, 2001, p. 106). Much like the courtly lover who makes the Woman his cause, the homosexual will not take a woman as a lover. He wishes her to remain in an idealised position.[16]

The male homosexual is also like the female hysteric. He is committed to the Other's jouissance, what Ragland calls "being-for-another" (2001, p. 114). The courtier is steadfast in his belief that the Woman does not lack and there is something *homosexual* about his belief in the Woman. Lacan notes that female hysterics know that men are often less interested in actual woman than they are in other men. This is to suggest that the male courtier of the medieval period reveals something *hommosexuelle* under the pretense of heterosexuality that corresponds to the hysteric's refusal to become a man's symptom-lover by proxy. As already explained, the object of the courtly lover's affections was often married to the man's Lord. Toril Moi writes that the "greatest threat to the lover's project of conquering the lady's favours, however, is posed by his rivals: constantly agonising in his neurotic fear of being rejected for another suitor, the lover is driven to despair by extreme jealousy" (1986, p. 22). This suggests that homoerotic competition between men may have been more significant than the object-Lady herself.[17]

In fact, Lacan notes that women were objects of exchange between men on the symbolic market. He observes what Eve Sedgwick (1985) would later elaborate upon in her queer reading of the English literary canon, a thinly disguised homoeroticism between men enabled by the mediating presence of a female character. In other words, the (male) homosexual and the courtly lover rely upon the Woman (as a fantasy ideal) and not a particular women. For Lacan, when one loves like a man there are no women involved. "The subject is the object of his or her own fantasy, the most cherished object being the maintenance of him- or herself as the object of a lost cause" (Ragland, 1995, p. 15). The lost cause is attached to the *object a* that causes desire. In Lacan's structuralist account the Lady of courtly love has "become a pure signifier that all the other signifiers derive their meaning from, but which itself signifies only "itself" – and therefore nothing. She provides sense to every gesture, every feeling, every word of the courtly poet, while emptying herself of all content" (De Kesel, 2009, p. 180). The Lady is, in other words, the anchor of all other signifiers, much like the phallus. Ragland explains that courtly love elevated "The Woman to a symbolic order signifier" (2001, p. 109), that is a phallic signifier.

The Lady, like the phallic signifier, prevents a torrential slide of signifiers by introducing a stopgap into a field of nothingness. The courtly lover does not attain the *Thing* he seeks but a Real emptiness. Courtly love is, for Lacan, a negative ethics whereby something is created out of nothing (*ex nihilo*). Let us remember that the sublimated object, the Lady of courtly love in this instance, exists outside the universe of symbols. What gets elevated to the status of the *Thing* (*das Ding*) has the marking of the Real and cannot be signified as such. The catch is that what is elevated to the dignity of the *Thing* is emptied of significance.

Lacan's point is not that women are insignificant but that there is a fault line in heterosexual love. What the institution of courtly love illustrates is that things relating to sex do not "mysteriously and almost miraculously work themselves out right" (p. 293). There is no unity or genital harmony foundational to what we might call the heteronormative good. Specifically, Lacan takes issue with what he calls "genital objecthood (*l'objectalité genitale*)" and unearths the perverse elements of masculine sexuality (which he describes as *hommosexuelle*) at the level of fantasy.[18] We cannot resolve the sexual impasse by consummating our desire or by having better (non-perverse) object relations. In his critique of psychological normalization Lacan could not be clearer, he says that "to aim for the fulfilment of what is known as the genital stage, that is, a maturation of the drive and object, which would set the standard for a right relationship to reality, definitely embodies a certain moral implication" (p. 302).

Not only do the standards of a right heterosexual relationship fall short, but Lacan tells us that the "*Thing* is that which in the real . . . suffers from the signifier" (2013, p. 118). It suffers because it is exempt from the signifying structure. Lacan turns to Freud's theory of the lost object to ask if it is an established fact that this object, discussed by Freud, is (or was) really lost. Lacan suggests that the loss of the object is a consequence of it having been re-found. The loss occurs with and alongside the re-found object, not before, or in absentia. Lacan then suggests we call the *Thing* the Other *Thing*. It is represented by something else. Here Lacan makes a quick turn to Picasso who says, "I do not seek, I find" (as quoted in Lacan, 2013, p. 118). What the subject-troubadour finds is, according to Lacan, the path of the signifier. The signifier takes us, like a troubadour, into the beyond. Our journey is from one signifier to another, none of which returns us, properly speaking, to the other sex.

Courtly Love and Hysteria

Part of what Lacan excavates in his discussion of courtly love are the multiple gender and sexual variances emerging in the medieval tradition involving hysteria and the *hommosexuelle* courtier. Let us first consider the *hommosexuelle* desire of the courtier. While the feminine position is attuned to the signifier of lack in the Other, the courtly lover actively seeks what he cannot have. If the male-courtier loves the Woman he cannot have in the form of the Lady, he is not unlike the *hommosexuelle* who, for Lacan, loves and remains true to the essence of the feminine (as opposed to a particular woman). "Heterosexual men tend to confuse Woman with a particular woman, while the *hommosexuelle* is faithful to Woman in figures or guises that hold out a hope of 'redemption' from lack through a jouissance of One-ness" (Ragland, 2001, p. 109). Of course, the heterosexual man may experience sexual jouissance with a particular woman (and a homosexual man may love a woman platonically), but the difference is in the way the *hommosexuelle* preserves the feminine as ideal.

For both masculine subjects, the feminine promises to rectify a lack in being operating at the level of the Real. As such, the Woman is idealised and untouchable. But like the phallus, the Woman cannot rectify a Real lack in being. This is why Lacan claims that we are all *nullisexual*, that is, "troubled by the void (*nulle*) that he aligns with the order of the real" (Ragland, 2001, p. 111). What the male courtier reveals through his unrequited declarations of love is much like what the *hommosexuelle* reveals through his decision to abstain from sex with women. Both reveal the impossibility of making love to the Woman in Lacanian terms (as distinct from having sex with actual women). In *Encore*, Lacan says "there is no chance that he [the man] will have *jouissance* of the woman's body, in other words make love with her" (1998, p. 143). Of course, he desires her, may have sex with her, but "what he approaches, is the cause of his desire, that I have designated the *object a*" (1998, p. 143). Another way to pose the problem is to say that heterosexual men can only experience sexual jouissance with a woman through fantasy.

Insofar as courtly love did not (usually) involve sex, it is not only a masculine undertaking but also something that must be interpreted on the feminine side. "Lacan locates the love of Woman on the feminine side of sexuation and the *act* of making love on the masculine side of lack" (Ragland, 2001, p. 107). But what is equally interesting is the way the male-courtier's position resonates both with the *hommosexuelle* and the hysteric. In fact, Bruce Fink asks if the courtly lover might not undergo a "form of hystericization; can I find or bring out a lack in another to which I myself correspond?" (2016, p. 139). Although Lacan does not speculate on the hysteria of the courtier in his exposition, the discourse of the courtier and the discourse of the hysteric are similar. In the same way the hysteric addresses her discourse to the Master the male-courtier addresses his discourse to the Lady's Master and to the love courts. It is also interesting to note that like the Victorian hysterics plagued by ailments defying medical explanation, the male courtiers of the Middle Ages claimed to be love-sick. They spoke of physical ailments caused by unrequited and tortured love. The troubadours referred to magic potions and to euphoric feelings that came over them arresting not only their capacity for restraint but their rational faculties.

Courtly lovers were dramatic and histrionic in their declarations of love. They ruminate about how they are lovelorn and palpably suffer from the cruelty, withholding, and emotionally callous actions of the Lady. The courtly lover embraces the signifier of lack, much like women (as sexuated subjects) do. Although men can be hysterics and Lacan was reluctant to put the hysteric on the feminine side of his graph of sexuation (Cavanagh, 2019), the questions, provocations, and complaints of the courtier resemble the discourse of the hysteric.[19] While the hysteric confounds the psychoanalyst with her enigmatic desire, the courtly lover is committed to the circularity of a discourse relating to a beloved beyond reach. Like the female hysteric who does not become a man or a woman (in Lacanian terms) and is more interested in equivocating upon sexual difference than resolving it (Cavanagh, 2019), the troubadour commits himself to the unattainable Woman (as Lady). Both know about the impossibility of love, the non-existence of the Woman, and are often antimatrimonial.[20]

If sexuation is a matter of how one responds to the Other's desire by being or having the phallus (as signifier), adopting a feminine or masculine solution respectively, we may say that the female hysteric and the male courtier refuse to choose. Lacan notes that the female hysteric is both undecided about sexual positioning and, also, that she "plays the part of the man (*faire l'homme*). . . being thus *hommosexual* or *beyondsex* themselves" (1998, p. 85). As already implied, the male courtier is, through his confessions of love and impotence in the face of the Lady, feminised. Neither is a woman or man in Lacanian terms, at least not exactly. In a way, the female hysteric of the Victorian era and the male-courtier of medieval France, make a perfect couple. Each exposes the a-sexuality foundational to phallic jouissance. The female hysteric wants to expose the man's lack and will not be what Colette Soler calls a "symptom by proxy" (2006, p. 64); this is to say she will not be the man's a-symptom. The male courtier is committed to his lack (the Lady he cannot have). Although he is not immune to masculine bravado, the courtier reveres a feminine ideal. Moreover, he is symptomatic and reveals his love-bound suffering to all who will listen.

The hysteric knows that the a-sexuality of the man divides her (Soler, 2006, p. 61), separates her from her desire, and that this splitting interferes with her being. In Soler's (2006) interpretation, the hysteric does not want to be the *object a* cause of desire, but to be desire itself. Like the courtier who commits himself to unsatisfied love, the hysteric prefers to leave the man's jouissance unsatisfied. Even when the hysteric knows what a man desires, she will not partake in a ritual whereby she becomes the object-*Thing* of his fantasy. Not only will she refuse his sexual advances, but she will achieve a little bit extra of being (*un plus d'être*), by refusing to be the object of his jouissance (Soler, 2006, p. 61). Like the courtier who is, in Lacan's assessment, not really concerned about the actual woman subject to his overtures, the hysteric knows that she is inconsequential to the man's desire. Also, like the hysteric, the courtiers know, or at least seek to know, something about love from the woman's side as evidenced in their poems, some of which read like psychoanalytic interpretations of feminine sexuality. The courtier who may, from the perspective of the present, be read as both "queer" and "campy" in his performative display of love, is not only masculine but feminine and/or hysteric. Ultimately, he insists upon his exceptionalism. His poems and speeches declare that he is worthy of the Lady's love, that he understands her desire, unlike other men. He is, like the Woman who does not exist, *the Man* who would exist if only the love courts would rule in his favour.

Lacan also notes that the Lady is not infrequently addressed in the masculine as, for example, *Mi Dom*. The Lady is referred to as the courtly lover's master or Lord. Feminist historians suggest that the occasional cross-dressing on the part of the Lady (woman) involved the "staging of complex love relations that push productively against the boundaries and expectations of normative heterosexuality" (Burns, 2001, p. 27). Burns observes that the positions of the Lady and the courtier allowed for gender variance (including cross-dressing), thereby providing opportunities for women to resist the fetishised and idolised positions they normally occupied in French medieval courting rituals (2001, p. 44). Historically speaking, it is unfortunate that so little is known about the female troubadours (*trobairitz*) (who sometimes mocked the male courtiers), the way women used the rituals of courtly love to instigate erotic liaisons of their own choosing, the way they formed lesbian liaisons, and chose to remain single in the period. The historical record shows that "A range of courtly women are joined in same-sex relations, whether homosocial, homoaffective, homoerotic, or more mystical and metaphorical, that offer paths of resistance to heterosexual courtly coupling" (Burns, 2001, p. 26). There is also much left to say about what feminist historians call the 'embroidery romances' between women, including the musical lyrics sewn into their needlework, both of which give rise to courtly patterns of love ignored by Lacan.

Conclusion

It is disappointing that Lacan does not elaborate upon the gender role reversals and the masculine address as applied to the exalted Lady in psychoanalytic terms. Nor does he say enough about the mother. We might surmise that it is difficult, as Lacan explains with respect to the Other jouissance, to say anything concrete about the feminine and the primary Other. As Ellie Ragland explains, the mother is "identified with the silence of the drives and the logic of sameness" (1995, p. 10). We may also recall that it was not until the early 1970s that Lacan turned his attention to the maternal discourse under the auspices of *lalangue* (fusing *langue* and *la*). Lalangue is not delimited by the rules of spoken language. Lalangue is unbound by a signifier and does not have associative links. Like the Woman (or Lady) who does not exist, the maternal discourse has jouissant-effects that cannot be said. In the mother's discourse there is a primordial signifier that cannot be conjugated.

Courtly love pays homage to this primary signifier tethered to the mother's body in Real and Imaginative ways. The courtier desires the Lady-*Thing* (as an a-element) in a way that involves *hommosexuelle* elements, as Lacan says, but also in a way that taps into the discourse of the hysteric as I have shown. In *Encore* Lacan notices that in what he calls (male) homosexual amusement and its decadence, something no longer works at all for the woman (p. 86), but the reader is left to wonder what, exactly, no longer works and how. Equally, Lacan does not theorize the desire of the woman subject to the adoration (and aggression) of the courtier. The ethics of psychoanalysis for Lacan concern the Real of the sexual impasse operationalised in the discourse of the courtier and the hysteric. Given the centrality Lacan places upon desire in the *Ethics* seminar and the fact that the mother (or primary Other) is the *Thing* around which desire circles, it is noteworthy that we must wait for his later seminars for a fuller treatment of the feminine, the hysteric and what he will later call the Other jouissance. What contemporary Lacanian studies must continue to do is interpret the vital role of the feminine in courtly love and in psychoanalytic ethics more generally to better understand the sexual impasse from the woman's side.

Notes

1 For Lacan the human drive pulls us away from nature. What counts as 'normal' love conceals perverse and destructive jouissance.
2 A troubadour was a travelling poetic performer, composer, and a satirist in the medieval period whose lyrics focused on chivalry and courtly love.
3 Lewis (1936) and de Rougemont (1939) contend that there is historical evidence to confirm that courtly love was an actual practice.
4 In Krueger's discussion of the *Lancelot* he observes that the idealized Lady is effectively written out of the text and her desire rendered problematic (1993). Douglas Kelly (1977) notes that the attributes of the courtly lover and the Lady seemed to be interchangeable, thus obscuring the author and addressee in courtly love poems.
5 In the Freudian case of the homosexual woman, her relationship with the Lady was passionate (and consummated). This raises questions about whether her love was courtly in the tradition established by the troubadours.
6 A knight was a warrior of impeccable manners and dress and of aristocratic birth.
7 Gabriele Rossetti suggests that medieval love originates with the Cathars (Boase, 1977).
8 We may pause here to consider what feminist psychoanalysts refer to as a legacy of mother-blaming in clinical practice, the long-standing problem of violence against women in intimate relationships, and the more recent sub-culture of male incels who, allegedly, want sex from women, feel entitled to it, but cannot have it. See https://www.newyorker.com/culture/cultural-comment/the-rage-of-the-incels for a discussion of incels.
9 As will become clear in Lacan's discussion of Antigone, the invisible law establishes a limit relating to pleasure and unpleasure. When the courtier approaches a limit, like an inaccessible Lady, he approaches something akin to the radiant splendour of Antigone: pure desire. The limit is Lacan's answer to the incest taboo and the pleasure principle theorized by Freud. He describes the limit thus: "I will have you note that it is avoidance, flight, movement, which in the beginning, even before the system starts to function, normally intervenes in order to regulate the invasion of quantity in accordance with the pleasure principle" (2013, p. 59). As such, the limit regulates the human subject. It

prevents us from getting too excited, too close to the mysterious *Thing* occupying the place of the void.

10 Bracha L. Ettinger (2006) elaborates upon the affect and aesthetics of the maternal body in her theorization of the matrixial borderspace.

11 In his discussion of courtly love in contemporary cinema, Slavoj Žižek (1993) makes a concordant assessment. Without disregarding the aggression and domination built into courtly love, he says that the "very semblance [of courtly love] provides women with a fantasy substance of their identity whose effects are real; it provides them with all the features which constitute so-called 'femininity' and define woman not as she is in her *jouissance feminine*, but as she refers to herself with regard to her (potential) relationship to man, as an object of desire" (Žižek, 1993, p. 108). Unfortunately, Žižek makes an argument against feminism on this basis. He says that feminists "undermine the fantasy support of . . . [their] own 'feminine' identity" (1993, p. 108). Additionally, he says that given the nature of the sexual impasse asymmetry between partners is inevitable and that the non-relation cannot involve "pure subjects" (Žižek, 1993, p. 108). What he does not consider is how in the contemporary cinematic vignettes the woman-object is not idealized in the way she was in the Middle Ages and, also, why femininity is, in his view, the only identity-based support available to woman.

12 In *Encore* Lacan writes that courtly love is a "highly refined way of making up for (*suppléer à*) the absence of the sexual relationship, by feigning that we are the ones who erect an obstacle thereto" (p. 69).

13 Another way to understand the *Thing* beyond the object is to consider what Kristeva (1987) calls the "ambiguities of courtly metaphor" (p. 283). Courtly lovers were nothing if not verbose. Their discourse overflows with nonmeaning, oppositions, and ambiguity thus creating "signification through *joi*" (p. 283). While Lacan notices how there is, in the discourse of courtly love, a suspension between the signifier and the signified, Kristeva attends to the semantic shifts, the "semantic as well as phonic uncertainty, reversibility, and contamination in signs, which carry the ambiguity of metaphorical meaning to its peak" (1987, pp. 286–287).

14 The a-sexuality in Lacanian theory must be distinguished from asexuality which in contemporary sexuality studies refers to a sexual identity and to a disinterest in sex (Przybylo and Cooper, 2014).

15 See Ragland (2001) for a discussion of the *hommosexuelle* in Lacanian theory.

16 See Schultz (2006) for a discussion of the heterosexual presumption in medieval studies of courtly love.

17 See Eve Sedgwick (2015) for a discussion of how women are used to mediate homoerotic desire between men in fiction. Rouben Cholakian (1990) and Sarah Kay (1996) discuss homoeroticism in the musical lyrics of the troubadours.

18 See Karma Lochrie (2005) for a discussion of the incongruity between contemporary definitions of heterosexuality and the "nature" of love in the Middle Ages. In his discussion of courtly love (and Shakespeare) Will Stockton (2010) argues that heterosexuality is one way to describe the sexual impasse theorized by Lacan and that it is a fantasy as opposed to an objective reality (or truth).

19 I would challenge De Kesel's (2009) contention that the courtly lover engages in a form of aesthetic sublimation that enables a creative engagement with lack whereas the (female) hysteric is repressed in an "unhealthy" way (De Kesel, 2009, p. 183). There is nothing to suggest that female hysterics, like male courtiers', cannot engage in aesthetic sublimation or that they are, by Lacanian definition, unhealthy.

20 Kay (1990) explains that the troubadour would sometimes express contrary ideas about love and marriage to the love courts while, also, insisting upon their entitlement to a Lady in matrimony.

Bibliography

Ali, H. M. (2013). The Abject Lover of the Courtly Love Era. *3L: Language, Linguistics, Literature*, 19(3): 11–19.

Benton, J. F. (1961). The Court of Champagne as a Literary Center. *Speculum: A Journal of Mediaeval Studies*, 36(4): 551–591.

Benton, J. F. (1968). Clio and Venus: An Historical View of Medieval Love. In F. X. Newman (Ed.), *The Meaning of Courtly Love* (pp. 19–42). Albany, NY: New York University Press.

Bloch, R. H. (1991). *Medieval Misogyny and the Invention of Western Romantic Love*. Chicago: University of Chicago Press.

Boase, R. (1977). *The Origin and Meaning of Courtly Love: A Critical Study of European Scholarship*. Manchester: Manchester University Press.

Burns, J. (2001). Courtly Love: Who Needs It? Recent Feminist Work in the Medieval French Tradition. *Signs*, 27(1): 23–57.

Butler, J. (2000). *Antigone's Claim: Kinship Between Life and Death*. New York: Columbia University Press.

Cavanagh, S. L. (2017). Antigone's Legacy: A Feminist Psychoanalytic of an Other Sexual Difference. *Studies in the Maternal*, 9(1). https://doi.org/10.16995/sim.223.

Cavanagh, S. L. (2019). Transgender, Hysteria, and the Other Sexual Difference: An Ettingerian Approach. *Studies in Gender and Sexuality*, 20(1): 36–50.

Cholakian, R. (1990). *Troubadour Lyric: A Psychocritical Reading*. Manchester: Manchester University Press.

De Kesel, M. (2009). *Eros and Ethics: Reading Jacques Lacan's Seminar VII*. Albany, NY: SUNY Press.

de Rougemont, D. (1939). *L'Amour et l'Occident*. Paris: Gallimard.

Denomy, A. J. (1965). *The Heresy of Courtly Love*. Gloucester: Peter Smith.

Donaldson, E. T. (1970). *Speaking of Chaucer*. New York: W. W. Norton & Company.

Ettinger, B. L. (1993). Woman-Other-Thing: A Matrixial Touch. In B. L. Ettinger (Ed.), *Matrix–Borderlines* (pp. 11–18). Oxford: Museum of Modern Art.

Ettinger, B. L. (2006). *The Matrixial Borderspace*. Minneapolis: University of Minnesota Press.

Fink, B. (2016). *Lacan on Love: An Exploration of Lacan's Seminar VIII, Transference*. New York: Polity Press.

Gaunt, S. (1990). Marginal Men, Marcabru and Orthodoxy: The Early Troubadours and Adultery. *Medium Aevum*, 59(1): 55–72.

Gaunt, S. (1995). *Gender and Genre in Medieval French Literature*. Cambridge: Cambridge University Press.

Kay, S. (1990). *Subjectivity in Troubadour Poetry*. Cambridge: Cambridge University Press.

Kay, S. (1996). The Contradiction of Courtly Love and the Origins of Courtly Poetry: The Evidence of the Lauzengiers. *Journal of Medieval and Early Modern Studies*, 26(2): 209–253.

Kelly, Joan (1977) "Did Women Have a Renaissance?" In *Becoming Visible: Women in European History*, Ed. Renate Bridenthal and Claudia Koonz, 37–64. Boston: Houghton Mifflin.

Kosofsky Sedgwick, E. (2015) *Between men: English literature and male homosocial desire*. Columbia university press.

Kristeva, J. (1987). *Tales of Love*. New York: Columbia University Press.

Krueger, Roberta (1993). *Women Readers and the Ideology of Gender in Old French Verse Romance*. Cambridge: Cambridge University Press.

Lacan, J. (1998). *The Seminar of Jacques Lacan (1972–1973): Book XX: On Feminine Sexuality, The Limits of Love and Knowledge*. Ed. J.-A. Miller. Trans. B. Fink. London and New York: W. W. Norton & Company.

Lacan, J. (2013). *The Seminar of Jacques Lacan (1959–1960): Book VII: The Ethics of Psychoanalysis*. Ed. J.-A. Miller. London: Routledge.

Lacan, J. (2015). *The Seminar of Jacques Lacan (1960–1961): Book VIII: Transference*. Ed. J.-A. Miller. Trans. B. Fink. Cambridge, UK and Malden, MA: Polity Press.

Lacan, J. (2016). *The Seminar of Jacques Lacan (1975–1976): Book XXIII: Le Sinthome*. Ed. J.-A. Miller. Trans. A. R. Price. Cambridge, UK: Polity Press.

Lacan, J. (2020). *The Seminar of Jacques Lacan (1956–1957): Book IV: The Object Relation*. Ed. J.-A. Miller. Trans. A. R. Price. Cambridge, UK and Medford, MA, USA: Polity Press.

Lewis, C. S. (1936). *The Allegory of Love*. Oxford: Clarendon Press.

Lochrie, K. (2005). *Heterosyncrasies: Female Sexuality When Normal Wasn't*. Minneapolis: University of Minnesota Press.

Moi, T. (1986). Desire in Language: Andreas Capellanus and the Controversy of Courtly Love. In D. Aers (Ed.), *Medieval Literature: Criticism, Ideology, and History* (pp. 11–33). London: Harvester Press.

Montefiore, J. (1987). *Feminism and Poetry: Language, Experience, Identity in Women's Writing*. London and New York: Pandora.

Morel, G. (2018). *The Law of the Mother: An Essay on the Sexual Sinthome*. London: Routledge.

Przybylo, E. and Cooper, D. (2014). Asexual Resonances: Tracing a Queerly Asexual Archive. *GLQ: A Journal of Lesbian and Gay Studies*, 20(3): 297–318.

Ragland, E. (1995). Psychoanalysis and Courtly Love. *Arthuriana*, 5(1): 1–20.

Ragland, E. (2001). Lacan and the Hommosexuelle. In T. Dean and C. Lane (Eds.), *Homosexuality and Psychoanalysis* (pp. 98–119). Chicago: University of Chicago Press.

Robertson, D. W. (1968). The Concept of Courtly Love as an Impediment to the Understanding of Medieval Texts. In F. X. Newman (Ed.), *The Meaning of Courtly Love* (pp. 1–18). Albany, NY: State University of New York Press.

Schultz, J. A. (2006). *Courtly Love, the Love of Courtliness, and the History of Sexuality*. Chicago: University of Chicago Press.

Sedgwick, E. K. (1985). *Between Men: English Literature and Male Homosocial Desire*. New York: Columbia University Press.

Söderbäck, F. (Ed.) (2010). *Feminist Readings of Antigone*. Albany, NY: SUNY Press.

Soler, C. (2006). *What Lacan Said about Women: A Psychoanalytic Study*. New York: Other Press.

Soler, C. (2016). *Lacanian Affects: The Function of Affect in Lacan's Work*. London: Routledge.

Stockton, W. (2010). How to do the History of Heterosexuality: Shakespeare and Lacan. *Literature Compass*, 7(4): 254–265.

Žižek, S. (1993). From Courtly Love to the Crying Game. *New Left Review*, I/202: 95–108.

Chapter 4

The Sublimation of Race

From the Courtly Lady to the Derelict White Body

Sheldon George

The first section of Jacques Lacan's Seminar VII, *The Ethics of Psychoanalysis*, comes to a close through Lacan's rhetorical deployment of a striking racial trope. While pivoting, at the end of chapter six, from a discussion of desire and the law to the focus on sublimation and the figure of the "Lady" in courtly love that would preoccupy the seminar's second section, Lacan first insists on the abiding influence of the law as it is articulated in the following commandment: "Thou shalt not covet thy neighbor's house, thou shalt not covet thy neighbor's wife, neither his man servant, neither his maid servant, neither his ox, nor his ass, nor anything that belongs to thy neighbor" (1997, p. 82). Lacan's playful assertion to the audience of his seminar is that this commandment makes many "smile" when it should not, and so he chastises those for whom "putting the wife between the house and the donkey", as the wording of the commandment does, suggests the "idea" that this law is a residue of "a primitive society – a society of Bedouins, 'wogs,' and 'niggers'" (p. 82).

But it would seem that Lacan here highlights the humorous responses of others to this commandment so that he himself can rhetorically invoke a scandalous reference to wogs (or nonwhites), Bedouins (or nomadic Arab tribes) and niggers.[1] Lacan's reference to these covetous primitives serves precisely to emphasise the law's lasting relevance to modern civilisation: "I don't agree" that the law is no longer pertinent, says Lacan, for the "law affirmed there", the "part concerning one's neighbor's wife at least, is still alive in the hearts of men who violate it every day" (p. 82). Strangely, then, it is race that, at least rhetorically, moves Lacan across these interconnected topics of desire, the law, courtly love, sublimation and, perhaps most significant, the Lady.

Lacan's ability to deploy race as a rhetorical launching pad for more pressing investigations into the Lady and ethics suggests Lacan's own ensnarement within the racial discourse of a period when the figure of the "nigger", or the "black", brought into particular alignment related questions of ethics, the law and the Lady. Lacan teaches the classes of this seminar from 1959 to 1960, a span of time when the Algerian war for independence from France had already raged for half a decade (1954–1962) and when the American Civil Rights movement would grant global attention to the plight of a group of people whose ethical demands for equality

DOI: 10.4324/9781003450795-4

rejected their reduction to the status of niggers. The American movement, in particular, responded to a history of slavery and Jim Crow segregation; and it recognised the barbaric laws and horrific practices of lynching that predominated the previous years as justified precisely by the idea that blacks are primitives driven by licentious, covetous desires that exceed the constraints of the law. Significantly, these desires were seen to be directed precisely at the (white) Lady.

Lacan's invocation of race and the Lady alongside of the law and desire aligns race and desire in ways that he failed to theorise. Lacan turns to the figure of the Lady to provide his audience with what he calls an "exemplary form, a paradigm, of sublimation" that retains "long-lasting influence" and "ethical ramifications that we still feel" (p. 128). For "a certain highly restricted circle", he suggests, courtly love is an "ideal" that serves as the "origin of a moral code, including a whole series of modes of behavior, of loyalties, measures, services, and exemplary forms of conduct" (p. 145). My interest is in articulating how race, too, functions to delineate a moral code of conduct that is anathema to an ethics of psychoanalysis, how it dictates modes of behaviours and loyalties that signal its status as a sublimated ideal.

Lacan speaks of the Lady as a produced image, a sublimation that transforms the flesh and blood Lady into an illusory manifestation of the Thing, the representative of the Real. My suggestion is that the figure of the black holds a similar relation to the Real, as a manifested Thing devoid of any personalised characteristics. This ascension to the status of Thing aligns the Lady and the black at the point of what Lacan calls Atè, as the gateway onto the Real. But where Atè designates a point of atrocious beauty, the Lady takes on the character of beauty that Lacan describes so clearly in his seminar, while the figure of the black is bound to the atrocity that makes that beauty emerge. Lacan associates the emergence of the beautiful with just such a background of atrocity, where something "decomposed and disgusting spreads out around" the beautiful (p. 273). The emergence of the beautiful white Lady in American history, and indeed the ascension of whiteness itself as a paradigm of beauty, marks a certain alignment and splitting of blackness and the Lady, whereby it is the atrocity brought to blackness, particularly through the practice of lynching, that sublimates the white Lady into the ascendent object of desire that cannot be touched.

Lacan notes that the ideal good that cannot be touched is easily transformed into the fantasy of a beauty that *must not* be touched (p. 239). It is precisely an interdiction against touching white women that, historically, has secured associations of whiteness with the beautiful. Here, I suggest, the white Lady serves as a sublimation of the Lacanian Imaginary that reconfigures the bodies of all white subjects. I will first engage the seminar's reading of the work of Melanie Klein to tie sublimation to race and the Lady. Then, I will trace the construction of the Imaginary white body within two primary regional and historical contexts: I shall present the emergence of Lacan's courtly Lady as framed within the historical moment of the Holy Crusades and their Christian war against brown Muslims; and I shall describe race in the American South as bound to myths of biblical patriarchs and embodied racial others who threaten an idealised white ego image. At issue with race is a struggle with the incapacities of the human body that white subjects have sought to overcome through reliance upon the figures of the (white) Lady and the embodied black other. What I shall show is that, starting with the Crusades, race itself emerges as a sublimation aimed at facilitating the white subject's Imaginary transcendence of the Real limitations of the body.

Sublimation and Race

Lacan's humorous reference to niggers would read like a hapax of the seminar if not for the fact that he again turns to race to discuss the body of the mother in section two of the text, titled "The Problem of Sublimation". This turn to race aligns race with sublimation in ways that Lacan fails to fully develop or integrate into the seminar. Though scholars such as Jacques-Alain Miller and Slavoj Žižek have found inspiration for their thinking on racism from ideas in this seminar, I wish to address specifically the seminar's implications for an understanding of race's relation to the body and sublimation. Lacan paves the way for his own discussion of the Lady as the sublimated Thing by engaging the work of Melanie Klein to refute Klein's positioning of the "mythic body of the mother at the central place of *das ding*", the place of the Thing (p. 106). Lacan critiques what he sees as the static nature of Klein's theory, the strict bond between the mother and the Thing, noting that Klein "locates the phases of all sublimation there" (p. 117). Klein discusses a patient named Ruth Kjar, whose mother's death leaves inside of her a sense of emptiness that is reawakened when her brother-in-law removes from her home a painting he had placed on the wall. Klein reads Kjar's efforts at replacing the missing painting with works of her own creation as a form of sublimation, seeing Kjar as transformed into an artist whose case confirms sublimation is linked to the mother's body. But Lacan critiques Klein by deploying race to expand the referential scope of a possible reading of sublimation.

Psychoanalytic critics like Jean Walton have read Klein's engagement with Kjar's case as emblematic of the ways that feminist psychoanalysts in the 1920s sought to reposition women at the centre of their inquires while ignoring the role of race in their patients' fantasies.[2] Lacan, however, seems for the moment to highlight race, pointing to Klein's lack of "astonishment" at the variety of painted figures that fill the wall: "First", he notes, "there is a nude negress, then a very old woman", and a number of other figures, ending with "the image of her own mother at the height of her beauty" (p. 117). Not only does the presence of the negress among a series of diverse representations emphasise a lack of correlation between sublimation and the mother for Lacan, but the otherness of the negress also helps facilitate Lacan's definition of sublimation as that which raises *any* object "to the dignity of the Thing" (p. 112). What Lacan thus explicitly unveils, but does not pursue within his own theory, is the potential for the racial other to be positioned by the subject in the sublimated place of *das Ding*.

Discarding race, Lacan's seminar instead engages the topic of sublimation through attention to the figure of the courtly Lady, who stands emblematically as the sublimated image of the *Ding*. In defining this *Ding*, Lacan makes a distinction between Freud's two German usages of the word thing: *die Sache* is the thing that is a product of human artistry or industry, such as a work of art or the idealised Lady of courtly poetry (p. 45); and *das Ding* is the alien Thing that is removed from all Symbolic representation. In courtly love, the Lady, as *die Sache,* is raised to the level of *das Ding*. This *Ding* is generated in the "original division" of the subject, at the point of the subject's initial emergence (p. 52). It is what flies off from subjectivity to produce the lack that constitutes the subject. The *Ding* is the excluded centre of subjectivity, an isolated absence that organises the subject's world in a series of signifying relations around it (p. 71). Lacan asserts that perception itself and all "adaptive development" of the subject are focused around the absent *Ding* (p. 53), such that reality is hallucinated in an effort to locate "pleasurable associations" that recall the *Ding* (p. 52). The mother and the Lady, as *die Sache,* are examples of such associations.

What we recognise through Kjar, however, is the added association of race with the *Ding*, race's ascension as a sublimated representative of the lost Thing. Lacan notes that in every form of sublimation emptiness is determinative (p. 129), for all art is a certain mode of organisation around an emptiness (p. 130). Kjar positions race precisely in this empty place left behind by the death of her mother, seeking to fill this emptiness through forms of racial whiteness and blackness that ultimately aim at allowing her entry into the world of art. Walton's reading of the role of the negress in facilitating this entry is useful. Walton describes Kjar's attempt at artistic creation as a potential threat to the patriarchal Symbolic that aligns true artistry with men like Kjar's brother-in-law. She cites the art scholar Lynda Nead to argue that to paint "a female nude" is to "seek legitimacy as creator of high art", for "more than any other subject, the female nude connotes Art", standing as a "shorthand for art more generally", as an "icon of western culture, a symbol of civilization and accomplishment" (p. 796). One may attain the culturally sublimated position of artist vis-à-vis one's relation to the female body, but Walton notes that this is specifically the white female body. Kjar is shrewdly able to deflect retaliation from men who reject her attempted entry into "the male domain of high art" by painting a naked black female, instead of a supposed raceless, white nude (p. 798). She disarms critique of her artistic aspirations and suggests the primitive, untutored nature of her artistry through the primitive nature of her subject matter: a female negress. Her sublimated status as painter thus relies upon an artistry that centralises race as the support of her white female identity.

Kjar's case is intriguing for the ways it positions the female body in artistic sublimations. If the nude white female body here retains in art the iconic status that prevailed centuries earlier for the Lady of courtly love, Walton's engagement with Kjar highlights a need to understand sublimation of the female form beyond the courtly past that centres Lacan's attention. And it suggests the need to expand Lacan's theory for inclusion of race in conceptualisations of sublimation. My own proposition is that, in spite of his disinterested deployment of race, Lacan's *Ethics* seminar traces the rudiments of a theory of racism, rudiments which can serve here as a foundation for a more expansive reading of race. Lacan's focus on the covetous neighbour ultimately sets the stage for what Derek Hook has referred to as "the theft of *Jouissance* thesis" that emerges in the works of Lacan's prominent followers, Jacques-Alain Miller and Slavoj Žižek (Hook, 2021, p. 36). Miller's reading is particularly useful for our purposes. In his essay "*Extimité*", Miller focuses on the extimacy of the Thing, or what Lacan describes in the seminar as its "intimate exteriority", the fact that the Thing that intimately structures consciousness is exterior to it (p. 139). It is this extimacy of the Thing that aligns the Lady with race.

Lacan views the Lady as marking the place of the absent Thing. She stands as the idealised "Sovereign good, which is das Ding, which is the mother, [and] is also the object of incest . . . a forbidden good" (p. 70). *Das Ding* is forbidden because it is upon the *Ding's* exclusion that the psychic apparatus of the subject is dependent. The Symbolic universe of the subject structures itself around this primal exclusion. The need to maintain the *Ding's* status as excluded centre is what fuels the artistry of the courtly love tradition. Centralised in the tradition is a sexual eroticism built on "techniques of holding back" (p. 152). The Lady stands within this tradition as an unattainable ideal, in pursuit of which one confronts only "detours and obstacles" (p. 152).

It is because the Thing must not be touched that the Lady raised to its level is bound to the covetous desires Lacan references in his discussion of the commandments. Lacan argues that the commandments function like the law, regulating "the distance between the subject and *das Ding*" (p. 69). But any law has a compounding effect upon the subject's transgressive desires (p. 83). The law is what designates the object that should not be coveted, but, in the process, it grants the object a hyperbolic character, tying to it an erotics and a desire that exceed the subject's moral restraints (p. 83). For Lacan, the subject's covetousness, agitated by the law, is not directed at any object the subject "might desire", but at an object that represents the Thing, at "a thing that is my neighbor's Thing" (p. 83). The subject is stirred to covet the neighbour's Thing by what Lacan calls *Lebensneid*, "the jealousy born in a subject in his relation to an other, insofar as this other is held to enjoy a certain form of *jouissance* or superabundant vitality" (p. 237). Racism, we can say, acts out this *Lebensneid*. The neighbour's enjoyment drives the racist beyond mere covetousness toward "the point of hatred and the need to destroy" because this enjoyment awakens the racist's recognition of a *jouissance*, bound to the neighbour's Thing, that the racist subject himself lacks (p. 237).

Miller's reading of racism aligns with my own understanding of *jouissance* as a pleasure imagined to be the possession of the other. The racial other's apparent moments of *jouissance*, the visible signs of his enjoyment, signal that he has accessed the lost Thing, or indeed that he has absconded with the subject's own Thing through a theft of *jouissance*. Here we recognise racism as, in Miller's words, "founded on what one imagines about the Other's jouissance" (p. 79); and this recognition has led Miller to clarify that, though "we cannot deny that races do exist", they only exist "insofar as they are, in Lacan's words, races of discourse" (1994, p. 81). But while Miller here centralises discourse, tying the Symbolic to the Imaginary through language, I would like to develop in the rest of this chapter a notion of the psychic link between the raced body itself – especially the white female body – and racism.

My focus here will resonate, though somewhat distantly, with a passing observation of Frantz Fanon's. The Martinique theorist, in one of his longest footnotes to his groundbreaking *Black Skin, White Masks*, enticingly suggests the need to investigate the impact of "the appearance of the Negro" upon the imago or imaginary image of a white child during "Lacan's mirror period" (1967, p. 161). Arguing that "the cycle of the biological" begins "with the Negro", Fanon speculates that we may note a bodily response to the racial other, an "imaginary aggression" emerging from the subject confronted by racial otherness (p. 161). I wish to trace this aggression, but I locate its roots – perhaps counter Fanon – not in the body of the racial other who stands before the subject, but in the psyche and physical body of the racist subject himself. At issue here is a bodily loss that is mediated at the level of the psyche by racial identity and racism.

Lacan describes jouissance as "the pound of flesh", or the sacrificed loss, that subjects must surrender upon entry into the Symbolic by way of language (1997, p. 322). Here Lacan's wording is instructive. What the Lacanian subject attains through language is a psyche stricken by lack, a consciousness depleted of all that escapes linguistic circumscription. But this loss exceeds language, for it is also written onto the body. The subject's anatomical loss, its pound of flesh, is what is symbolised by the phallus, which is always seen, by subjects of any gender, as an absent object preventing completion of the bodily image. The body itself lacks, and according to Lacan, this is the cause of a psychic sense of utter dereliction that plagues each subject.

The body is carved into erogenous zones of pleasure that can never compensate for lost jouissance. The Thing, which can be fantasised as the mother or the Lady but fully exceeds each of these, stands as the primordial loss that can never be recovered. Existence within the Symbolic means existence within the dereliction of the body; it means isolation from *das Ding* in a "world" that finally "is our body" (1997, p. 93). This is the world that Lacan ties to religious fantasies of the fall of man, who is cast out of the garden and forever loses access to the divine *Ding* positioned as his god. In conceptions like these, the subject and his Symbolic are "united with the diabolic", says Lacan, as fallen man seems to be given over to "the figure who was for a long time known as the prince of the world, Diabolus himself" (p. 92). Thus, for Lacan, it is perhaps Luther who best voices the feeling of dereliction germane to the subject and articulated in certain overriding religious sensibilities: "You are that waste matter which falls into the world from the devil's anus" (p. 93). It is in contention against such dereliction that race is brought onto the scene.

Historicising Sublimation: The Birth of Race

Lacan's focus on courtly love begins a process of historicising the dereliction of the body that I would here like to continue through attention to race, racism and race-based slavery. Lacan reads the sublimation of the Lady in courtly love as a culturally sanctioned expression of the drive that emerges "at a certain histori-cal moment" in time (1997, p. 112). Sublimation satisfies the drive in its aim at the *Ding* by providing the object as a substitute for the unattainable Thing. But sublimation privileges only certain objects, those that are valorised and esteemed by society. Because sublimation channels the drive through the agency of the dis-courses of the Symbolic, what sublimation allows us to do, I argue, is historicise the psyche and its drives. Sublimation displays correlations between the psychic struggles of groups of people and manifested historical and cultural phenomena. Lacan reads courtly love as a discourse that fashioned the Lady as representative of the Thing starting "probably" at "the middle or at the beginning of the eleventh century, and continu[ing] into the twelfth or even, in Germany, to the beginning of the thirteenth" (p. 145).[3] I point to race as a supplementary discourse about subjec-tive dereliction from *das Ding* that begins during the Crusades and stabilises with the rise of the slave trade in the sixteenth century. Through this discourse, we are able to chart something of the history of the racist Western psyche.

The Crusades occur during the Dark Ages, in the very centuries when we see the rise of courtly love.[4] Significantly, this historical moment is when we first witness a formalising of race as a category of difference among groups of people of different skin colour. What characterises the Crusades is religious fervour that fuelled racial strife. The Crusades occurred at the turn of the first millennium, one thousand years after the death of Christ, at the time when the biblical Book of Revelation proph-esied the coming of God's Kingdom. The popular belief of the period was that the judgement day would soon arrive: after being bound for a thousand years, Satan would be set loose upon the earth, and the Antichrist's final defeat by Jesus would bring about the end of the world. As scholar and psychoanalytic theorist Farhad Dalal has argued, this sociohistorical context "cathected" the psyches of a God-fearing people with intense "fear and hope" (p. 146). The Bible outlined a terrify-ing present in which the world could end at any moment and all who are judged to be wanting would be damned forever. But the Crusades and their Holy War against racial others would promise an attainable route to salvation.

The Crusades themselves become a sublimation that was sanctioned by the church as a means toward escaping earthly dereliction. Lacan argues that sublima-tion is located at the level where man fashions a signifier to represent and manage the emptiness that is *das Ding* (p. 121). The signified object attains hermeneutical value, allowing the subject to address the existential question of his dereliction and his ultimate place in the world. Through his Lady, for example, the courtly lover measures his distance from a seemingly attainable ultimate good. The lover's quest, and the little tasks or heroic feats he performs for his Lady, function as impediments and tangible barriers outlining the borders that must be crossed to reach the unimaginable *Ding*.[5] Running parallel with the tradition of courtly love, the Crusades position the racial other, for the first time, as barrier to *das Ding*, and the quest that this other impedes is a divine Crusade sublimated as the earthly path toward the Kingdom of Heaven.

The first Crusade begins in 1095, when Pope Urban II initiates a Holy War against Turkish Muslims. As Dalal explains, "the Holy war was a war of the forces of light against the forces of darkness" (p. 150). It marked the period when the blackness of one's skin came to be equated with the darkness of one's soul (p. 142), and the Crusades themselves "resulted in Europe starting to define itself as Christian and white" (p. 151). Contrastingly, people of the Middle East were equated with the "Devil and his forces of evil", making the killing of brown people by whites come to be "seen not only as a moral duty, but also as a divine act sanctified by God", a sublimated act of penance that would guarantee entrance into God's Kingdom at the turn of a new millennium (p. 151). The Crusades thus produced race in answer to an existential quandary concerning one's dereliction from God's presence, and they simultaneously established racism and the killing of racial others as a return route to the jouissance of *das Ding*.

In sublimation, it is the very process of signifying the emptiness of the *Ding* that makes possible the hope of filling it. In the Crusades and extending into the emergence of slavery, race promised to fill an extimate lack that is internal to the subject but positioned in the beyond. Lacan himself notes, in *Seminar XVII*, a discursive shift that allows for a new relation to the *Ding* in the sixteenth century, one that I suggest coincides with the rise of race-based slavery. Whether "because of Luther, Calvin or some unknown traffic of ships around Genoa, or in the Mediterranean Sea", says Lacan, at a certain point in history, "jouissance became calculable, could be counted, totalised" (p. 177). Lacan identifies this traffic of ships as the moment when "capital begins", the moment when jouissance becomes tied to possible objects of exchange, but he fails to acknowledge that what was being trafficked in these ships at the birth of capital was not merely goods but also, quite often, enslaved bodies-as-goods (p. 177).

This conjoined emergence of slavery with capitalism is not surprising from the perspective of the psyche's relation to the body and *das Ding*. Lacan alerts us at the start of the *Ethics* seminar that at the end of his inquiry into ethics we will find the "structure embodied in the imaginary relation", whereby "narcissistic man" becomes a "double" of some other (1997, p. 14). This other, Lacan argues at the end of the seminar, is the father, or any "imaginary other", who is seen to hold the power "to deprive" the subject of what he wants (p. 234). In the *Ethics* seminar, Lacan ties lack and covetousness to the subject's psychic body image, as it develops in the Imaginary, and to privation within the Symbolic. This covetousness is bound both to the sense of being deprived, at the level of the body, of something needed to complete the self, and to the desire for the power to deprive others of the objects that signal power and jouissance in the Symbolic. Where, in the sixteenth century, capital comes to be tied to power and slaves come to be transformed into forms of capital – into fungible objects situated within a system of monetary exchange – race-based slavery gives rise to powerful discourses that refute dereliction with rooted fantasies about the core being of varieties of racialised subjects.

In *Seminar XX*, Lacan presents the religious concept of the human soul as based upon fantasies of being, fantasies that we can recognize as often intersecting historically with race. Lacan defines being in *Seminar XI* as the jouissance or pound of flesh lost to the subject in the Vel, that forced choice by which subjects gain subjectivity through meaning but give up being, or jouissance (p. 219). Religion, argues Lacan, provides subjects a means of recuperating this lost being and tolerating "the intolerable in [their derelict] world" (1997, p. 84) by constituting the soul as a "semblance of being", as an echo of the being possessed by the Supreme Being (p. 92). With the rise of slavery, race provided a means of obfuscating dereliction and calculating one's relation to being through race's articulation within various prevailing religious and philosophical understandings of the world, including within the famous concept of the Great Chain of Being.

This concept, which originates with Plato and Aristotle, established a hierarchical structure for the Symbolic, vertically arranging all levels of being from God, through the various orders of angels, to animate and inanimate earthly objects. And, as Henry Louis Gates, Jr. has noted, "by 1750, the chain had become individualized" with a subdivided "human scale" (p. 45) that positioned blacks "as the 'lowest' of the human races, or as first cousin to the ape" (p. 46). The chain established notions of racial superiority by pinning dereliction to blackened peoples whose dark souls seemed devoid of some quality of being, some full humanness, and who could thus be relegated to enslavement and to commodification as objects of exchange. By establishing race as an external sign of one's internal relation to being, the chain sublimated race and racial difference as governing concepts that unveiled the very structure of God's universe. Not only could race help explain God's plans for the derelict world and the Kingdom to come, but it introduced whole new ways for measuring being and modulating one's relation to lost jouissance. Race thus rooted subjects in a novel relation to *das Ding*, a relation that could only be secured through recurrent insistences upon racial fantasies of being that would structure social reality across the multiple centuries to come.

The Body of the Mythical Patriarch

We have seen that Lacan's *Seminar VII* reads courtly love as an erotics that prevailed until the thirteenth century but generated ideals for "exemplary forms of conduct" that had lasting social impact (p. 145). Still, for Lacan, what finally roots moral propriety and stands as ultimate support for the law and its super-egoic rules of conduct is the mythical death of the father. Here I wish to extend my historical reading of race by focusing on race as a mediator of psychic lack that conjoined the myth of the father's death with sublimation of the Lady in the particular location of the American South in the 1800s. I will read patriarchal metaphors and moral codes of honour that emerge in the antebellum and postbellum South as expressive of an Oedipal myth that binds southern gentility and morality to unethical acts of racism. Through rereading Freud's Oedipal complex in relation to Lacan's *Ethics* seminar, I will first display the psychic fears of castration that drive, equally, the bodily images of patriarchal, genteel southerners and the race-relations that structure antebellum America. I will then highlight a shift from a mere sublimation of race, in antebellum attempts to access jouissance, to a more active embrace of transgression as a direct route toward confronting the *Ding* in postbellum American practices of lynching black men and women.

Our attention to the American South and its Oedipal myths allows for a Lacanian corrective to flawed hierarchal readings of raced individuals and their psyches that appear in the theories of Sigmund Freud. The core notion presented in concepts such as the Great Chain of Being, that groups of human beings can be stacked vertically according to race, helped produce ideas of biological recapitulation that would shape Freud's work in *Totem and Taboo*. As one of "the most influential ideas of late nineteenth-century science", recapitulation held that the various stages of a *species'* development are recapitulated or repeated in the *individual's* growth from childhood to adulthood (Gilman, 1995, p. 27). This concept helped spur Freud's attempt to reconstruct the violent past of human history through analysis of children and so-called savages who seemed, to Freud, to be situated at an earlier stage of psychic development (1989c, p. 3). Freud articulates a flawed conception of the Oedipus complex through reliance upon the myth of a prehistoric past and the murder of the father of the primordial horde, a story that Lacan himself calls nothing but "Darwinian buffoonery" (2007, p. 112). Lacan's dismissal of the evolutionary pseudo-science that, in Freud's times and in his work, established developmental variations in the psyches of Western men and savages, allows us to strip away some of the racial assumptions imbedded in conceptions of the Oedipal complex.

Lacan asserts that whenever he talks about the complex it is always in relation to the paternal metaphor (2007, p. 112). The paternal metaphor is a metaphor for the function of language itself, which introduces lack and strikes being, in equal measure, from the psyches of all subjects, despite their race. But in antebellum America, we find that lack is refuted by white subjects through paternal imagery buttressed by notions of religion and race. Though the kinds of scientific racism I reference above were popular across the globe and held especial sway in Europe, they were overshadowed in the American South by a centering, patriarchal biblical narrative of race: the story told in Genesis 9 of the curse placed upon Ham by his father, Noah. This story is important both because it was the central biblical justification for slavery and because it helped refit the derelict body of southerners through idealised glorifications of biblical patriarchs whose stories reinforced the imago, or psychic body image, of members of a mannered gentile southern society.

Ham's story is precisely about the body of the patriarch. For witnessing his drunken father's nakedness and failing to cover him, Ham is cursed by Noah with the promise that his descendants will be slaves to the children of Ham's brothers, Shem and Japheth. For centuries this narrative was turned to in efforts to explain the emergence of varieties of human beings and to justify slavery. Though the Bible never specifies the races of the three brothers, their status as descendants of Noah

at the time of the flood – when God cleansed the world of all life not safely seques-
tered on the arc – positioned them in popular readings as the forefathers of three
races: whites, blacks and Asians. During the "ninth and tenth centuries", in the
midst of the Crusades and traditions of courtly love, race first came to be used to
sanction slavery as the biblical curse placed on Africans as putative descendants of
Ham (Haynes, 2002, p. 7).[6] This association set the stage for southern justifications
of slavery by rooting slavery in race and in the biblical shaming of the white body.

The narrative of Noah's curse inverts Freud's myth of the father of the primordial horde to signal a threat to the white body. A myth, Lacan stipulates, is "a chron-
icle expressing in an imaginary way the fundamental relationships characteristic
of a certain mode of being human at a specific period" (1979, p. 408). Variations
within myths introduce cultural and historical specificity to narratives that express
what Lacan calls the castration of the subject – the severing of that pound of flesh –
but in the Western world these myths are primarily articulated around notions of
the depriving father who, in an unforgivable act of privation, stakes claim to the
mother and bars the subject from jouissance. Freud's myth of the father of the primordial horde, for example, displays Freud's own succumbing to the fantasy of a
savage, apparently racialised being who escapes castration and accesses absolute
jouissance through possession of all the women of the tribe. In Freud, it is the
revolt of the sons who bring an end to the father's jouissance. This fantasy of a
possible escape from castration, and of belligerent sons who introduce lack, is also
what we see in the southern embrace of the story of Noah. But here it is specifically
the black son who brings lack.

As Stephen Haynes has argued, core to readings of Ham's story "were Noah's
exaltation as a righteous and obedient patriarch and Ham's deprecation as a worthless son" (p. 69). Southern principles of honour and gentlemanly conduct framed
such readings. Noah's curse was seen as justifiably resulting from "filial dishonor",
from mocking not just a parent but a patriarch chosen by God (p. 73). Revising
Freud's story of the murdered father, the two most popular *European* explanations
for the severity of Noah's curse were that Ham had either castrated his father or
rendered him impotent with a magic spell (p. 35). But such images of castration
seem to hold an extimate, excluded status in the narratives of the South. What figured this castration, doing so both powerfully and obliquely, was the nakedness of
the disrobed patriarch whose function was to serve as a model imago, or Imaginary
image, of southern patriarchy.

The popularity of this story emerged from its ability to justify slavery while
simultaneously exalting a reinforcing egoic image for genteel slave holders. Southern slaveholders regarded "themselves as patriarchs in the tradition of Noah" and
demanded respect from their families as well as from slaves, who were seen as
falling under the protective authority of the patriarch (Haynes, 2002, p. 79). To a
society that prized honour and highly valued external appearances of grace that
signal internal merit, Ham's act was a severe effrontery marking a shameful dis-
robing of a primordial father. As Haynes explains, "Noah is figuratively stripped
under Ham's gaze, while his brothers reclothe their father in an attempt to preserve

his threatened honor" (p. 79). It is this action by Ham, as forefather of the black race, that justifies his descendants' slavery, a condition that, as Haynes explains, is defined in the South "as a life without honor, and thus worse than death" (p. 81). The story registers white psychic fears over the instability of the fantasy ego image that framed southern society. It uses race to reinforce the very hierarchical class structures, based on a culture of gentility, that are figured within the narrative as threatened by the gaze of the racial other.

This other allowed for both a modification of southerners' mythical relation to the primordial father figured through Noah and a weakening of the prohibitions against jouissance that are typically instated by the death of the father. Freud's myth shows the murder of the father giving rise to civilisation, as this murder unifies the sons in a patricide that produces super-egoic feelings of guilt (1989a, p. 93). What both Lacan's *Ethics* seminar and southern culture itself highlight, however, is a splitting of the figure of the father, which, in the South, allows for a certain avoidance of guilt. In focusing on the function of the father as metaphor and myth, Lacan differentiates the "real father", as an embodied other of the real world, from the "imaginary father", who frames the child's self-image (p. 308). In southern society, the Imaginary father, Noah, was split in three, manifesting as forefathers to three respective races; but to the southern psyche, it was the black forefather, Ham, who was critically significant and who framed a relation to jouissance.

Lacan explains that it is access to the mother, as Lady or as symbol of jouissance, that elevates the real father to the godly status of the Imaginary father. This father emerges as a mythical father whose idealisation ensures he exists only as a dead father, as an ideal – like Noah – that neither the child nor the real father can embody (1997, p. 308). What this ideal father does embody, instead, is the loss the child has suffered at the levels of his body and his psyche, and it is thus toward the idealised Imaginary father that the child usually expresses his "hatred for the creator", who not only deprives him of enjoyment but also made him "such a weak and inadequate creature" (p. 309). Ham stood, however, as an Imaginary forefather who did not create the white race but yet is hated and held responsible for its lack. Ham took unto himself all of the aggression typically addressed to the Imaginary father by the child, thus facilitating the ascension of figures like Noah, who frame an Imaginary ego that rooted southern patriarchy. Simultaneously, he allowed for a guiltless expression of violence toward Ham's descendants. As embodied racial others, it is these descendants who take the place of Lacan's real father, figuring as the "rival" who Lacan maintains is held responsible for the subject's castration (1997, p. 307). Where Ham is only unconsciously imagined as castrating Noah and threatening the patriarchal ego image that framed southern gentility, especially postbellum blacks come to embody this rival who aims to deprive the subject of the Lady as his source of jouissance.

After the Civil War, in the postbellum South, we witness another coalescing of racial violence with sublimation of the Lady, and just as sublimation made violence a social ideal during the Crusades, the Lady here functioned as accomplice to an externalisation of aggression tied to subjective embodiment. The Civil War forestalled efforts to explain black subservience through the figure of Ham by bringing slavery to an end; but the freedom of blacks made more urgent the white southern effort to segregate racial members of the emergent postbellum society. In this era, it was the figure of Ham's grandson, Nimrod, that dominated and that thus helped frame a white Imaginary ego. In this moment of new freedoms for blacks, Nimrod was viewed as "the primordial human rebel", conceived as a patriarch of the black race who defied God's will by building the Tower of Babel (Haynes, 2002, p. 113). God's angered response, in confusing the language of the builders, was proof to postbellum southerners that God's plan demanded a separation of groups and races, and it also helped to establish the image of Nimrod as "a shameless miscegenist" bent on uniting the races (p. 113). Through Nimrod, southern society channelled its anger over the actual shattering of its patriarchal ego image that had been tied to plantations and cultural structures now decimated by the war. Nimrod, in his rebelliousness toward patriarchal authority and his desire for race mixing, facilitated southern efforts to direct aggression over psychic and social losses toward blacks occupying the postbellum South.

In Freud's model, the Oedipal murder of the father redirects aggression toward the self because it generates both guilt and the super ego. The guilt-ridden child comes to identify with the father, and the "aggressiveness" that he feels toward the father who deprives him of jouissance is introjected and aimed at the child's own ego; this aggression is then taken on by a portion of the ego that "sets itself against the rest of the ego as a super ego" or a "conscience" (1989a, p. 84). But what we have in the South is a weakening of the agency of the super ego, precisely because aggression that should be directed inward finds expression externally upon the racial other. Lacan argues that the only thing that bars the subject from the aggression awakened by his pursuit of jouissance is the fear of "assaulting the image of the other" through which the subject was "formed as an ego" (1997, p. 195). It is this reverence for the unifying ego image that generates "the leveling power of certain laws of equality" in a given society, establishing that "common denominator of the respect for certain rights" that seems to prevail in American society (p. 195). But, as Lacan notes, this sense of equality generated by a unifying ego image can yet "take the form of excluding from its boundaries, and therefore from its protection, everything that is not integrated into its various registers" (p. 195). What we find in the South is a society rooted in an ego image that found its ultimate support in the physical differences of raced bodies.

Such differences did more than secure an Imaginary white egoic body image. They also agitated antebellum southern practices of lynching tied to the white Lady but aimed at the *Ding* of the Real. It was the supposed covetousness of the black man – whose "bestial propensities" (Wells-Barnett, 1991, p. 31) ever threatened to defile the "honor" of white women – that ostensibly justified southern postbellum acts of lynching (p. 30). The number of African Americans lynched in the 1880s and 1890s averaged over one hundred per year (p. 3). This proliferation of lynching in the postbellum South speaks to lynching's psychic import, which exceeds any true relation to the Lady; what it speaks to is lynching's ability to manifest the

Ding as an attainable object, an object often circulated through collections of body parts taken from the corpses of lynch victims. As James Allen's *Without Sanctuary* allows us to see – through a striking compilation of lynching postcards that were popularly disseminated across the South – the "dismemberment and distribution of severed bodily parts as favors and souvenirs to participants and the crowd" were common practices at lynchings (p. 14). Whether the lynching involved hanging or burning black bodies, everything from "teeth" to "ears, toes, fingers, nails, kneecaps, bits of charred skin and bones" was collected as "trophies" that "might reappear as watch fobs or be displayed conspicuously for public viewing" (p. 14). Through these collections of body parts and circulated postcards, we see southerners' sublimation of not just the Lady but also the black body in their attempted approach to the *Ding*.

In a notable moment in *Seminar VII*, Lacan speaks of proliferation of objects, particularly those that are collected, as demonstrating a distinction between an "imaginary fixation" directed at the object itself (the sublimated Lady, for instance, or the severed body part) and the "revelation of the Thing beyond the object" (p. 114). Lacan describes a friend with an extensive collection of empty matchboxes, arguing that it is the matchboxes' "wholly gratuitous, proliferating, superfluous" and "imposing multiplicity" that points to their "thingness as match box[es]" (p. 114). Lacan's discussion of the empty boxes is what brings him to his reading of Klein in the following chapter, and of the emptiness that is replaced by the image of the negress. For Lacan, what is involved in this proliferation of matchboxes is a creation *ex nihilo*, a creation out of nothing, where the boxes or any created object may fill the function of representing the Thing (p. 119). The empty object, Lacan says, creates the void and thereby introduces the possibility of filling it (p. 120). Through lynchings, white southerners attempted to adumbrate the *Ding* within a proliferation of violence that reduced black lives and black subjecthood to empty nothingness.

Lacan notes that when a subject in radical pursuit of the *Ding* "approaches that central emptiness" through which "*jouissance* has presented itself" to him, the other's "body breaks into pieces" (p. 202). But what is at issue in this breaking is the inferiority of the subject's own body to that of the other, whether this other is figured as the real father, as the savage father of the primordial horde, or as the bestial black man who pilfers the Lady as lost object. Lacan argues that the "form of the body, and especially its image", represents "the relationship of man to his [own] death", as the ultimate object that restricts his full access to *jouissance* (p. 298). This body image, apprehensible in the other, presents itself as "a barrier to the Other-thing that lies beyond" (p. 298). And so, when the other is established in relation to the *Ding*, as barrier to the Thing, the body of the other rises up to confront the subject as a "total object", as a whole, uncastrated other who is "silhouetted there" in the midst of a "charnel house figure", in the midst of the crumbled, enfeebled form of the subject's own body (p. 202).

It is for this reason that the savage, bestial black man must be destroyed, precisely because what is silhouetted in his sublimation as emptied body is, paradoxically, "the indestructible character of the Other" (p. 202). The insistent, repetitive nature of lynchings, their progression from castrations to a severing of body parts and finally to hangings or burnings, mark the black body as an indestructible object. This body rises up to veil the *Ding*, sublimated as an embodied impediment that must be destroyed over and over again with each new lynching. Through constituting the black man as a savage manifestation of the primal body, southern whites sought, truly, to transcend their own imprisoned embodiment. By first establishing the body of this other as the manifested barrier to the *Ding*, they made possible the prospect of accessing this *Ding* – which is denied by their own bodies – through the gruesome process of shattering the black bodies of racial others.

Beauty and Transgression

This relation I have traced between the *Ding*, the racialised body and Oedipal myths that inform cultural understandings of sublimation challenges the discrete distinctions Lacan's seminar makes between art and religion. Where the work of art fashions a signifier – the sublimated Lady, for instance – that "represents" the Thing, religion "displaces" the Thing, for Lacan, manifesting the Thing in an object that stagnates desire (p. 131). But our reading of the Lady in relation to race suggests a coalescing of the functions of religion and art. In keeping with Lacan's reading of the lost "pound of flesh" as "precisely the thing that religion undertakes to recuperate", race, as we have seen, draws upon religion to compensate for lack (p. 322). Simultaneously, however, race makes possible an artistic sublimation of the Lady as a figure of beauty. Particularly in later discursive constructs of the Lady that are ignored in Lacan's focus on courtly love, the Lady becomes the white Lady, and she stands as reification of the beautiful. It is through the Lady's beauty, I wish to now show, that the (white) body itself is recuperated as a symbol of plenitude, as an ideal of a white physical form that defies subjective dereliction.

The distinction Lacan makes between religion and works of art is apparent from his discussion of the image of Jesus Christ on the crucifix and his reading of Antigone as a literary figure whose beauty redefines an audience's relation to *das Ding*. Lacan presents the image of the crucifixion as a sublimation that evinces religion's ability to displace desire onto an object that actively stagnates desire. The crucifixion is the apotheosis of a sadism, says Lacan, the divinisation of a limit in which a being remains in a state of suffering (p. 261). One notes a similar divinisation of suffering in acts of lynching, where masses of people congregate around a sacrificed victim whose death becomes a great good, a glorious communal attestation that structures – more so than the Lady whose honour was only pretext for the slaughter to come – the moral conduct of a barbarous society. With their accompanying memorabilia and postcards of black bodies in endless suffering, such racist acts aimed at eternalising a particular relation to the *Ding*. If, as Lacan says, religion has been crucifying man in holiness for centuries, race has been sanctifying white men and women in racism since at least the Middle Ages (p. 262).

White racism stagnates desire, fixating it at the limit-point that Lacan calls Atè. This Atè is precisely where Lacan positions the crucifixion. Tied to the word atrocious, the Atè is a simultaneous barrier and lure to the destructive jouissance we aim at in the beyond. It stands at the threshold, as a limit that protects us from and yet binds us to the impossible jouissance of the beyond by attracting to itself all the threads of our desire (p. 261). What I wish to suggest is that both race and racism intersect with religion to take on a cross-historical function as Atè, wherein the racialised black other stands as barrier to a fantasised white *jouissance* that reshapes subjective desire into white racial desire. Additionally, I maintain, the racial other, as barrier, functions simultaneously as lure, exciting not just desire but also the drive. While racial desire facilitates production of the white body as an object of beauty – one that, I argue, is somewhat at odds with Lacan's conception of the beautiful – the drive aims at an end to all forms of embodiment.

For Lacan, the beautiful is apprehended at "the very point of the transition between life and death" (p. 297). The beautiful rises up to mark the place of Atè, solidifying Atè in its function as limit, as barrier to the life-destroying Thing. Lacan presents beauty itself as an effect of this *Ding*: the beautiful radiates with the "unbearable brilliance" of the Thing, achieving its most determinative function when, "only in a blinding flash", it unveils "man's true relation to his own death" (p. 29). As Lacan shows in his reading of Antigone, such unveiling occurs if one breaches the limit of Atè and enters into the zone of the *Ding*. From here, says Lacan, "the beam of desire", for those who witness such an atrocious crossing, "is both reflected and refracted" to produce the inherently pacifying "effect of beauty on desire" (p. 248). Rather than stagnating desire, as religion does, beauty purifies desire, disrupting its relation to the atrocity of the Thing. Such disruption is what Lacan isolates in his focus on Antigone, a figure of beauty who, in breaching the barrier of Atè by burying herself in her brother's tomb, makes visible the limit that should not be crossed. Lacan argues that through her crossing of the Atè Antigone purifies the audience's desire for such atrocity by perpetuating, eternalizing, and immortalising that Atè (p. 283). But the sublimation of an eternally suffering black body does not pacify the lyncher, and, unlike Antigone, the beautiful white Lady does not redirect desire away from its aim toward the atrocious.

What we find through engagement with the history of race is a modification of the Lady in her function as the beautiful. Lacan's Lady of courtly love both represents the Thing and sustains the fantasy of its attainment through tasks and obstacles that make her inaccessible; unlike Antigone, who redirects desire by making manifest the Atè that stands in place of the Thing, the courtly Lady functions as an object of desire. But the racialised white Lady (of the South, for example) is an object of desire that makes visible the limit of Atè for the very purpose of breaching this limit. She allows for the glorification of race as an image of the beautiful and for an erection of racism as the sublimated atrocity, or the Atè, that both bars and lures entry into the zone of *das Ding*. She agitates not only a resolute racial desire but also a drive-level insistence on breaching all boundaries of the atrocious. Here, the line of the limit is drawn so that it can be transgressed, and the body of the racial other emerges as the very site of an atrocity, as reification of a penetrable, raced Atè barring entry onto the jouissance of the Thing. As Lacan himself explains, without transgression there is no access to jouissance. Mere sublimation, of the kind the subject embraces in directing desire to a Lady or a stagnating Atè, only binds subjects to fantasy, offering "no direct satisfaction" from the Thing (p. 94). But transgression functions as what Lacan calls "the all-terrain vehicle" that breaks the subject free of the well-trodden satisfactions to which he is ethically limited (p. 177). Transgression allows for a self-destructive confrontation with the Thing of the Real.

Lacan's seminar, taught in the end of the 1950s during the peak of the American Civil Rights movement, does not account for this relation between transgression, race and the Thing; but African American writers who are contemporary to Lacan bear witness to both this relation itself and the violence that ensues from it. In particular, James Baldwin, in his 1965 short story *Going to Meet the Man*, presents an incisive illustration of the racialised white Lady's ability to generate both white phallic desire that defies castration and transgressive racism that defies the pacifying function of beauty outlined by Lacan. Baldwin's story focuses on the erotic implications of a lynching as they play out upon a white deputy sheriff named Jesse. Tying desire to race, the text begins with Jesse lying in bed with his wife, unable to achieve an erection. The narrative conveys that Jesse's sexual difficulties are linked to his obsession over his inability to break the will of an imprisoned black Civil Rights protester. But Jesse's recalling of the violence he commits upon the protester takes him back to a lynching he witnessed during his childhood, as an 8-year-old boy seated on top of his father's shoulders. As a child, Jesse recognised that his father was carrying him "through a mighty test" and revealing "to him a great secret which would be key to his life forever" (p. 248). The experience initiated Jesse into his racial whiteness. Simultaneously, it generated the structures of (racial) desire and the modes of accessing jouissance that would later repeat for Jesse through the violence of the prison and his sexual difficulties with his wife.

Jesse's induction into whiteness starts with his relation to a blackness that is terrifying, a blackness embodied by a black man who is accused of raping a white woman. The man holds an incomparable power. In seeing the man's stripped black body, Jesse focuses on "the nigger's privates", which are "cupped" in the hands of a white man with a knife as if they are a "remote" piece of "meat being weighed in the scales" (p. 247). Jesse is convinced that the phallic pound of flesh is "much heavier" and "much bigger" than his "father's flaccid, hairless" genitals (pp. 247–248). The man's genitals are "the largest thing he had ever seen till then, and the blackest" (p. 248); but far from reinforcing any psychic sense of castration held by Jesse, the fact that white hands wield the blade that severs the biggest Thing imaginable drives Jesse toward a psychic identification with whiteness.

Significantly, during the event, Jesse watches his mother's white face together with the lynching. In one signal moment, Jesse turns to note that his mother "was more beautiful than he had ever seen her", and he simultaneously feels "a joy he had never felt before" as he also "watched the hanging, gleaming body, the most beautiful and terrible object he had ever seen till then" (p. 247). In this moment, we witness racial whiteness and blackness both emerge as objects of beauty for Jesse, as they come to radiate with an unbearable splendour derived from their proximity to death. Lacan shows that Antigone's appearance as "victim and holocaust" at the "center of the anamorphic cylinder" of the play produces a perspectival shift, allowing the audience to confront and forestall their desire for death (p. 282). But here the suffering body of the lynch victim allows Jesse a certain defiance of death. Jesse recognises that "it was they [the white men] who held death" (p. 247), and it is as the adult-Jesse thinks finally of the man in the cell, the body in the fire and the knife in white hands that he grabs himself, feeling his own erection and demanding that his wife love him "just like [she would] love a nigger" (p. 249).

Jesse takes on the physicality of blackness, in the specific form of its supposed sexual prowess, while remaining a member of the beautiful white race. Here both the beauty of the white Lady and the renewed tumescence of Jesse's glorious white physique (and phallus) emerge from the "black charred" corpse that once radiated with a vitality that could be cupped in white hands (Baldwin, 1993, p. 248). Jesse confronts the charred Thing and takes in its vigour as a jouissance he approaches through a transgressive encounter with death. We are told that at the climax of the lynching the crowd had "rushed forward, tearing at the body with hands, with knives, with rocks, with stones", and as "the crowd screamed" so too had "Jesse screamed" (248). Melding his passions with that of the white throng set upon the black body, Jesse did not simply fantasise a relation to the *Ding* but actively accessed the *Ding* in the form of a jouissance derived from death, embracing this jouissance as a libidinous upsurgence that, from childhood, agitates both his desire and his drive. Lacan notes that it is the *Ding* that structures our "choice of neurosis", defining our "subjective orientation" by framing the pathologies, desires and drives through which we compensate for lack at an unconscious, psychic level (1997, p. 54). Here we see the charred Thing as the *Ding* that determines Jesse's particular mode of jouissance, binding him to a cyclical return to racism as the specific mechanism through which he aims repeatedly at an overcoming of his psychic condition of lack.

This overcoming is both insistent and, at best, momentary, veiling Jessie's psychic turmoil behind the mask of an established manhood that ever reveals its lack. Jessie achieves a phallic identity, a racialised masculinity that is rooted in the intangible *Ding*. But, more so than the beauty of a white Lady – a mother, a wife – it is the big black phallic Thing that localises the jouissance of the *Ding* for Jessie, rising insistently for him, from childhood into manhood, to the level of the *Ding*. Tellingly, Jessie's sexual impotence at the story's beginning coincides with homoerotic desires his body itself announces in the prison before he returns to his beautiful wife: there, in the prison, he watched in "horror" as his penis "violently stiffen[ed]" while he beat the protestor (p. 235). Jessie's body betrays him, and the lost pound of flesh, the phallus that promises him a sustained jouissance, is most properly possessed by another man. Whether lynched or beaten, the black men Jessie encounters bring him manhood through a *Lebensneid* that melds jealousy with homoerotic, racial violence. Jessie's arousal in the prison thus complicates the very term "man" featured so prominently in the story's title: *Going to Meet the Man*. Not only does it signal Jessie's violent brutality, but it also queries the very structure of Jessie's homophobic, racialised, white manhood.

What Jessie aspires to with this manhood, ultimately, is an impossible construction of the white body as a site of wholeness, as an idealised, beautiful form vibrant in its abnegation of lack. Lacan notes classical historical periods in which the human body was presented as "ideal", as "the limits of the possibility of the beautiful" and, indeed, as a "divine form" (1997, p. 289). Such impossible divinity is what whiteness aims at attaining in the face of subjective dereliction. For Lacan, the body is the seat of the imaginary, the "cloak of all possible fantasms of human desire" (p. 298). The form of the body itself stands in the place of Atè, as the "site of desire insofar as it is desire of nothing", desire for an all-consuming jouissance that is promised in an abyssal beyond (p. 298). Race agitates such desire because, in the progression of our long historical embrace of racism, race – even as heteronormative whiteness – has come to highlight the fact of our embodiment, a fact which of itself already marks "the relationship of man to his own lack of being", to the bodily loss which he suffered in emerging into subjectivity (p. 298). What idealisation of race atrociously aims at, therefore, is destruction of the body, both one's own and that of the racial other. Race, in its dominance as our contemporary mode of visible difference, not only stagnates desire but also agitates the death drive, seeking annihilation of both the other and the subjective self through union with the *Ding*.

Conclusion

In the *Ethics* Seminar, Lacan affirms that for speaking beings plagued by castration, "the whole achievement of happiness turns on the genital act" (1997, p. 300). Such achievement is what eludes Baldwin's character Jesse in his struggles to consummate this act with the Lady he claims as his wife. It is possible, explains Lacan, "to achieve for a single moment in this act something which enables one human being to be for another in the place that is both living and dead of the Thing" (p. 300). In such a moment, the lover "may simulate with [their] flesh", and in their body, what they are "not under any circumstances" (p. 300): they may rise to the status of sublimated representative of the lost *Ding*. But Jesse, and the racism he manifests, rejects sublimation by seeking after the *Ding* itself, forgoing desire and embracing, instead, the immediacy of the drive.

In analysis, the subject may acquire something even the lover cannot guarantee: the analyst may bequeath the analysand access to the analyst's own desire, which is an experienced desire built on recognition that one cannot "desire the impossible" (p. 300). I have shown race and racism to be tied to just such an impossible desire, the desire to overcome the dereliction of the body. I have traced a historical insistence on race and racism at the levels of both desire and the drive by positioning the Lady as a central figure in the constitution of imagoes of the body that frame racial whiteness. And I have shown how this lady, as manifestation of the beautiful, agitates a racism aimed at breaching the barrier of Atè. Race and racism, I suggest, stand in direct opposition to what Lacan calls an ethics of psychoanalysis, giving ground on the subject's inherently metonymic desire by stagnating desire upon deep-rooted cultural sublimations of race that urge fervent embrace of transgressive drives toward destruction (p. 319). Where it is desire that provides the unconscious theme of each of our subjectivities, race roots us in paths not our own, laying out routes to excesses of jouissance that bind us psychically to centuries-long histories of violence.

A true Lacanian analysis allows a subject to arrange and organise his instinctual drives. It allows a subject to establish a safe distance from a permanent, eternal Atè that "began to be articulated before him in previous generations" (p. 300). By engaging the long history of race's ties to *das Ding*, what this chapter has attempted to facilitate is the raced subject's ethical distance from the racial Atè that has come to radiate in the place of the Thing. However, rather than eternalise this barrier – as Lacan shows Antigone to do for the audience who, through her, can mark its reestablished limit – I have attempted a necessary devaluation of race and racism as sublimated reifications of an enticing and all-too breachable Atè. What this chapter aims at is a crucial rejection of the Atè of race, which today yet trammels our desires and drives to enduring sublimations of beauty and atrocity rooted in the violence of our Western past.

Notes

1 The French publication of the seminar reads, "d'une société primitive – des bédouins, des bicots, des ratons" (Lacan, 1997, p. 100). The final word, *ratons*, translates as rats, not "niggers", but the combination of these terms justifies the use of "niggers". In addition to defining *raton* as a young rat ("*jeune rat*"), the French dictionary *Le Petit Robert*, lists *raton* as a racist ("*raciste*") term dating from 1937 for a North African (*Nord-Africain*) and lists *bicot* as its synonym, which it also defines as Nord-Africain. Significant for my discussion of the Crusades, the dictionary also lists the term *Ratonnade*, which emerged in 1955 and refers to a punitive or brutal expedition exercised by Europeans against North Africans ("Expédition punitive ou brutalités exercées par les Européens contre des Nord-Africains"). An article on BBC.com pointedly notes that "the campaign waged against Algerians in Paris", which in one case in 1961 resulted in at least 100 Algerian protesters for independence being "thrown [to their death] into the River Seine" by police, "was unofficially called the 'ratonnade,' meaning 'rat-hunting'" (Rouaba, 2021, parts 3 and 25).
2 See Walton's "Replacing Race in (White) Psychoanalytic Discourse".
3 Scholars tie courtly love to the "poet-composer-performers" called the Troubadours who dazzled Southern French and neighbouring European courts with their songs from the eleventh to the thirteenth centuries (Gaunt and Kay, 2003, p. 1).
4 Scholars like John Jay Parry have argued that "courtly love is a fusion of Latin and Moorish elements" (12), maintaining "that the troubadours were influenced by the culture of Moslem Spain", which had fallen under the Califate of Cordova until 1031 (7).
5 Kay notes that the Lady herself is commonly figured as a "quasi-divine creature" in courtly love, as an "all powerful" presence in front of whom the lover "humbles himself" (2003, p. 216).

6 Interestingly enough, Haynes suggests that it is not white Europeans but Muslims in the Near East who first make this association between Africans, slavery and Noah's curse (2002, p. 7).

Bibliography

Allen, J., Als, H., Lewis, J., and Litwack, L. F. (2004). *Without Sanctuary: Lynching Photography in America*. Santa Fe, NM: Twin Palms Publishers.

Baldwin, J. (1993). *"Going to Meet the Man": Going to Meet the Man: Stories*. New York: Vintage Books.

Dalal, F. (2002). *Race, Colour and the Processes of Racialization: New Perspectives from Group Analysis, Psychoanalysis and Sociology*. New York: Routledge.

Fanon, F. (1967). *Black Skin, White Masks*. Trans. C. L. Markmann. New York: Grove Press.

Freud, S. (1989a). *Civilization and Its Discontents*. Trans. J. Strachey. New York: W. W. Norton & Company.

Freud, S. (1989b). *Group Psychology and the Analysis of the Ego*. Trans. J. Strachey. New York: W. W. Norton & Company.

Freud, S. (1989c). *Totem and Taboo*. Trans. J. Strachey. New York: W. W. Norton & Company.

Gates, H. L., Jr. (1992). *Loose Cannons: Notes on The Culture Wars*. New York: Oxford University Press.

Gaunt, S. and Kay, S. (2003). *The Troubadours: An Introduction*. Cambridge, UK: Cambridge University Press.

Gilman, S. L. (1995). *Freud, Race and Gender*. Princeton, NJ: Princeton University Press.

Gould, S. J. (1981). *The Mismeasure of Man*. New York: W. W. Norton & Company.

Haynes, S. R. (2002). *Noah's Curse: The Biblical Justification of American Slavery*. New York: Oxford University Press.

Hook, D. (2021). Pilfered Pleasure: On Racism as "the Theft of Enjoyment". In S. George and D. Hook (Eds.), *Lacan and Race: Racism, Identity and Psychoanalytic Theory*. Abingdon, UK: Routledge Press.

Kay, S. (2003). Desire and Subjectivity. In *The Troubadours: An Introduction*. Cambridge, UK: Cambridge University Press.

Lacan, J. (1979). The Neurotic's Individual Myth. *Psychoanalytic Quarterly*, 48(3): 405–425.

Lacan, J. (1986). *Le Séminaire De Jacques Lacan: Livre VII L'éthique De La Psychanalyse 1959–1960: Texte établi par Jacques-Alain Miller*. Paris: Éditions Du Seuil.

Lacan, J. (1997). *The Seminar of Jacques Lacan Book VII: The Ethics of Psychoanalysis*. Trans. D. Porter. New York: W. W. Norton & Company.

Lacan, J. (1998). *The Seminar of Jacques Lacan Book XI: The Four Fundamental Concepts of Psycho-Analysis*. Trans. A. Sheridan. New York: W. W. Norton & Company.

Lacan, J. (2007). *The Seminar of Jacques Lacan Book XVII: The Other Side of Psychoanalysis*. Trans. R. Grigg. New York: W. W. Norton & Company.

Miller, J. A. (1994). Extimité. In M. Bracher, M. W. Alcorn, R. J. Corthell, and F. Massardier-Kenney (Eds.), *Lacanian Theory of Discourse* (pp. 74–87). New York: New York University Press.

Parry, J. J. (1990). Introduction. In *The Art of Courtly Love by Andreas Capellanus*. New York: Columbia University Press.

Rey, A. and Rey-Debove, J. (1990). *Le Petit Robert 1: Dictionnaire Alphabétique Et Analogique De La Langue Française*. Montréal, QC: Les Dictionnaires Robert.

Rouaba, A. (2021). How a Massacre of Algerians in Paris was Covered Up. *BBC.com*, October 17, 2021. https://www.bbc.com/news/world-africa-58927939.

Walton, J. (1995). Re-Placing Race in (White) Psychoanalytic Discourse: Founding Narratives of Feminism. *Critical Inquiry*, 21(4): 775–804.

Wells-Barnett, I. B. (1991). *On Lynchings*. Stratford, NH: Ayer Company, Publishers.

Chapter 5

Ethics Amid Commodities

Das Ding and the Origin of Value

Todd McGowan

Escaping the Object

Perhaps the most shocking aspect of Jacques Lacan's *Seminar VII* on the ethics of psychoanalysis is the disappearing act that *das Ding* performs. When one begins the seminar, one has the sense, given its prominence, that this concept will provide the key to interpreting the ethics of psychoanalysis. But if it is the key, Lacan hides the lock. After spending the majority of the seminar introducing and exploring the concept of *das Ding*, Lacan stops referring to it once he begins to talk about *Antigone*, the play that will exemplify his ethics. What's more, when it comes time to provide a pithy statement of his ethical position – "the only thing one can be guilty of is giving ground relative to one's desire" – he makes no reference at all to *das Ding* (1992, p. 321). Lacan sets up his discussion of the ethics of psychoanalysis by identifying the centrality of *das Ding* in the subject and in the subject's relationship with others but then leaves it behind when it comes to theorizing the ethical position. But its disappearance places an ethical imperative on us. In order to make sense of what the ethical position inherent in psychoanalysis might be, we must trace the role that *das Ding* plays in its absence. We must locate *das Ding* in the constitution of ethics as such.

When examining the fate that *das Ding* undergoes in the course of *Seminar VII*, one might say that Lacan is enacting in the form of his seminar what he's discussing in the content. *Das Ding* is itself an absence, the void existing inside a vase, to cite the example that Lacan himself explores (ibid., pp. 119–123). After establishing *das Ding* as the fundamental absence that structures our subjectivity, he forces those listening to him to confront this absence at the precise point where they expect the answer. In this sense, the absence of *das Ding* in discussion of *Antigone* represents a way of revealing it. One detects *das Ding* through its effects on other objects. There is no way to confront it directly. We must piece together its role from the implications that Lacan leaves behind.[1]

This obtrusive disappearance of *das Ding* in the ethics seminar paves the way for its vanishing in Lacan's thought after this seminar. He mentions it only a handful of times in subsequent seminars, as a focus on *das Ding* gives way to an emphasis on the *objet a*. The contrast between these two objects is important: whereas *das Ding*

DOI: 10.4324/9781003450795-5

is the void that opens beyond the signifier, the *objet a* is the curvature of symbolic space, the distortion that desire produces within the signifier. There is thus a certain danger involved in speaking about *das Ding*, a risk of implying that when referring to it one is attempting to step outside of language while continuing all along to speak.[2] We might postulate that this is why Lacan turns away from it.

Lacan runs this risk in *Seminar VII* and then backs away from it in the years afterward, although he never returns to the question of ethics to reformulate his ethical position in light of the turn away from *das Ding*. Ethics disappears along with the Thing. This seminar thus represents Lacan at his boldest, the point at which he hazards a line of thought with an explicit ethical claim to it. At the same time, it marks, I contend, one of the most significant missteps of his intellectual career. This misstep lies in associating the Thing (and the enjoyment of it) with transgression. While recognizing the ethical potential of the psychoanalytic project, Lacan also manages to confine this ethical position to perpetual defiance of the law, which resembles perversion a bit too much to be a convincing form of ethics. In what follows, I will attempt to separate the wheat from the chaff, to interpret the role of *das Ding* in the ethics of psychoanalysis while distancing this ethical position from Lacan's misstep. Perhaps such a surgical effort will lead to the death of the patient. It is often the case that one's greatest insight depends on one's error and would dissolve without it. But even if that is the case here, it's worth looking to see.

The central innovation of *Seminar VII* – and one could even say in all of Lacan's life – concerns sublimation. Lacan defines sublimation in a way that runs counter to Freud's conception. For Freud, sublimation, which he contrasts with repression, involves the full satisfaction of the drive, but it is a satisfaction that occurs through a socially acceptable object.[3] It creates a detour of the drive that produces satisfaction in a nonsexual object. For Freud, sublimation enables me to experience sexual satisfaction while fighting fires or selling light bulbs. As he does with castration, Lacan broadens Freud's concept (2014, p. 136).[4] When he theorizes sublimation in *Seminar VII*, it ceases to be a special way that we satisfy the drive and becomes *the* way that the drive satisfies itself. There is no satisfaction of the drive without sublimation because sublimation creates an object for the drive to enjoy. Such objects do not just exist but must emerge through the sublimating act.

There are no natural objects of the drive, not even sexual organs, nothing satisfying for the subject's drive in itself. Instead, sublimation produces such objects. Lacan's explanation of the process of sublimation has become one of his most famous statements. He proclaims that sublimation "raises an object . . . to the dignity of the Thing" (1992, p. 112). By lifting an ordinary object out of circulation and treating it as an end in itself, one provides an orientation for one's drive. This is the key to sublimation: it arrests the generalized exchangeability of objects by subtracting an object from the field in order to establish it as the foundation for the subject's enjoyment.

This enjoyment has no end outside of itself, which means that the value of the object lies in itself, not in its exchange value. Sublimation is an ethical struggle against exchange value. Although sublimation is necessarily unconscious – we can't consciously determine what will function as our Thing – it defines the singularity of the subject by giving the subject a relation to a point that transcends the realm of objects. *Das Ding* provides the subject with an orientation for its existence, an orientation that enables it to establish a transcendent value in the form of the sublimated object that becomes the Thing.

Whereas Freud views sublimation as one of the vicissitudes of the drive, Lacan rightly sees sublimation as drive's *sine qua non*. It is through sublimation that the drive acquires an object worthy of its pursuit. This is what leads Joan Copjec to claim that "sublimation is not something that happens to the drive under special circumstances; it is the proper destiny of the drive" (2002, p. 30). Without sublimation, the drive could not function. Lacan's reformulation of the concept of sublimation marks his most radical transformation of Freud's theory, a transformation that enables him to denaturalize the drive beyond what Freud himself thought possible. It also enables him to construct an ethics of psychoanalysis.

Sublimation is at work throughout the spectator's relationship to *Antigone*. She herself becomes a sublime object through Sophocles' depiction of her, which is what gives her the splendour that Lacan finds so appealing. At the same time, Antigone as a character in the play enacts the process of sublimation relative to her brother. She insists on burying Polyneices because he has the status of *das Ding* for her. She experiences an ethical duty toward him that trumps all other incentives. Antigone is an example of the ethics of desire because she elevates an object to the dignity of *das Ding* and then never wavers in her commitment to this object. Her act of sublimation is what gives her a sublime aura for those regarding the play.

Even though Lacan doesn't mention sublimation in his discussion of *Antigone* or in his formulation of the ethics of psychoanalysis in the final session of the seminar, sublimation is clearly evident in what Antigone does and in how we respond to her. Given the language that he uses to describe her, Lacan himself undoubtedly considers Antigone a sublime figure, an instance of the beautiful that puts us on the track of the real of our desire. She is a sublime figure because of her own sublimation. She attains a sublime value for us as spectators through her insistence that Polyneices has a sublime value for her.

What stands out in Lacan's analysis of Antigone is the position that she comes to occupy in the play. Her insistence on burying Polyneices regardless of the consequences places her beyond the limit that governs the realm of the good, a realm that Lacan calls the service of goods. This reveals to us the result that inheres in the act of sublimation. Sublimation and the drive that accompanies it place one beyond the pleasure principle and beyond the service of goods. While *Antigone* predates the capitalist socioeconomic system by approximately two thousand years, Lacan finds himself drawn to the play and to Antigone because her sublimation places her at odds with the capitalist system, a system that functions by reducing every object to its exchange value.[5] The ethics of psychoanalysis that he identifies is an ethics that tries to navigate a path beyond capitalist relations of production.

Capitalizing on Sublimation

The signifying order has the effect of levelling out all values. If every signifier acquires its value in relation to all other signifiers, then there is no room for transcendence as long as we remain strictly on this plane.[6] Signification functions through a system of differences that doesn't leave the plane of the signifier. This levelling process becomes exacerbated when we turn from the realm of signification to that of the market. The fundamental impulse of the market is to reduce all commodities to a position of possible exchange. No commodity can resist the market's levelling process and remain a commodity, since its exchangeability defines it as a commodity. There is no such thing as a transcendent commodity.

This is the situation that Karl Marx probes in *Capital*. In the first chapter of the first volume, Marx describes a universe of commodities in which the principle that predominates is that of exchange. In order to exist as a commodity, an object must be able to be exchanged with every other commodity. According to Marx, we know the value of the commodity through its potential exchange with other commodities. What counts is only its exchange value, to the extent that Marx eventually defines exchange value as simply value as such. The commodity has no value outside of the exchange relation (1976, p. 46).[7]

Capitalist society is built on the rejection of singularity. It reduces all objects to a machine of equality that is market exchange. From the perspective of capitalist society, one can always equate the most valuable object and the least valuable. As Marx puts it, "all commodities, when taken in certain proportions, must be equal in value" (ibid., p. 136).[8] Even though we value some commodities (such as gold) above others, all of them are fundamentally capable of being exchanged with each other, as long as one has them in the correct proportions. This generalized exchangeability has the effect of reducing every object to the same level. The capitalist universe is a universe in which nothing stands out.

The logic of the commodity that reduces each object to every other object does not leave subjectivity out of its calculus. Within capitalist society, every subject becomes a commodity and thereby loses its own status as a Thing. The subject's opacity to itself, which is its Thing quality, ceases to have any value. Stripping the Thing from the subject is the fundamental capitalist operation. Once capitalist society takes *das Ding*, the subject loses its resources for challenging the commodity. The subject becomes commodified in the form of labour time and in this way ceases to be fundamentally different from other commodities traded on the market. This is what Marx means by what he calls commodity fetishism (even though he wouldn't put it this way): the subject loses its Thing and becomes just another commodity.

Marx wants to change this situation with a political revolution. He imagines a proletariat with nothing to lose but its chains would be capable of desiring outside of the logic of the commodity. But what this solution misses is that the path outside of capitalism requires a Thing, which the proletariat abandons by commodifying itself in the form of labour time. Lacan envisions a response that takes the Thing as its starting point, a form of living that refuses the capitalist blackmail and insists on a value that cannot be exchanged. This ethical position is not divorced from politics but provides the foundation for any possible anti-capitalist political struggle. One must break from the prevailing commodity logic if one is to access an alternative to capitalism.

When Lacan opposes the ethics of psychoanalysis to the service of goods, his target is the realm of capitalist exchange. By reducing all objects to their exchange value and to the logic of the commodity, capitalism completely obfuscates our relationship to the sublime. We cease to recognize how we enjoy, since our enjoyment depends on what defies exchange. As Franck Chaumon puts it, "The concept of enjoyment comes . . . in opposition to the social link defined as sharing, understanding, contract. It is that which in the human resists passing into the logic of exchange" (2004, p. 77). Enjoyment depends on the sublimity of *das Ding*, a sublimity that the process of exchange eliminates.

Capitalism doesn't do without sublimation. It uses sublimation to create value and then obscures it behind the façade of the commodity. By creating a universe in which we rely on the sublime without ever becoming aware of our encounter with it, the capitalist system tends to generate right-wing populist reactions, reactions that promise a restoration of the sublime. This is why Donald Trump, for instance, invests himself in fighting for statues of great figures of the past and why Adolf Hitler inveighs against the levelling effects of Judeobolshevism. In both cases, these leaders respond to the absence of the sublime with promises of its reintroduction into society. Such leaders emerge in response to the capitalist levelling process and make a fallacious promise of a future sublimity that will come with devotion to their person.

Capitalism's relationship to *das Ding* is conflicted. On the one hand, it ruthlessly reduces every object to a commodity and thereby squelches *das Ding*. It demands the submission of all objects to the field of exchange value, a field in which nothing can stand out. Capitalism permits no object to remain singular. But on the other hand, value within the capitalist system depends on the erection of *das Ding*. Without the sublimation that creates *das Ding*, no one would buy a commodity. Desire for any commodity stems from the residue of sublimation that remains in it.

Capitalism relies on sublimation and also relies on its disavowal. The disavowal of *das Ding* hides the source of the commodity's value. The price of a commodity is not equivalent to its value, as Marx notes. It is the necessary obstacle that prevents one from having an unlimited quantity of the commodity. But the commodity itself, even if it is not a vase, contains *das Ding*, which confers value on the object. Its value stems from the collective sublimation that occurs with it. This sublimation raises an everyday object to the dignity of the Thing and thereby makes it desirable on the market.

If we look at the case of Coca-Cola, we can even see how the Thing is written into an advertising campaign. Advertisements proclaim that Coke is "the real Thing," thereby removing it from the ranks of everyday drinks and giving it an transcendent status. When one goes to drink a can of Coke, one senses that it is more than just a drink to quench thirst, that it is specifically an object to be enjoyed (which is why cans often include the admonition, "Enjoy Coke!"). But what one enjoys in this manner is never present. If one is to enjoy Coke as *das Ding*, one must enjoy what one cannot name or grasp. One must enjoy what isn't there present in the flavoured drink.[9]

When the object becomes the Thing, its value consists in what is not there, in the absence that characterizes the Thing. This is precisely what no one within the capitalist relation can avow. Treating the object as a commodity is the way that we disavow the absence of the Thing. It allows us to desire the Thing without confronting its nothingness. In this sense, commodity fetishism functions as a substantialization of the fundamental absence that defines *das Ding*.

The ubiquitous reach of the commodity and the logic of exchange transforms every object into a fetish. This process is just as necessary for capitalism as the process that turns an everyday object into *das Ding*. For Marx, the fetishism of commodities

> reflects the social relation of the producers to the sum total of labour as a social relation between objects, a relation which exists apart from and outside the producers. Through this substitution, the products of labour become commodities, sensuous things which are at the same time supra sensible or social.
>
> (1976, p. 165)

Fetishism obscures the labour that produces commodities and causes them to appear as if they simply appeared on the market, as if their value inhered in the object rather than in the Thing.

Lacan's project in *Seminar VII* is an attack on commodity fetishism and its deleterious effects on subjectivity. By placing the emphasis on the Thing, he poses sublimation as a critical response to the capitalist system. Although capitalism requires sublimation in order to reproduce itself, it demands that we incessantly retreat from the sublimated Thing to the exchangeable commodity. By sustaining the path of sublimation and continuing to recognize *das Ding* instead of the commodity, we chart a path out of capitalist relations, which depend absolutely on an unrelenting fetishism. *Das Ding*, as the void that undermines all presence, resists fetishism absolutely. It is the anti-fetish, the absence that fetishism attempts to obscure.

Our conformity derives from the abandonment of sublimation. When the subject sublimates and holds fast to the void of *das Ding*, the grasp of the symbolic structure over this subject dissipates. The subject that sustains its relationship to *das Ding* is not vulnerable to the incentives and enticements that the symbolic structure offers. Such a subject recognizes that its value lies in *das Ding* and not in the variety of objects that symbolic authorities try to ply the subject with. Sublimation puts one in a position beyond the reach of symbolic authorities and beyond the appeal of the commodity. *Das Ding* acts as a barrier to this appeal. But the result is that the subject can no longer hope for symbolic advancement. Attaching oneself to one's Thing entails going beyond.

Antigone shares this position with the rest of the heroes in the seven extant plays of Sophocles, save Oedipus in *Oedipus Tyrannus*. In the middle of his discussion of *Antigone*, Lacan takes a detour to run through these plays. The plays share a conception of heroism in which the hero lives beyond the limit that defines the existence of everyone else. These heroes enter into a zone beyond symbolic constraint where they can no longer impact the world. They cease to have a symbolic identity.

This position beyond symbolic constraint is one without the hope of symbolic advancement. Lacan describes this as the destiny of all the Sophoclean heroes. He states,

> If there is a distinguishing characteristic to everything we ascribe to Sophocles, with the exception of *Oedipus Rex*, it is that for all his heroes the race is run. They are at a limit that is not accounted for by their solitude relative to others. There is something more; they are characters who find themselves right away in a limit zone, find themselves between life and death.
>
> (1992, p. 272)

To put it in terms that Lacan would employ later, the Sophoclean heroes all experience their symbolic death.

We would be wrong to consider this position too extreme for us to occupy. The Sophoclean hero has a paradigmatic status for all subjectivity. This not because everyone is, like Antigone in her tomb or Oedipus at Colonus, on the verge of death. It is because there is no consistent or substantial authority that can grant us recognition within the symbolic structure. The race is run for us, as it is for the Sophoclean heroes, because there is no one waiting at the finish line to reward us for finishing first (or even to give us a participation trophy).

The path to recognition is the path of the commodity. We accumulate commodities and even turn ourselves into commodities in the hopes of achieving recognition as a valuable one. This is the fantasy that governs relations within capitalist society. But it is a fool's errand because there is no symbolic authority out there that could decide on our worthiness. The commodity remains an indifferent object. No matter how attractive a commodity I become, there will be no one there to tell me when I have arrived. Thus, I will spend my entire existence striving for a recognition that is constitutively impossible to obtain. The fruitlessness of this search leaves an opportunity for the intervention of a psychoanalytic ethic.

Sublimation is an alternate course. By sublimating and maintaining our relation to the Thing, we elevate an object above the fray and give it a value that doesn't rely on any symbolic authority. When we hold fast to the project of sublimation and the Thing that it produces, we lay out a path beyond the commodity. Our commitment to sublimation represents an ethical alternative to the commodification of everything. It affirms both the singularity of our object and our own subjectivity.

The Creation of the Singular

Antigone refuses to accede to Creon's order that no one bury Polyneices because she elevates her brother to the status of *das Ding*. This act of sublimation defines her character and propels her beyond the limit that governs everyone else in *Antigone*. Her act of sublimation forms the connection between Lacan's elaboration of *das Ding* and his analysis of the play. It is the reason why Lacan chooses this play to provide the exemplify his conception of ethics.

Antigone defends herself against Creon by invoking the singularity of her brother, a singularity that she contrasts with that of a potential husband or child. Whereas she could have replaced a husband or a child with another, her brother is irreplaceable because her father and mother have died. The strangeness of this claim shocks Goethe and other readers. It is a scandalous passage, so scandalous that Goethe wishes it was a late addition and not properly part of the play. The scandal of this passage bespeaks its appeal. It disturbs Goethe and others insofar as it marks the point at which Antigone departs from what is expected. Lacan states, "In the end, precisely because it carries with it the suggestion of a scandal, this passage is of interest to us" (1992, p. 256). Psychoanalysis pays attention to the disturbances in the text or the points, like this one, where the text disturbs those who read it.

The disturbance goes so far in some cases that it triggers a repression. There are editions of *Antigone*, including what was for a time the most popular English translation, that simply omit Antigone's claim that she would defy the law for her brother but not for her child. Editors Dudley Fitts and Robert Fitzgerald claim that the text itself is spurious, despite acknowledging the fact that Aristotle refers to it without doubting its propriety. Then they claim that even if Sophocles did write this passage, "it is dismal stuff. Antigone is made to interrupt her lamentation by a series of limping verses whose sense is as discordant as their sound" (1966, p. 240). Antigone's act of sublimation simply makes no sense to Fitts and Fitzgerald, so they take the extraordinary step of excluding it from the play. But this repression indicates the passage's importance. It shows us that sublimation and the Thing it produces cannot fit within the world of signification without disrupting that world.

For Lacan, it is important that Antigone does not defend herself by appealing to the authority of the gods or even the authority of unwritten laws. She disdains Creon's interrogation and never tries to escape condemnation. Her only attempt at a justification for her act refers to who Polyneices is. From the beginning of Creon's interrogation of her to the end, she appeals only to the singularity of her brother. Lacan summarizes her position in this way:

> My brother is what he is, and it's because he is what he is and only he can be what he is, that I move forward toward the fatal limit. If it were anyone else with whom I might enter into a human relationship, my husband or my children for example, they are replaceable.
>
> (1992, pp. 278–279)

The bizarreness of this claim is integral to its appeal. Lacan hones in on Antigone's specific defense of her action because it sounds so strange to our ears. What sounds strange are the words of sublimation.

To hear Antigone claim that she values her brother over a potential son because she could always have another son seems to violate our sense of how anyone would value things. What she says does violence to our common sense. It does so because she is talking about her own act of sublimation. Sublimation always cuts against common sense by creating a value that matters for the subject and no one else. Polyneices has this extreme value for Antigone insofar as he functions as her Thing. But what her explanation makes clear is that it is impossible to understand sublimation and its erection of *das Ding* from the outside. To the outsider, valuing the Thing above everything else appears insane. But it is not insanity; it is subjectivity. One asserts oneself as a subject through the devotion to the Thing, a devotion nicely captured when we say of someone, "That's her thing."

Every subject is a Thing. It is as a Thing that the subject is opaque to itself. One relates to this opacity by identifying it in the world of objects, through the act of sublimation that raises some object to the status of the Thing. How we relate to the Thing that we create is at the same time how we relate to the Thing within. By insisting on the burial of Polyneices, Antigone reveals herself as a Thing. She becomes a Thing for the spectator through her absolute commitment to her Thing.

Her extreme commitment shows that Marc De Kesel must surely be wrong when he distinctly separates Antigone's treatment of Polyneices from *das Ding*. If we don't understand Polyneices as Antigone's Thing, her act in the play makes no sense. In *Eros and Ethics*, De Kesel writes, "Polyneices's value for Antigone is not of the order of the natural, nor of the real in the Lacanian sense (and thus does *not* derive from what Lacan called *das Ding*), but of the order of the signifier" (2009, p. 218). De Kesel makes this claim because he doesn't want to envision Antigone as an ethical model. The fact that she goes too far, the fact that she ends up killing herself after being buried alive, makes her too extreme to function as a model for everyone to follow – or so De Kesel sees it. But that she goes to such extremes indicates that she has taken up a relationship to *das Ding*. Even though the value of Polyneices transcends the natural world, he has this rank due to Antigone's elevation of him. Signification places her next to him as a sibling, but her reaction to this situation, her sublimation of Polyneices, transcends the order of the signifier.

Antigone's act of sublimation is correlative with her drive. Even though Lacan sees her as an exemplar of the ethics of desire, she is from beginning to end a driven subject. As a result, she never pursues what's good for her. She simply attends to her Thing. As Alenka Zupančič says in *Ethics of the Real*, "Her starting point is an unconditional 'must'– Polyneices must be buried" (2000, p. 57). Antigone lets nothing interrupt this unconditional drive.

The burial of Polyneices marks his status as *das Ding*. This is the role that burial always plays and is the reason why we insist on it not just for Polyneices but for everyone. Burial (or cremation) takes the body of the subject out of circulation, affirming that the body is not just another object but contains *das Ding*. By leaving the body of Polyneices out to rot in the elements, Creon doesn't just treat him as an enemy of the country – one buries the dead of the enemy – but attempts to strip him of his subjectivity, to act as if he is just another object. As unburied, it is as if he has no Thing.

The Thing is an absolute singularity. It is a dark spot within the subject, the point at which the subject does not know itself. *Das Ding* enthralls others because no one, not even the subject, can make sense of it. There is a sense in which calling the Thing a "Thing" is misleading. As Richard Boothby points out, "A primary danger in speaking of '*das Ding*'. . . is the way that it inclines us toward reifying or over-substantializing what is involved." In light of this danger, Boothby adds a clarification. He continues, "*Das Ding* has no objective existence whatsoever. If it is not an object, nor is it any sort of prehistorical perceptual givenness. It is rather a locus of pure lack, a zone of something unknown."[10] It is the point at which the subject confronts what drives it but what it cannot integrate into its personality. The Thing defies interpretation.

The obscurity of the Thing lies in its link to enjoyment. No one can explain why the subject finds satisfaction in the specific Thing. In order to illustrate the concept, Lacan turns to his friend Jacques Prévert, who collects matchboxes. There is nothing particular about matchboxes that makes them enjoyable. And yet, Prévert's collection of them exhibits his Thing. And as his Thing, they evince his singularity as a subject (Lacan, 1992, pp. 113–114).

We cannot will the Thing into existence. Sublimation doesn't work automatically when I express my devotion to something. I must pay the price with a conspicuous sacrifice. Sacrifice attests to the value of the Thing, but more than that, it constitutes the object as a Thing by giving it the value of what I have given up. There is no shortcut to the creation of *das Ding*, nor a shortcut to enjoyment. It always passes through the subject's sacrifice because sacrifice elevates the object from the realm of all other objects. Sacrifice lets us know that we can find the subjectivity of the subject in this object. This is what Boothby is getting at when he says that "the being of the sacrificer emerges for the first time only with the loss effected by the act of sacrifice" (2001, p. 247). To find the essence of the subject we need only look for evidence of its senseless sacrifices. Antigone does not have a monopoly on these. Everyone partakes in senseless sacrifices insofar as everyone enjoys.

The sacrifice that produces the Thing cannot have an ulterior motive. I can't make a lot of money or gain fame as a result of the sacrifice. By sacrificing for the sake of something that has no utility whatsoever, I produce the Thing. This sacrifice most often takes the form of devoting great quantities of time to the Thing. I neglect the chance to earn more money or to act productively in order to sacrifice my time for *das Ding*. This sacrifice is evident even in Jacques Prévert's matchboxes. The time that he spends tying them together and arranging them is time that he cannot spend usefully. The Thing emerges out of what he gives up.

The creative power of sublimation gives the subject a way to orient itself. The orientation occurs through the sacrifice of utility. One gives up one's good and the prospects for advancing it in order to organize one's enjoyment. This mode of enjoyment centers around *das Ding*, although it is the *objet a* that provides the directional arrow that points toward this absolute singularity.

From *Ding* to *objet a*

Das Ding and the *objet a* are a bit like Clark Kent and Superman. When looking through Lacan's works, we almost never see them together, which prompts those who are suspicious, like Lois Lane, to wonder if they are not just two names for the same thing.[11] Perhaps Lacan begins theorizing the object that causes our desire as the abyssal *das Ding* and later comes to see this cause as a fissure in the perceptual field, which he names the *objet a*. Unlike *das Ding*, the *objet a* doesn't seem so radically foreign to the signifying order. It indicates a revelatory disturbance rather than a gaping void. But the key to understanding the importance of *das Ding* is mapping its relationship to the *objet a*, a concept that threatens to replace it.

In his earlier seminars, Lacan mentions something that he calls the *objet a*, but prior to *Seminar VII*, it is always just an imaginary object. That is, the *objet a* of the early seminars has nothing to do with what would become the *objet a* understood as the object-cause of desire. The first theorization of the *objet a* as the real object-cause of desire arrives in *Seminar IX*, the seminar devoted to identification.[12] Toward the end of this seminar, he states,

> It is at the point where all signification is lacking, is abolished, at the nodal point of the desire of the Other, at the phallic point, insofar as it signifies the abolition as such of all significance, that the *objet petit a* comes to take up its place.[13]

Lacan theorizes the *objet a* as what is missing in the field of signification. This absence functions as a barrier to what we desire.

Both *das Ding* and the *objet a* are absences. The *objet a* is a barrier that the subject confronts. This barrier triggers the subject's desire by obscuring *das Ding*, the point of transcendence that introduces value into the subject's existence. The Thing lies beyond the realm of signification. This beyond is nothing but a void, a nothingness that the subject cannot have. But the *objet a* enables the subject to relate to this void. It establishes the path through which the subject can remain faithful to its Thing.

Slavoj Žižek often speculates on the relationship between the Thing and the *objet a*. In *Plague of Fantasies*, he writes, "*das Ding* is the absolute void, the lethal abyss which swallows the subject; while *objet petit a* designates that which remains of the Thing after it has undergone the process of symbolization" (1987, p. 81). This way of putting it has the advantage of highlighting the link between *das Ding* and what lies beyond the symbolic structure. What lies beyond, in Lacan's early thought, is the mother.

The turn from *das Ding* to the *objet a* in Lacan's thought represents his gradual turning away from granting the Oedipus complex a central position in the psyche. As the *objet a* becomes the featured object, mentions of the Oedipus complex become far less frequent. Whereas every iteration of *das Ding* recalls the original mother Thing, the *objet a* has no specific relationship to the mother. It is rather a little piece of the subject itself that has broken off and kick-started the subject's desire.

Although Lacan doesn't articulate it (because he has yet to develop his concept of the *objet a*), one of his examples of *das Ding* in *Seminar VII* has the merit of illustrating both the *objet a* and *das Ding*. The first example that Lacan uses to clarify *das Ding* is the vase, a variation of the object that Martin Heidegger chooses to explicate *das Ding* in his eponymous essay on the topic.[14] The material of the vase is the *objet a*. It places an obstacle between the subject and *das Ding*, which is the void inside the material, and it constitutes this void as a void. Without the materiality of the vase, there would be no absence within. In the same way, without the obstacle that the *objet a* erects around *das Ding*, there would be no Thing. The nothing of the Thing emerges only through the obstacle of the *objet a*. While it is tempting simply to choose between them, to opt for *das Ding* or *objet a*, an understanding of how subjectivity relates to others requires both.

Without *das Ding*, what we lose is the indication of the subject's inability to fit within a universe of generalized fetishism. This universe where the logic of the commodity reigns is that of capitalist society. The Thing not only allows us to make sense of how capitalism makes use of sublimation but also gives prominence to what refuses the commodity's reign. In our senseless sacrifices made on behalf of our Thing, we testify to the insufficiency of the commodity. This is why Lacan initially turned to the *das Ding* and why we must sustain it theoretically in the way that Antigone does practically.

The Contingency of Criminality

Antigone's insistence on burying her brother leads to her death. This insistence occurs in defiance of the law that Creon pronounces and thereby incurs his wrath. While Lacan rightly associates Antigone's burial of her brother with her act of sublimation, he unfortunately doesn't leave it at that. According to Lacan's interpretation of *Antigone*, her desire in relation to her brother emerges in opposition to the law. In fact, desire, as Lacan conceives it in *Seminar VII*, is necessarily constituted in opposition to the strictures of the law. The law's prohibition functions as the vehicle through which desire satisfies itself. Without the law, there would be no path for desire and no possibility for enjoyment.

It is here that we can identify the great misstep of *Seminar VII* that we must probe while assessing its theoretical importance. This seminar marks the first moment where Lacan identifies enjoyment as real. It is a real possibility for the subject, and it exists beyond symbolic and imaginary constraints. Enjoyment is no longer just the product of fantasy but resides in what the subject does. So far, so good. But Lacan locates enjoyment in the act of transgressing the law, which creates serious problems.

Antigone becomes the representative of enjoyment insofar as she goes beyond what the law allows. In his essay on the trajectory of enjoyment throughout Lacan's theoretical development, Jacques-Alain Miller claims that in this seminar enjoyment

> is structurally inaccessible, except through transgression . . . . It is moreover the great figure of Antigone who appears here at the forefront as crossing the barrier of the city, the law, the barrier of the beautiful, in order to advance up to the zone of horror that entails enjoyment.[15]

Miller sees that the seminar locates Antigone's enjoyment in her transgression of the law. This prompts us to ask the question, "What if Creon did not enact this law against burying the traitor?" Antigone's enjoyment, it seems, comes to depend on the contingent fact of Creon laying down a law that arouses Antigone's desire to transgress it. Everything turns around the law's prohibition.

The point of the law, as Lacan conceives it in *Seminar VII*, is to provide the subject with a limit to transgress in order to enjoy. He lays his cards on the table in a remarkable passage that theorizes the law as a vehicle for the enjoyment that derives from transgressing it. He states,

> We are, in fact, led to the point where we accept the formula that without a transgression there is no access to jouissance, and, to return to Saint Paul, that that is precisely the function of the Law. Transgression in the direction of *jouissance* only takes place if it is supported by the oppositional principle, by the forms of the Law.
>
> (1992, p. 177)

As Lacan conceives it here, the symbolic law exists in order to be broken. It provides enjoyment for us because it gives us a limit to transgress.

The problem with this insistence on the role of the law in constituting the possibility of enjoyment is that it ignores what Lacan himself says earlier in the seminar about the role of sublimation. He simply cannot have it both ways. Either sublimation raises ordinary objects to the dignity of the Thing or the law creates *das Ding* through its prohibition. There is no way to reconcile these two positions. Their coexistence in *Seminar VII* leads various theorists to express dissatisfaction with the seminar as a whole. This alternative derails the seminar and ends up creating the impasse that causes Lacan to prematurely turn away from *das Ding*. He abandons *das Ding* because he mistakenly links it to prohibition rather than remaining true to his insight that it is the product of sublimation.

One way out of the impasse would be to say that we only sublimate what the law prohibits. In this sense, prohibition would not inherently create the Thing but would lay the groundwork for its creation through the sublimating process. The problem with this tidy solution is that Lacan's own example of sublimation – Jacques Prévert's matchboxes – has nothing at all to do with the law's prohibition. No one, not the most authoritarian ruler, has ever prohibited the collection of matchboxes or even had the idea to do so. Sublimation works because it ignores the symbolic context, not because it focuses on what the symbolic law interdicts.

This conception of enjoyment as necessarily linked to transgression not only contradicts Lacan's statements on enjoyment in later years but runs counter to the example of Antigone. Antigone does not enjoy her defiance of Creon. It is clear, instead, that her defiance of Creon follows from her drive and the satisfaction that she derives from it. When Antigone talks with Creon, she expresses a disregard for him and his law. This disregard – a result of her commitment to her Thing – is the source of the splendour that so enraptures Lacan. Antigone encourages Creon to go ahead and execute her. She views his law as a stubborn fact, not as a site for enjoyment through transgression. After he says that he will execute her, Antigone replies, "Why do you wait, then?" (Sophocles, 1991, p. 544). Antigone does not defy the law for the sake of her desire but on account of the value that she accords to Polyneices. The defiance of Creon is incidental to her relationship with *das Ding*. If we pay close attention to Antigone's trajectory during the play, her example has the effect of correcting Lacan's own theoretical misstep on the question of desire and enjoyment.

What Lacan misses is just how little Antigone cares about Creon or his law.[16] He rightly draws attention to her insistence on the absolute singularity of her brother, but he muddies this insight by identifying her with the enjoyment of transgression. Antigone finds enjoyment in devoting herself to her Thing, to Polyneices. What is remarkable about her character is how little it changes from the beginning of the play to the end. Antigone is devoted to her Thing. She vows to bury him and honour his singularity regardless of what Creon commands, not to defy Creon's command. This distinction has the utmost importance and determines how we categorize Antigone.

It is clear that Lacan's discussion of the Marquis de Sade earlier in *Seminar VII* leads him astray when talking about Antigone. He associates Sade's perversion – his enjoyment of defying the law and provoking the symbolic authorities – with Antigone. As Lacan ultimately conceives it, Antigone must be a pervert, someone who gets off on the defiance of the law.[17] His claim is that the defiance of Creon pushes Antigone into the position of symbolic death, the position where the race is run. But Antigone ends up in this position not because she is in love with defiance but because she is devoted to her Thing.[18] She enjoys her Thing while remaining indifferent to the law.

Lacan fails to see the independence of enjoyment from the law because he associates *das Ding* with the mother. He remains caught within the structure of the Oedipus complex, where the father's interdiction plays the decisive role in establishing the mother's retroactive desirability. As Lacan conceives it here, the symbolic prohibition of the mother turns her into a desirable Thing. The law creates *das Ding* as a site beyond symbolization. If *das Ding* is the mother, it must be outside the symbolic structure. Jacques-Alain Miller identifies the problem that Lacan runs into with this initial conception of *das Ding*, which is why Lacan must largely abandon it. He claims that the seminar produces "an impasse in isolating the Thing as outside of symbolization."[19] Later, Lacan will recognize that the failure of symbolization doesn't involve an outside but is internal to it. The signifier stumbles over itself, and this internal fissure is what he will call the real. The notion of a real outside to the signifier becomes the result of an imaginary misrecognition that captures Lacan himself at this point. But this error makes him reluctant to talk about the Thing at all, which results in the exile of one of his most important insights.

Seminar VII marks simultaneously the high point of Lacan's theorizing and the low point. His insight into the role that sublimation plays in constituting the drive represents a major innovation. It enables him to conceive of *das Ding* as the radical absence that acts as the gravitational source around which the drive forms. But at the same time, this seminar advances a cockeyed conception of enjoyment located only in transgression. Lacan couldn't see that, while the symbolic law is a necessary condition for the drive and the enjoyment that results from it, this enjoyment is in no way concerned with rebellion against the symbolic law. Enjoyment proceeds on its own terms without referring itself to the law. The seminar ends up apotheosizing pointless acts of rebellion that do nothing but reinforce the symbolic structure that they revolt against.

This gets to the heart of Slavoj Žižek's thoughtful objection to the seminar as a whole on political grounds. He claims, "Beneath this mask of flirting with radicality it is basically this conservative vision, you know, we have these moments of self-obliterating encounters with truth, but then we return to normal life, servicing the good, and so on" (2010, p. 426). For all Lacan's celebration of Antigone's act of defiance, he envisions no staying power to it. She defies Creon but doesn't point the way forward politically, which is why Žižek sees Lacan's vision here as basically conservative. Lacan's hostility to the law in *Seminar VII* produces a political dead end, one that has seduced many in its wake.

But the other possibility birthed in this seminar should lead us to avoid committing it to the flames too quickly. Here, for the first and only time, Lacan provides a rigorous formulation of sublimation. He identifies sublimation as the key to the structure of the drive and as the key to taking up an ethical position in the midst of enforced commodification. The only path out of the logic of the commodity lies in holding fast to the emancipatory power of sublimation. Sublimation creates *das Ding*. It is only by confronting the fundamental absence of *das Ding* – including its absence in the conclusion of *Seminar VII* – that we can free ourselves from the blandishments of the commodity.

Notes

1 Perhaps the origins of Lacan's emphasis on *das Ding* lie in the seminar that he gave just prior to the one on the ethics of psychoanalysis. In the seminar on *Desire and Its Interpretation*, Lacan devotes considerable attention to *Hamlet* in an effort to explain the structure of desire. This seminar has seven sessions on *Hamlet*, including a discussion of Hamlet's description of the King's body. In a discussion with Rosencrantz, Hamlet famously states, "The body is with the King, but the King is not with the body. The King

is a thing . . . Of nothing." William Shakespeare, Hamlet, in *The Riverside Shakespeare*, 2nd ed., ed. G. Blakemore Evans (Boston: Houghton Mifflin, 1997), Act IV, scene ii, 27–30. Hamlet's recognition in this line marks the beginning of his turn to action. Here, Hamlet grasps that there is nothing substantial to the King, that the source of the King's authority resides in the absence, the nothing, that gives him his sublimity. This sublimity does not simply accord to the King but is the result of the act of sublimation, the act of the King's subjects granting him his sublime status.

2 Richard Boothby provides a thorough account of the danger of substantializing *das Ding*. See Richard Boothby, "What Is Religion?" (unpublished manuscript).

3 Freud explains sublimation at different times. An early explanation occurs in the essay " 'Civilized' Sexual Morality and Modern Nervous Illness." There, Freud writes, "This capacity to exchange its originally sexual aim for another one, which is no longer sexual but which is psychically related to the first aim, is called the capacity for *sublimation*." Sigmund Freud, " 'Civilized' Sexual Morality and Modern Nervous Illness," in *The Standard Edition of the Complete Psychological Works of Sigmund Freud*, ed. J. Strachey, trans. E. B. Herford and E. C. Mayne (London: Hogarth, 1959), 187. Despite the changes that the concept of the drive would undergo in Freud's thought, his understanding of sublimation remains basically the same. It is against this conception that Lacan would formulate his own in *Seminar VII*.

4 In his seminar on anxiety, Lacan says directly, "Castration . . . is symbolic." Jacques Lacan, *The Seminar of Jacques Lacan, Book X: Anxiety*, ed. J.-A. Miller, trans. A. R. Price (Malden, MA: Polity Press, 2014), 136.

5 Before Lacan's ethics seminar, Martin Heidegger wrote an essay devoted to distinguishing between objects and *das Ding*, although Heidegger never linked *das Ding* to sublimation in the way that Lacan does. But it is significant that this is the only of Heidegger's works that Lacan translated into French. See Martin Heidegger, The Thing, in *Poetry, Language, Thought*, trans. A. Hofstader (New York: Harper and Row, 1975), 161–180.

6 The claim that signifiers have no other value than that which emerges from their relation to other signifiers is, of course, the basic claim of Ferdinand de Saussure. In effect, Saussure identifies the structure of signification along the lines of commodity relations. Just like signifiers, commodities have value only in their relation to other commodities. For an attempt to trace the implications of this homology, see Jean-Joseph Goux, *Symbolic Economies: After Marx and Freud*, trans. J. C. Gage (Ithaca: Cornell University Press, 1990).

7 This is what Marx is getting at when he says, "when commodities are exchanged, their exchange-value manifests itself as something totally independent of their use-value." Karl Marx, *Capital: A Critique of Political Economy*, vol. I, trans. B. Fowkes (New York: Penguin Books, 1976), 46.

8 Marx, *Capital*, 136.

9 Slavoj Žižek often points to Coke as the *objet a*: it is the embodiment of a nothing – it has no nutritional value, and it doesn't quench thirst – that nonetheless functions as a lure for desire. What he doesn't mention is the role that *das Ding* necessarily plays in the constitution of the commodity. *Das Ding* is the site of the genuine enjoyment that the commodity produces for the subject, but it is an empty space within the commodity, not a positive presence.

10 Boothby, "What Is Religion?"

11 This is the position of Daniel Cho, for instance. He writes, "objet a [is] the schematization or formalization of *das Ding*." Cho warns against treating the two "as separate concepts" Daniel Cho, private communication, January 30, 2020.

12 *Seminar VIII* on the transference provides a hint of what will become the *objet a* when Lacan identifies the agalma as the object within Socrates that causes Alcibiades to desire him. There is a clear through-line from agalma to *objet a*, as many theorists have noted.

13 Jacques Lacan, "Le Séminaire IX: L'Identification, 1961–1962" (unpublished manuscript, session of June 27, 1962).
14 Heidegger uses the jug, not the vase, as the example. But what both objects have in common is the absence that constitutes them (and that they constitute).
15 Jacques-Alain Miller, Les six paradigms de la jouissance, *Ecole de la cause freudienne*, 2015. http://www.causefreudienne.net/wp-content/uploads/2015/04/JAM-Six-paradigmes-jouissance.pdf.
16 Yannis Stavrakakis sees Antigone's act as void of any political content because her desire is inextricably related to the law that it defies. See Yannis Stavrakakis, *The Lacanian Left: Psychoanalysis, Theory, Politics* (Albany: SUNY Press, 2007).
17 In his account of Lacan's interpretation of the character of Antigone, Charles Freeland insists on the importance of Antigone's negative relationship to the law. He writes, "Her death drive is the transgression of the limit of the law commanding the pleasure principle and the good for all." Charles Freeland, *Antigone in Her Unbearable Splendor: New Essays on Jacques Lacan's* The Ethics of Psychoanalysis (Albany: SUNY Press, 2013), 167.
18 This is Mari Ruti's point in *Distillations*, where she develops an ethic that borrows from Antigone. Ruti writes, "Antigone acts against the Other (Creon's system) but not against the other (Polyneices)." Mari Ruti, *Distillations: Theory, Ethics, Affect* (New York: Bloomsbury, 2018), 73. It is crucial, for Ruti, that Antigone is not simply opposing the Other but, even more importantly, embracing the other, the one she has installed as the Thing.
19 Miller, Les six paradigms de la jouissance.

Bibliography

Boothby, R. (2001). *Freud as Philosopher: Metapsychology After Lacan*. New York: Routledge.

Chaumon, F. (2004). *Lacan: La loi, le sujet et la jouissance*. Paris: Éditions Michalon.

Copjec, J. (2002). *Imagine There's No Woman: Ethics and Sublimation*. Cambridge: MIT Press.

De Kesel, M. (2009). *Eros and Ethics: Reading Jacques Lacan's Seminar VII*. Trans. S. Jöttkandt. Albany: SUNY Press.

Fitts, D. and Fitzgerald, R. (1966). *Sophocles: The Oedipus Cycle*. Ed. and Trans. D. Fitts and R. Fitzgerald. San Diego: Harcourt Brace.

Freud, S. (1908). Civilized: Sexual Morality and Modern Nervous Illness. In *The Standard Edition of the Complete Psychological Works of Sigmund Freud* (Vol. IX). London: Hogarth.

Heidegger, M. (1975). The Thing. In *Poetry, Language, Thought* (pp. 161–180). Trans. A. Hofstader. New York: Harper and Row.

Lacan, J. (1961–1962). Le Séminaire IX: L'Identification, 1961–1962. Unpublished Manuscript.

Lacan, J. (1992). *The Seminar of Jacques Lacan, Book VII: The Ethics of Psychoanalysis, 1959–1960*. Ed. J.-A. Miller. Trans. D. Porter. New York: W. W. Norton & Company.

Lacan, J. (2014). *The Seminar of Jacques Lacan, Book X: Anxiety*. Ed. J.-A. Miller. Trans. A. R. Price. Malden, MA: Polity Press.

Marx, K. (1976). *Capital: A Critique of Political Economy* (Vol. I). Trans. B. Fowkes. New York: Penguin Books.

Miller, J.-A. (2015). Les six paradigms de la jouissance. *Ecole de la cause freudienne*. http://www.causefreudienne.net/wp-content/uploads/2015/04/JAM-Six-paradigmes-jouissance.pdf.

Ruti, M. (2018). *Distillations: Theory, Ethics, Affect*. New York: Bloomsbury.

Sophocles (1991). Antigone. In *Sophocles I*. Trans. D. Grene. Chicago: University of Chicago Press.

Stavrakakis, Y. (2007). *The Lacanian Left: Psychoanalysis, Theory, Politics*. Albany: SUNY Press.

Žižek, S. (1997). *The Plague of Fantasies*. London: Verso.

Žižek, S. (2010). Unbehagen and the Subject: An Interview with Slavoj Žižek, Interview with Maria Aristodemou, Stephen Frosh, Derek Hook. *Psychoanalysis, Culture & Society*, 15: 418–428.

Zupančič, A. (2000). *Ethics of the Real: Kant, Lacan*. New York: Verso.

Chapter 6

On Tragedy and Desire in the Ethics of Psychoanalysis

Dany Nobus

Introduction

The original French text of Lacan's 1959–1960 seminar at Sainte-Anne Hospital in Paris was first published in September 1986 as *Séminaire VII, L'éthique de la psychanalyse* (Lacan, 1986).[1] I cannot remember when exactly I first read the book from cover to cover, but I do recall checking the table of contents at the back of the volume, skimming through the 375 pages of text, reading the extract from the fifteenth lesson on the back cover, admiring the glorious reproduction of Man Ray's 1938 *Portrait imaginaire de D. A. F. de Sade* on the front cover, reading the titles and sub-headings of the various lectures (all of which added by the editor, Jacques-Alain Miller), and being simultaneously fascinated and intimidated by Lacan's choice of source materials. I also recall how my preliminary encounter with the text generated a panoply of questions around the contents and structure of Lacan's seminar, and how my first approach of *Seminar VII* stretched my own elementary instruction in Lacanian psychoanalysis towards previously ignored or unexplored philosophical horizons whose concrete clinical or practical significance was everything but clear.

Since this chapter mainly serves an introductory and expository purpose, and is strictly confined to Lacan's reading of Sophocles' *Antigone* in *Seminar VII*, my own questions at the time pertaining to this particular part of the text might still offer the best guide for structuring my line of reasoning.[2] Without being so presumptuous as to think that all new readers of *Seminar VII* will raise exactly the same questions, here is what I asked myself. What place do *Antigone* and its tragic heroine occupy in a discussion on the ethics of psychoanalysis? What could have prompted Lacan, towards the end of his seminar, to devote no fewer than three entire lectures to the study of this particular tragedy? What could an interpretation of *Antigone* contribute to the (formulation of an) ethics of psychoanalysis? How did Lacan approach Sophocles' text? What interpretative models or methodologies did he employ when he analysed and presented *Antigone* to his audience, which mainly consisted of psychoanalytic trainees?[3] Which conceptual tools did Lacan rely on when demonstrating the meaning and relevance of *Antigone* for (the ethics of) psychoanalysis? Which conclusions did Lacan arrive at? How do these conclusions affect (the

DOI: 10.4324/9781003450795-6

ethics of) psychoanalysis? What did *Antigone* and Antigone teach Lacan about (the ethics of) psychoanalysis? If psychoanalytic clinical practice requires an ethical framework and *Antigone* may help establish this framework, how does a practicing psychoanalyst stand to benefit from Lacan's reading of it? At which points does *Antigone* connect with the clinical concerns of psychoanalytic practitioners?

When Lacan announced to his audience, on May 18, 1960, that he would pursue his enquiry into what human beings desire, and what they defend themselves against, with a reading of *Antigone* (Lacan, 1992 [1986], p. 240), he was evidently in a very different position than me when I picked up a copy of *Séminaire VII* in September 1986. As I will demonstrate, Lacan was far from naïve when it came to the question of ethics and already exceptionally well informed as regards the interpretative traditions that had crystallised around Sophocles' tragedy. In principle, this should not have stopped him from articulating all or some of the aforementioned questions, yet it simply was not in Lacan's nature to do so.

In what follows, I shall keep to the chronology of Lacan's three lectures on *Antigone* instead of attempting a retroactive reconstruction of its arguments, because this is undoubtedly how most readers will access the text, starting with Lecture 19 and ending with Lecture 21.[4] However, my chapter will inevitably be more than a mere description and explanation of Lacan's commentary on *Antigone*, because the nature and style of his work require a high degree of interpretation in order to generate a coherent and consistent narrative. What follows therefore constitutes an interpretation of a commentary that is in itself an interpretation of a tragedy, which is also an interpretation of an ancient Greek myth. I shall leave it to others to decide whether my own interpretation is justified and correct, yet as far as Lacan's interpretation is concerned, I believe it definitely necessitates interpretation but not necessarily criticism – *pace* the factual, transcription and translation errors that mar the text and which I shall highlight whenever necessary – because it is essentially a reading of a work of art, perhaps the most magnificent tragedy ever produced, and thus the outcome of a specific, subjective encounter, which is as valid as the result of any other interpretative act. In the process, one should of course also be mindful of how, in this case, interpretation is crucially predicated upon translation, from the ancient Greek into French, and from the ancient Greek and French into English.

Background and Context

It is rather odd, given the centrality of the Oedipus saga and the eponymous complex throughout Freud's theory of psychoanalysis, but when Lacan started relaying his views on *Antigone* – in the nineteenth session of *Seminar VII*, on May 25, 1960 – he was the first psychoanalyst in history to express a serious interest in it.[5] At the end of the previous week's lecture, Lacan had announced that he would pursue his enquiries into ethics by focusing on a tragedy in which the 'underlying structure' (*la sous-structure*) of the 'morality of happiness' (*la morale du bonheur*) is presented on the surface, in full view, whereby he insinuated that this tragic revelation of the hidden structure of human happiness in *Antigone* also constitutes the main reason why it had preoccupied so many people over the centuries, including some of the world's greatest minds.[6] To grasp Lacan's point, here, I need to provide the reader with a brief summary of his arguments in *The Ethics of Psychoanalysis* until then, if only because the lessons on *Antigone* cannot be separated from a series of questions and issues Lacan had been advancing since the start of his seminar.

From the very beginning of *Seminar VII*, Lacan was adamant that any serious critical analysis of human desire, which he himself had conducted in *Seminar VI*, on *Desire and Its Interpretation* (Lacan, 2019 [2013]), inevitably leads to the question of ethics, as the consideration of what human desire is aimed at, what it is hoping and expected to achieve, what it is geared towards. Hence, much like Aristotle had suggested in the opening lines of his *Nicomachean Ethics*, Lacan conceived the question of ethics as an investigation into the goals, aims and objectives of human desire. Concurrent with a philosophical tradition going as far back as Plato, he also acknowledged that an investigation into the goal of human desire would not only generate questions about ethics, but also invoke the field of aesthetics, since the 'morally good' had consistently been associated with the 'beautiful'.[7] Hence, to Lacan, the term 'ethics' pertained to questions concerning the goal of human desire, and these questions would not only be important for the development of a proper understanding of the human condition, but also for the conception of the psychoanalytic treatment, on at least three distinct levels. First, insofar as it is the patient's suffering that brings her or him to see a psychoanalyst, to what extent is this suffering fundamentally related to a certain disparity between the (aims of the) patient's desire and what he or she has, or has not accomplished? Second, assuming that it is indeed a disparity between desire and its aims that has induced the suffering, what can a patient hope for in terms of the outcome of the treatment process? And third, since the treatment process is facilitated by the psychoanalyst, how should the latter's own desire be conceptualised as a professional clinical force that is aimed at the realisation of a certain outcome? For Lacan, 'the ethics of psychoanalysis' should thus be understood in the subjective as well as the objective sense of the genitive: it is a psychoanalytic consideration *of* ethics that leads to the formulation of an ethics *for* psychoanalysis. It needs to be underscored, here, that Lacan was in no way concerned with the development of a deontology, a regulatory framework or a list of dos and don'ts that could serve as a manual for psychoanalytic practitioners. The question of the ethics of psychoanalysis refers to what the psychoanalytic treatment process – the patient going through it and the psychoanalyst directing it – is aimed at, and as such to requisite reflections upon the end, the termination and the finality of the treatment.

In the opening session of *Seminar VII*, Lacan conceded that he was by no means the first to think about the preferred outcome of a psychoanalytic treatment. However, most of his predecessors had defined this outcome – much like the philosophers before them – as a set of ideals, such as genital love, authenticity, and independence (Lacan, 1992 [1986], pp. 8–10). The problem with these ideals is not only that they are exactly that – ideal, and therefore unattainable goals – but also that they are generally more indicative of ideological norms and moral values than of what concrete human beings want, and what is most likely to make them happy (Lacan, 1992 [1986], p. 302). On this basis, Lacan set out to articulate a radically different perspective on psychoanalytic ethics, which not only challenged firmly established views on treatment outcomes, such as the sublimation (and concurrent de-sexualisation) of the patient's drives, but also integrated the numerous, often controversial contributions Freud had made to our understanding of the human condition: the seemingly irreducible impact of the death drive (Freud, 1955 [1920g]), the insistent human discontents in civilisation (Freud, 1964 [1930a]), the recurrent problem of masochism (finding pleasure in one's own pain and misery) (Freud, 1961 [1924c]), and so on. Considering these classic Freudian observations, Lacan questioned how could anyone still advance an ethical doctrine that is exclusively predicated on the principle that the highest moral good is not only achievable, but also desirable? Given these Freudian principles, how could anyone continue to believe that human happiness is conditioned by the desire for, or the realisation of, a concrete state of perfection, which would be as good as it is beautiful, and which should orient, regulate, and direct all aspects of our human existence? How could an analyst still think that the ultimate confluence of moral goodness and spiritual beauty is what patients want, what could make them happy, and what they themselves, as clinical 'facilitators', could deliver?

At this point in his disquisition, Lacan resolved to be led by *Antigone* and Antigone, in order to demonstrate (1) how the object (goal, aim) of human desire does not coincide with the perfect realisation of a sovereign good, because it is impossible to know exactly what this sovereign good entails; (2) how human happiness does not stem from the ultimate fulfilment (satisfaction) of desire; and (3) how the radical emancipation of human desire from all its socio-symbolic constraints is an unequivocal recipe for disaster. These three axes frame the tragic 'underlying structure' of the 'morality of happiness', and they basically show how this 'morality of happiness' is hopelessly fraught with countless inconsistencies. In revealing this dialectical, 'underlying structure' of desire, Lacan argued that Sophocles' *Antigone* – the play which Hegel had designated as "the most perfect" tragedy, although, in Lacan's opinion, "for the worst reasons" (Lacan, 1992 [1986], p. 240, translation modified) – does not only expose the fallacies of the 'morality of happiness', but also paints a more accurate picture of the trials and tribulations of human desire, from which the theory and practice of psychoanalysis can take their lead.[8]

The Cathartic Effect of Antigone's Brilliance

Initially, Lacan's audience may have wondered why he decided to begin his commentary on *Antigone* with a lengthy reflection upon the purpose of tragedy in general. Even so, the first lecture in Lacan's own trilogy already offered, in no uncertain terms, the fundamental thesis to which his meticulous reading of Sophocles' play had led him. I shall unpack it in all its idiosyncratic features below, yet it can be captured in a single sentence: as the central figure of the tragedy, Antigone comes to represent a focal point of exceptional brilliance, which is both the main source of the play's cathartic effects upon the audience and the problematic place where human desire finds its ultimate fulfilment. Lacan constructed this thesis upon the resonances of two separate small passages in *Antigone*: a few lines spoken by Antigone herself shortly before she is led away to the cave in which she will be buried alive (909–912), and one verse sung by the chorus just before Antigone is brought before Creon for the last time (795–797).[9] Lacan highlighted Antigone's own words at the end of his first lecture, whereas for the chorus's song his audience would have to wait until the following session. In relying on these fragments, Lacan explicitly distanced himself from Hegel's interpretations of the play, whilst simultaneously endorsing the authenticity of verses which many scholars had considered unworthy of Sophocles, and conceivably as interpolations by another playwright, since the early nineteenth century.

During the first part of his lecture, Lacan recalled how *Antigone* constitutes a tragedy (as opposed to a comedy) and how ancient Greek tragedy had not only proven to be important for psychoanalysis owing to Freud's extraction of the Oedipus-complex from Sophocles' *Oedipus the King*, but also because of Freud's reliance on the defining purpose (aim, objective) of all ancient Greek tragedies for his conceptualisation of the goal of clinical interventions, even before his adoption of psychoanalytic treatment principles. As Aristotle had put it in the sixth section of his *Poetics*, the purpose of tragedy is the catharsis of emotions, which is being accomplished δι' ἐλέου καὶ φόβου, "through pity and fear" (Aristotle, 1999, pp. 47–48).[10] Since this particular part of Aristotle's book does not include a definition of catharsis – maybe because Aristotle deferred his explanation of it to other chapters of the *Poetics*, those that have not survived – it is impossible to gauge from the *Poetics* what Aristotle meant by catharsis. However, the philosopher was quite explicit about the nature of catharsis at the very end of his *Politics*, where he stated that it involves "a pleasant feeling of purgation and relief" (Aristotle, 1962, p. 314). In other words, catharsis coincides with pleasure, which made Lacan wonder aloud about the nature of "this pleasure to which one returns after a crisis that occurs in another dimension, a crisis that sometimes threatens pleasure" (Lacan, 1992 [1986], p. 246).

When Breuer and Freud adopted the term catharsis in their 1893 'Preliminary Communication' to the *Studies on Hysteria*, they translated it as *Abreagiren*, a process they described as the patient's putting into actions or words the troublesome affective quantities that are attached to repressed memories (Breuer and Freud, 1955 [1895*d*], p. 8). This process of purgation and purification, whose name James Strachey translated as 'abreaction', thus coincides with the point in the treatment when the patient succeeds in liberating the affect from its unconscious representations and proceeds to discharging it verbally (or otherwise), which then results in an alleviation of the clinical symptoms.[11] Ancient Greek tragedy, of which *Antigone* is one of the best examples, is therefore closely related to the psychoanalytic treatment, because Breuer and Freud inscribed its purpose literally into their account of how the treatment unfolds. Catharsis, as the characteristic purpose of tragedy, reappears in the endgame of psychoanalytic clinical practice, and it is therefore intimately related to the ethics (the aims and objectives) of the treatment. It is important to note, here, that over the years Freud came to think rather differently about what a psychoanalytic treatment should be aimed at, yet he never went so far as to discard catharsis completely as an erroneous, misguided or insufficient goal (see, for example, Freud, 1959 [1926d], p. 167). When reconstructing these connections, Lacan emphasised that, at least in principle, Breuer and Freud had replaced the original ethical and aesthetic connotations of catharsis with a strictly medical meaning, by which they had taken advantage of a long tradition of classical and other scholarship, in which Aristotle's original notion had been extrapolated to include ideas pertaining to the palpably therapeutic impact of the purification of the psyche.[12]

So where does catharsis emanate from in *Antigone*? Which part(s) of the play render it possible? Where is it to be situated? Here, Lacan argued that it is to be found specifically in the distinctive place Antigone occupies at the end of her final appearance, before she is taken away. This argument is first of all based on Lacan's conviction that Antigone is the undisputed protagonist of the play. This may strike the reader as an emphatically trivial point, yet in rendering his own position explicit in this way, Lacan not only showed once again that he had familiarised himself with the scholarly literature and the associated debates on the tragedy, but also that he was prepared to take a stand against all those who had claimed that the central figure of *Antigone* is Creon and that any discussion of the play's ethical dimensions should therefore be focused on the new ruler of Thebes rather than on his niece Antigone.[13] Putting Antigone at the heart of *Antigone*, Lacan averred that, at the high point of her presence, she epitomises the target (*le point de visée*) of desire, notably that which desire is aimed at.[14] Insofar as catharsis is the overall aim and the defining feature of tragedy, this effect is generated by how Antigone herself appears, in her final moment on stage, as the prototypical personification of what commands fear and pity. This, for Lacan, is the place where the ethical truth of the tragedy is to be located.

The heart of *Antigone* having been identified as such, Lacan then approached it from a wide range of different angles, offering various descriptions of this ethical truth along the way. First and foremost, he designated it as Antigone's "unbearable brilliance" (*éclat insupportable*), a source of high-intensity luminosity which is not at all intolerable to herself, but hugely insufferable to everyone who is confronted with it (Lacan, 1992 [1986], p. 247).[15] It is important to reiterate, here, that Lacan was not interested in the meaning of Antigone, let alone the function she serves at that particular point in the play, but rather in what the place she occupies represents for the nature and structure of human desire. Finding alternative designations for it, he suggested that it is a place of sublime beauty, which is simultaneously fascinating and horrifying, and which does not appease the senses but induces a complex admixture of captivation and trembling, terror and enchantment, pity and fear. It is a place of turmoil (*émoi*), the place which the fictional Pope Pius VI – one of the libertines in Marquis de Sade's *Juliette* – could have explained as the point of the 'second death', where the natural cycle of the endless regeneration of life is itself radically abolished after the 'first death' of an individual's living substance.[16] Implicitly employing Heideggerian terminology, Lacan also pointed to this locus of unbearable brilliance as "the place where the metamorphoses of 'that which is' [*das Seiende*] are being separated from the [naked, pure] 'position of being' [*das Sein*]", so that the latter stands out in the full advent of its unfathomable presence (Lacan, 1992 [1986], p. 248, translation modified).[17] Additionally, drawing on Kant's transcendental philosophy of pure reason (Kant, 1998 [1781]) and Freud's posthumously published 'Project for a Scientific Psychology' (Freud, 1966 [1950a]), he referred to it as an existential twilight zone, where the only factor coming into play is the perfectly thinkable, but radically unknowable Thing (Lacan, 1992 [1986], p. 253).

As I indicated at the beginning of this section of my chapter, Lacan derived the textual evidence in support of his argument from two small passages in *Antigone*: a tiny part of Antigone's final lament and an even tinier invocation from one of the chorus's songs. The lines (909–912) spoken by Antigone run as follows:

πόσις μὲν ἄν μοι κατθανόντος ἄλλος ἦν,
καὶ παῖς ἀπ' ἄλλου φωτός, εἰ τοῦδ' ἤμπλακον,
μητρὸς δ' ἐν Ἅιδου καὶ πατρὸς κεκευθότοιν
οὐκ ἔστ' ἀδελφὸς ὅστις ἂν βλάστοι ποτέ.

In the English translation of *Antigone* by Hugh Lloyd-Jones, they are rendered as: "If my husband had died, I could have had another, and a child by another man, if I had lost the first, but with my mother and my father in Hades below, I could never have another brother" (Sophocles, 1998, p. 87).[18] The context in which this sentence appears is worth recalling, here, because it adds poignancy to the tone and significance of Antigone's words. Antigone is brought before Creon one last time, and she is both reflecting upon her fate and contemplating her reasons for defying Creon's injunction that Polynices must not be buried. Whereas previously Antigone had explained her 'criminal act' with reference to the unwritten, divine law that elevates kinship far above the written rules and regulations of the city, now she justifies her decision to honour her dead brother in a different way. Whereas earlier she had exposed Creon's order as a decree running counter to the laws of Hades (Sophocles, 1998, p. 51) – putting herself in the position of a dutiful, compliant servant of the gods – now she acknowledges another law. She is no longer speaking to Creon, nor to anyone else for that matter but, as Bernard Knox has put it, she is engaging in a "lonely, brooding introspection, a last-minute assessment of her motives, on which the imminence of death confers a merciless clarity" (Knox, 1984, p. 46). And when she has finished articulating the true motive of her act, she addresses herself directly to the dead body of Polynices: "Such was the law for whose sake I did you [Polynices] special honour, but to Creon I seemed to do wrong and to show shocking recklessness, O my own brother" (Sophocles, 1998, pp. 88–89). Whatever the divine laws may have encouraged her to do, in the final instance Antigone concedes that she decided to perform funerary rites for her dead brother, and sacrifice herself in the process of doing so, because he is quite simply irreplaceable. Faced with death, she suddenly sees that she relinquished her own life for Polynices owing to his absolute, incommensurable uniqueness.

I shall elaborate on Lacan's reasons for situating Antigone's 'unbearable brilliance' at this particular point of the play in the next section of my chapter, yet for now it should already be clear that the source of Antigone's most advanced rationale for breaking Creon's law is exceptionally difficult to describe. Making abstraction of her outspoken reliance on the unwritten, divine laws, it is much easier to encapsulate and render intelligible her antagonistic 'No' to Creon than to pinpoint the root source of her 'Yes'. In fact, the immense challenge of trying to make sense of Antigone's words at 909–912 has prompted numerous scholars since the early nineteenth century to consider them interpolated, and in his seminar Lacan demonstrated that he was very much aware of the debate they had sparked (Lacan, 1992 [1986], pp. 254–256).

In a sense, it had all started in 1821, with a classical philologist called August Ludwig Jacob, who argued, in the first volume of a massive compilation of 'Sophoclean questions', that "Antigone, as she is called, is so apt in claiming that her brother is irreplaceable, that she becomes utterly ridiculous" (Jacob, 1821, p. 366). In subsequent years, scholars such as August Böckh and Hermann Hinrichs categorically opposed Jacob's arguments, whereby they (sometimes implicitly) rekindled Hegel's famous analysis of *Antigone* in *The Phenomenology of Spirit*, in which 909–912 are mentioned without any suspicion concerning their genuineness being raised (Hegel, 2018 [1807], p. 264; Böckh, 1824, 1828; Hinrichs, 1827).[19] However, serious doubts remained and continue to linger until this day.[20] On Wednesday March 28, 1827, none other than Johann Wolfgang von Goethe, the greatest mind of his generation, confessed to his friend Johann Peter Eckermann: "In *Antigone* [909–912], for example, there is a passage that always jars with me, and I would give a great deal for some eminent scholar to come along and prove that it is not original, but a later interpolation by somebody else"; "as she [Antigone] is going to her death at the end, she suddenly comes out with a motive so implausible that it verges on the comical" (Eckermann, 2022 [1823–1831], pp. 507–508).

From Lacan's detailed presentation of the controversy, it can be inferred that he knew very well how 909–912 had appeared in nearly identical form in the *Histories* by Sophocles' contemporary Herodotus – with the proviso that in this episode the 'chosen brother' is still alive (Herodotus, 2014, p. 243) – but also that he fully endorsed the main argument against the hypothesis according to which verses 909–912 must be spurious: Aristotle (mis)quoted 911–912 in his *Rhetoric* without questioning their authenticity, even though the philosopher indicated that in this case Antigone's argument is quite 'hard to believe' (ἄπιστον) (Aristotle, 2020, pp. 446–447, translation modified).[21] Erudition aside, the fact that Lacan discovered the truth of *Antigone* in verses whose genuineness was highly disputed is already highly instructive with regard to his methodology.

Having told his audience that, as psychoanalysts, they would be expected to pay attention to the circulations of the signifier, whether in the words of a patient or the written text of a document, rather than applying one or the other key concept as an "intellectual talisman", he proceeded to focus not on the most outstanding, thematically prominent signifiers, but on those emerging in the margins of the play – disruptive and disturbing signifiers, words that do not seem to fit into the overall picture of the narrative tone and dramatic action, verses so strange and unusual that a plethora of eminent scholars had concluded that they must be inauthentic.[22] In doing so, he implicitly embraced a classic Freudian *modus operandi*, which I have designated elsewhere as the 'Zadig-Morelli method' (Nobus, 2000, p. 58). In his 1914 essay 'The Moses of Michelangelo', Freud had compared psychoanalytic technique to the innovative method for establishing the authorship (and authenticity) of a painting which had been introduced by the Italian art critic Giovanni Morelli during the late nineteenth century: rather than looking at the central composition of the work, one needs to pay careful attention to the smallest of details, because this is where the true identity of the artist would reveal itself (Freud, 1958 [1914b], p. 222). As to the act of psychoanalytic 'divination' itself, this would generally adopt the format of what Thomas Huxley dubbed a 'retrospective prophecy', an *ex post facto* hypothesis which explains how, on balance of probability, the rubbish heap had come to pass, and for which Voltaire's fictional character Zadig provides the paradigmatic illustration (Voltaire, 1964 [1747]; Huxley, 1894 [1880]). In singling out verses 909–912, Lacan quite literally took the 'despised features' of *Antigone* as one of his starting points for developing a psychoanalytic interpretation of Sophocles' tragedy. Of course, Lacan's assertion that the truth of the entire play is to be situated in just a few easily overlooked, barely noticeable or deliberately discarded verses is also methodologically reminiscent of Heidegger's approach to *Antigone* in his 1935 lecture course *Introduction to Metaphysics* (Heidegger, 2000 [1953], pp. 112–126) and, more poignantly, in his 1942 lectures on Hölderlin's hymn 'The Ister' (Heidegger, 1996 [1984], pp. 51–122), in which he concentrated almost exclusively on just a few words in the first and especially the second choral odes of the play (332–333).[23]

Before I move on to a discussion of Lacan's arguments in the two other sessions he devoted to *Antigone*, I should also comment briefly on his recurrent criticism of Hegel's interpretation of the tragedy. In all likelihood, Lacan first encountered Hegel's analysis of *Antigone* when attending Alexandre Kojève's lectures on *The Phenomenology of Spirit* (Hegel, 2018 [1807]) during the 1930s in Paris. Although the transcription of Kojève's courses is incomplete, we know that he addressed the sixth chapter of *The Phenomenology of Spirit* – in which the ethical dimensions of *Antigone* are being discussed (Hegel, 2018 [1807], pp. 253–267) – during the academic year 1935–1936 (Kojève, 2017 [1947], pp. 122–123).[24] In sum, Hegel's entire conception of the tragedy revolves around the dialectical opposition between the law of the state, as represented by Creon, and the law of the family, as embodied by Antigone, which reaches its climax in the emergence of "equality by *justice*", which is "the simple spirit of he who has suffered wrong" (Hegel, 2018 [1807], p. 266). As Hegel put it in his *Aesthetics*:

> Everything in this tragedy is logical; the public law of the state is set in conflict over against inner family love and duty to a brother; the woman, Antigone, has the family interest as her "pathos", Creon, the man, has the welfare of the community as his.
>
> (Hegel, 1975 [1820–1829], p. 464)[25]

Throughout his discussion of *Antigone*, Lacan expressed his disagreement with Hegel on two separate matters. First, he argued that Hegel's portrayal of Creon and Antigone as two opposing polarities is too uni-dimensional (Lacan, 1992 [1986], p. 254). In other words, Lacan criticised Hegel for failing to appreciate the intrinsically conflicted nature of both Creon and Antigone – their insecurities, their fragility and, ultimately, their self-doubt. Second, Lacan distanced himself from Hegel, because he felt that neither *Antigone* nor *Oedipus at Colonus* culminate in some form of reconciliation between the opposing forces (Lacan, 1992 [1986], pp. 249–250).[26] To Lacan, the dialectical drama of the two antagonistic principles is not resolved in a higher synthesis but left wide open, which is exactly why *Antigone* is a sublime tragedy. Whether these criticisms are entirely justified is a question that would require a separate chapter, yet I think it is fair to say that Hegel was much more subtle in his analysis of *Antigone* than Lacan's disparaging remarks intimate. In addition, as I shall show below, there is at least one point where Hegel's critique reconnects with Lacan's interpretation, so that Lacan was perhaps more Hegelian in his reading than he would have wanted his audience to believe.

Beyond Desire and What Antigone Found There

In this section of my chapter, I shall present a combined reading of lessons 20 and 21 of Lacan's *Seminar VII*, partly because Lacan himself announced that the second of these lessons would be an in-depth continuation of the first (Lacan, 1992 [1986], p. 269), partly because the two lessons revolve around the same set of questions. I shall also include some observations derived from the so-called Supplementary Note (Lacan, 1992 [1986], pp. 284–287), which should have been included into the transcription of the seminar as a stand-alone lesson, and thus as lesson 22, because it concerns a completely separate session.[27]

Let me start with Lacan's key statement that Antigone comes to inhabit a place of 'unbearable brilliance'. How does she get there? Lacan's answer was exceedingly simple: she manages to reach her destination by crossing a certain line, exceeding a limit, breaking a rule, transgressing a boundary. However, in order to understand what this limit consists of, it needs to be approached from two different angles:

from the viewpoint of Creon and from the perspective of Antigone herself. Indeed, the limit Antigone crosses is not the same for Creon as it is for her. Even though the end point is identical, the perception of the actions and motives that lead up to it differs depending on the character defining the limit that has been exceeded. If we approach the transgression from Creon's point of view, the limit is as inflexible as it is unequivocal: the dead body of the traitor Polynices shall not be honoured with funerary rites. Accordingly, in Creon's opinion, Antigone has become *persona non grata* because she has dared to disobey his orders – not once, but twice.[28] In the eyes of Creon, the fact that she did what he had formally prohibited makes her a criminal and fully warrants her receiving the death penalty. However, Lacan argued that, for Antigone herself, there is much more at stake than breaking an official edict. Much as she despises Creon's law because she believes it ignores the unwritten laws of the gods, Antigone takes advantage of the opportunity presented to her (to break the law and commit a criminal act) in order to cross another limit. For Lacan, Antigone antagonising Creon by burying Polynices is just a means to another, much more important objective, notably her breaking the dreadful spell that has brought innumerable misfortunes upon her family (the House of Labda-kos), ever since the days the Delphic oracle had told her grandfather Laius that under no circumstances he should father a child. Whereas Creon's limit is the law that Polynices must not be buried, Antigone's limit is the law that has brought hor-rendous suffering upon her family. The former law is a written policy of the city; the latter law is an unwritten malediction called ἄτη.

The term ἄτη is exceptionally difficult to translate in any modern language and Lacan did not even venture to suggest a concise French equivalent (Lacan, 1992 [1986], pp. 262–263). Over the years, English translators of *Antigone* have tried to capture ἄτη with a cornucopia of different words, ranging from madness, fantasy and delusion to bewilderment, chaos, ruin and disaster, all of which being context-dependent and relaying slightly different aspects of the term, depending on the nature and style of the discourse in which it features. Because my chapter is not intended as a philological study of *Antigone*, and at the risk of attracting the wrath of various classicists and Hellenists, I shall render it as 'curse'.[29] Hence, for Lacan, Antigone reaches the place of 'unbearable brilliance' not merely on account of her having defied Creon's law, but also because she has broken the curse that has dev-astated the House of Labdakos for so long.

In his seminar, Lacan drew his audience's attention to the fact that ἄτη is easily overlooked, even though it is mentioned in various parts of the tragedy (Lacan, 1992 [1986], p. 262). However, of all the occurrences of ἄτη in the play, the one that Lacan was most interested in features at the very end of the second strophe in the third choral ode, which constitutes the bridge between Antigone's taking sole responsibility for her crime in front of Creon, and Creon being confronted by his son Haemon, who tries to convince his father that he needs to reconsider his orders, if only because they do not accord with the will of the people. Reflecting upon the curse that has thrown the House of Labdakos into disarray, the chorus sings about the unfathomable, omnipotent power of the gods, compared to which the will of earthly mortals must remain forever diminutive and insignificant. Enthralled by its grandiose encomium, the chorus then proclaims its own law (611–614):

τό τ' ἔπειτα καὶ τὸ μέλλον
καὶ τὸ πρὶν ἐπαρκέσει
νόμος ὅδ'' οὐδὲν ἔρπει
θνατῶν βιότῳ πάμπολύ γ' ἐκτὸς ἄτας.

In Lloyd-Jones's translation: "For present, future and past this law shall suffice: to none among mortals shall great wealth come without disaster [ἐκτὸς ἄτας]" (Sophocles, 1998, p. 61).[30] The conventional reading of this law suggests that disaster (ἄτη) is inevitable if ordinary mortals aspire to great wealth. However, Lacan's interpretation was markedly different, insofar as he considered ἐκτὸς ἄτας not as signifying 'without' or 'in the absence of' disaster, but rather as connoting 'outside', 'beyond' or 'on the other side of' disaster. To Lacan, the chorus's law therefore conveys another sense, and another injunction: no mortals shall ever acquire great riches unless they succeed in going beyond disaster. And since ἄτη is precisely the limit Antigone wants to cross, ἐκτὸς ἄτας is the point at which her desire is directed (Lacan, 1992 [1986], p. 263).

Lacan intimated that Antigone reaches this 'otherworldly' place, 'beyond the curse', as soon as she has broken Creon's law, but that Creon himself remains ignorant of Antigone's true purpose. In the eyes of Creon, his niece has committed a heinous crime, yet to Antigone herself she has only done something that is morally good. As Lacan put it: "something beyond the limits of *Atè* [*sic*] has become Antigone's good" (Lacan, 1992 [1986], p. 270).[31] What Creon is expecting to hear as an explanation of his niece's crime thus enters Antigone's speech as a justification of her well-doing. What Antigone is hearing in Creon's defence of his own ordinance is not the explanation of a just law, but the motive of a criminal act in its own right.

At this particular point of the perilous juncture between Creon and Antigone – whereby the latter has not only broken the former's law, but also the curse of the House of Labdakos, yet without Creon being aware of this second transgression – Lacan detected the multi-dimensionality, the trials and tribulations, the dilemmas and the internal conflicts of the play's two principal characters. At first, Creon defends his decree on the basis of an entirely reasonable principle, which could have only been appreciated by the theatregoers as a fair and just decision: murderous traitors who are intent on destroying both their own city and their kin do not deserve any kind of honours when they perish on the battlefield, because they have become enemies of the state. In considering this principle, Lacan went so far as to say that its purportedly universal, unconditional validity would make it fit rather well as a classic, paradigmatic example of a Kantian categorical imperative (Lacan, 1992 [1986], p. 259; Kant, 1997 [1788], p. 28). Yet it is not in Creon's act of formulating this law that his ἁμαρτία – the 'error of judgement' which Aristotle designated as the cardinal trait of all tragic heroes (Aristotle, 1999, pp. 70–71) – needs to be situated.[32] If Creon epitomises ἁμαρτία, it is because he involuntarily allows his law to become contaminated with at least four kinds of lethal poison, and it is through these confusions and aberrations that his weakness of character transpires. Lacan did not mention each and every source of contamination, and one could undoubtedly write a separate chapter on why he 'forgot' to include some of them, yet they can be summarised as follows. First, Creon erroneously believes that the written law he has passed is *de facto* in accordance with the unwritten laws of the gods, and that his sense of justice (δίκη) is synonymous with the gods' spirit of moral order and fair judgement (162–210) (Sophocles, 1998, pp. 19–23; Lacan, 1992 [1986], pp. 276–277). Second, whereas Creon has ruled that all those who break his law shall be put to death by public stoning (29–36), when he discovers that Antigone is the perpetrator, he abandons his own 'fixed penalty' in favour of a much harsher punishment, so that her suffering can be prolonged – sustained and extended for as long as possible (773–780) (Sophocles, 1998, p. 77; Lacan, 1992 [1986], pp. 260–262).[33] Third, when Creon hears from his son Haemon that Antigone's death sentence does not represent the will of the people, he does not hesitate to reaffirm his decision on the basis of a self-proclaimed autocratic position: the city belongs to the ruler and I, Creon, can do whatever I want (736–738) (Sophocles, 1998, p. 71). Finally, Creon states on two occasions that he is not prepared to compromise, let alone pardon the perpetrator, because he cannot accept his sovereign masculinity to become unsettled through the actions of a woman (525, 680) (Sophocles, 1998, pp. 51, 65).[34] Only after his eyes have been opened by the blind prophet Tiresias, and he is consumed by pity, fear and self-doubt, does Creon realise that he has made a tragic mistake, but at that point the damage has already been done: Antigone is dead, Haemon will follow her to Hades, and so will his wife Eurydice.

As far as Antigone herself is concerned, she too is conflicted, but for completely different reasons than Creon. Lacan conceded that, unlike Creon, Antigone experiences neither pity nor fear until the very end. In fact, he argued that it is precisely because she never gives in to pity and fear that she commands pity and fear in the audience and that her ultimate appearance is cathartic (Lacan, 1992 [1986], p. 258).[35] But she is torn in another way, which may not be emblematic of ἁμαρτία, but which nonetheless leaves her in a state of turmoil and self-doubt. Lacan insinuated that Antigone's own conflicted state of mind comes to the fore most strongly when she stops saying 'No' to Creon, relinquishes her attempts to justify her 'criminal act' in front of the ruler of Thebes, and goes in search of answers to the question of her own transgression, that of the trans-generational ἄτη. As long as Antigone is immersed in her defence vis-à-vis Creon, she remains headstrong, but when she distances herself from this defence (and from Creon), towards an exploration of what has prompted her to say 'Yes' to her own desire to break the curse, she becomes unsteady and unsure, hesitant and tentative, so much so that her words are verging on the irrational. It is in this moment, which Lacan located in the disputed verses 909–912 and which, to him, constitute the true core of the play (as opposed to a spurious interpolation), that Antigone acquires her 'unbearable brilliance', because she is no longer interested in revolting against a written law, but fully taken up by the mystery of her own acquiescence, the motive behind her desperate desire to break the curse.[36]

Lacan thus differentiated between Antigone's uncompromising allegiance to the unwritten laws of the gods – as what motivated her 'crime' – and her sudden moment of "lonely, brooding introspection" (Knox, 1984. p. 46), in which she searches for an answer to her own question about the source of her desire to break the curse. Both parts of Antigone's oration are equally important – and so the second part should by no means be considered as totally unworthy of the tragic heroine, as Goethe and others had done – but they contrast radically in contents, style and tone, because they refer to completely different psycho-social registers. In the first register, Antigone is being interrogated by the ruler of Thebes about how she could have gone so far as to give up her own life for the burial of a dead traitor. In this sphere, Antigone keeps repeating that she merely acted in accordance with the divine laws, and Lacan did not hesitate to attribute her fearless self-sacrifice to her spiritual membership of the divine contingent of Ares, which Socrates explains in Plato's *Phaedrus* as a state of mind that can easily drive someone who is enamoured (with another human being or with the gods) to commit murder or self-sacrifice (Plato, 2005, p. 33[252c5]; Lacan, 1992 [1986], p. 260).[37] In the second register, Antigone moves away from Creon and interrogates herself about her motives for crossing the limit of ἄτη. And here the answers do not flow freely, nor do they come across as rational, understandable and acceptable. The only thing Antigone can think of, the only thing that occurs to her, is that Polynices was irreplaceable, yet this reveals much less about her brother than about the fact that their parents are dead and therefore cannot produce another brother for her. What she is attempting to say is that, ultimately, she did what she did because she loved her brother deeply. However, she cannot bring herself to finding the right words, as if they might actually exist.[38] In this particular instance, Lacan's reading of *Antigone* does chime with Hegel's interpretation of the play, because in his *Aesthetics*, Hegel too asserted that in verses 909–912, Antigone is animated by "her holy love for her brother" (Hegel, 1975 [1820–1829], p. 221).[39]

In any case, because Antigone struggles to articulate the motive behind her desire to break the curse, what she is left with is a state of confusion, uncertainty and self-doubt. And so the firm ethical stance that she adopted vis-à-vis Creon dissipates and transmutes into an episode of sublime beauty, which is greatly intensified by the fact that Antigone also realises that she will only learn afterwards – after her own death – whether her actions were in keeping with the gods' will. Antigone's 'unbearable brilliance' is therefore concurrent with the (rather awkward and altogether failed) expression of the source and origin of her deepest desire. She is transformed into a dazzling point of high-powered luminosity, because the inexpressible force of her own desire suddenly erupts onto the stage in all its blazing purity.

However, Lacan identified another moment in the tragedy when Antigone becomes one with the birthplace of her desire. In this case, the moment is not part of Antigone's own discourse but included in the fourth choral ode, which follows the end of Haemon's futile attempt at changing his father's mind. After the famous opening strophe in which the chorus pays tribute to the invincibility of romantic love (Ἔρως ἀνίκατε μάχαν, 781), they pursue the antistrophe with a paean to Antigone herself (795–800):

νικᾷ δ᾽ ἐναργὴς βλεφάρων
ἵμερος εὐλέκτρου
νύμφας, τῶν μεγάλων
πάρεδρος ἐν ἀρχαῖς
θεσμῶν. ἄμαχος γὰρ ἐμ-
παίζει θεός, Ἀφροδίτα.

Lloyd-Jones translates these verses as: "Victory goes to the visible desire [ἵμερος ἐναργὴς] that comes from the eyes of the beautiful bride, desire that has its throne beside those of the mighty laws; for irresistible in her sporting is the goddess Aphrodite" (Sophocles, 1998, p. 79). In this sentence, the words that mattered the most to Lacan are ἵμερος ἐναργὴς, because they indicate how Antigone's desire has become clearly discernible, distinctly perceptible – in no uncertain terms, in all its immediacy, naked in the pure presence of its implacable being (Lacan, 1992 [1986], pp. 268, 281). Lacan also deservedly emphasised, here, how Sophocles did not employ the more common ancient Greek word for desire (ἐπιθυμία) but the word ἵμερος, which has less pejorative connotations than ἐπιθυμία and which quite literally refers to elements that flow together in a stream of longing, craving or yearning, as Socrates again explains in Plato's *Phaedrus* (Plato, 2005, p. 32; Lacan, 1992 [1986], p. 268).[40]

For Lacan, ἔστ᾽ ἀδελφὸς ὅστις ἂν βλάστοι ποτέ (912), which conjures up the irreplaceability of Polynices, and ἵμερος ἐναργὴς (795–796), which renders Antigone's desire visible, thus constitute the essence of the place beyond ἄτη, where nothing is left of Antigone, other than the immaculate presence of the core of the desire that has taken her to the other side. However, even though the leader of the chorus praises Antigone for having gone there "by virtue of her own law" (αὐτόνομος, 820) (Sophocles, 1998, p. 81, translation modified), Lacan was not particularly keen to ascertain in the tragic heroine a paragon of free will (Lacan, 1992 [1986], p. 282). Likewise, he remained rather sceptical about the idea that Sophocles' tragedy exemplifies the basic principles of humanism: the emancipatory value of self-determination, the liberating force of freedom of thought, the inexhaustible resource of human willpower, the strength of the human spirit to realise its full potential in conscious, confident acts of self-assertion.[41] In Lacan's reading, Antigone's being called αὐτόνομος does not mean that she is the sole author of the law that drives her. As the theory of human desire Lacan had constructed over the years would suggest, Antigone's desire to take advantage of Creon's edict, in order to break the curse of the House of Labdakos, had probably already been mediated by another desire, yet here Lacan did not go any further than obliquely designating it as the desire of the Other, whilst insinuating that this 'Other desire' may in fact find its origin in the desire of Antigone's mother Jocasta (Lacan, 1992 [1986], pp. 282–283).[42]

Before I bring my chapter to a close, there are two other matters that deserve some attention – one interpretative, the other methodological. As far as Lacan's interpretation of Antigone's desire goes, the place beyond ἄτη she comes to occupy after having broken both Creon's decree and the curse of the House of Labdakos is not a grand realm of unsullied, 'prelapsarian' bliss. Antigone's life ἐκτὸς ἄτας is everything but cheerful and tranquil, even though she would have had every reason to feel completely satisfied, given how she has succeeded in fulfilling her deepest desire. One could argue, of course, that she would not have ended up in this state of turmoil had it not been for Creon's unwillingness to compromise and his obstinate refusal to pardon her for performing funerary rites on the body of Polynices. Yet this is counterfactual history and moreover Antigone already knew before she did the deed that she would probably be punished harshly for it. Antigone's state of mind ἐκτὸς ἄτας is a place of profound solitude, where she is morally disconnected from her only surviving sibling (Ismene) and cannot even find solace in the arms of her beloved Haemon.[43] On two separate occasions, Lacan described Antigone in her insular space ἐκτὸς ἄτας as "running on empty" (à-bout-de-course): she takes full responsibility for the consequences of her act, yet she is struggling to find meaning in her new-found freedom and is forced to acknowledge that she cannot even be entirely sure that the 'moral good' she endeavoured to achieve is as significant and valuable as she thought it was.[44] Paraphrasing the title of one of Lacan's earlier essays, one might say that, once she is outside ἄτη, Antigone exists in a state of 'anticipated certainty' (Lacan, 2006 [1945]), because only after her death will it be revealed whether she was right or wrong. Only after she herself has entered Hades will she know the truth (see verses 925–928 above) (Sophocles, 1998, p. 89). Finally, as if all of this was not enough, Antigone also concedes that the nature of her death sentence has put her in a highly troublesome 'ontological position' (850–852):

ἰὼ δύστανος, βροτοῖς
οὔτε νεκρὸς νεκροῖσιν
μέτοικος οὐ ζῶσιν, οὐ θανοῦσιν.

Lloyd-Jones translates these verses as: "Ah, unhappy one, living neither among mortals nor as a shade among the shades, neither with the living nor with the dead!" (Sophocles, 1998, p. 83). Here and later on, in her final lament (916–920), Antigone refers to herself explicitly as the 'unhappy one' (δύστανος), because she is now dead amongst the living and will soon be alive amongst the dead.[45] In his seminar, Lacan referred to Antigone's state of mind as "being shut up or suspended in the zone between life and death" (Lacan, 1992 [1986], p. 280), and subsequently one of the participants would suggest the term 'between-two-deaths', which Lacan gladly adopted.[46]

As regards Lacan's methodology, it is interesting to see that throughout the period of his commentary on *Antigone*, he engaged in a conversation with Claude Lévi-Strauss, whose structuralist method for interpreting myths is mentioned on various occasions in the course of the seminar. Engaging in a conversation should be taken literally, here, because every so often Lacan would tell his audience about Lévi-Strauss's views on one or the other aspect of the tragedy (Lacan, 1992 [1986], p. 274), and at one point he even took credit for persuading his interlocutor to re-read Sophocles' work (Lacan, 1992 [1986], pp. 282, 285). The motive for Lacan's personal discussions on *Antigone* with Lévi-Strauss should probably not be attributed here to the mere fact that Lévi-Strauss and Lacan entertained a close friendship, and were in the habit of spending time together at Lacan's country house in Guitrancourt (Lévi-Strauss and Eribon, 1991 [1988], pp. 66, 109).[47] I think the motive is rather to be found in the contents of Lévi-Strauss's 1955 essay 'The Structural Study of Myth' (Lévi-Strauss, 1955), a French translation of which had been included in *Anthropologie Structurale* (Lévi-Strauss, 1958 [1955]), a generous collection of papers released in 1958, just a year before Lacan started his seminar *The Ethics of Psychoanalysis*. In that essay, Lévi-Strauss had presented an innovative, structuralist reading of the Oedipus-myth, in which it was situated within a much broader mythological framework, reorganised in its orthogonal diachronic and synchronic dimensions, and reduced to a set of structurally invariant units (mythemes) (Lévi-Strauss, 1963 [1955], pp. 213–217).[48] In Lévi-Strauss's interpretation, Antigone's decision to bury the body of her dead brother Polynices appeared as a diachronic transmutation of Oedipus marrying his mother Jocasta and, higher up the mythological ladder, Cadmos going in search of his sister Europa (Lévi-Strauss, 1963 [1955], p. 214).

When Lacan disclosed to the participants at his seminar that Lévi-Strauss had told him personally that Antigone represents a place of synchrony in opposition to the diachronical position of Creon (Lacan, 1992 [1986], p. 285), it was thus Lévi-Strauss's methodology and terminology from 'The Structural Study of Myth' that had been extended to inform a closer look at *Antigone*. However, despite his unmistakable enthusiasm for Lévi-Strauss's interest in *Antigone*, Lacan's own reading of the tragedy does not fit into the structural(ist) study of myth, if only because Lacan approached the play primarily as a work of art rather than the transfiguration of an ancient Greek myth. Yet in addition to this, he was not particularly interested in extracting from *Antigone* the elementary symbolic schemes that contribute to the construction of subjective positions and which underpin the binary dialectical oppositions within and between psycho-social relations of property and exchange, as he had done with great success a few years earlier in his seminal reading of Edgar Allan Poe's 'The Purloined Letter' (Lacan, 2006 [1956]). For all the exceptional value of kinship in the tragedy's unfolding intrigue – as the driving force behind Creon's decree and Antigone's defiance of it – Lacan was not particularly interested in extracting its elementary structures. In fact, the only time he allowed himself a little foray into the structural study of the Antigone-myth was when he considered the mystery of Antigone's death at her own hands. "Antigone hanging in her own tomb evokes something very different from an act of suicide," Lacan posited, "since there are all kinds of myths of hanged heroines . . . [O]ne finds there a whole ritual and mythical background, which may be brought back to resituate in its religious harmony all that is produced on the stage" (Lacan, 1992 [1986], p. 286).[49]

Conclusion

Let me return now to the questions I posed in the introduction to my chapter and endeavour to formulate some answers. Lacan resolved to devote his 1959–1960 seminar to the age-old query as to what human desire is geared towards, and to how these goals, aims and objectives of desire play out within the space of a clinical psychoanalytic encounter. This project would have followed naturally from his having spent an entire year investigating the meaning and function of desire, both in the human mind and in the act of psychoanalytic interpretation. Lacan intended his investigation of the aims of desire to be theoretical as well as practical, and for it to be of direct relevance to the psychoanalytic trainees attending his seminar. Accordingly, *The Ethics of Psychoanalysis* would not only be a seminar on the aims of desire, in the broadest sense of the word, but also on the aims (goals, direction, finality) of the psychoanalytic treatment, insofar as the latter is conceived as a particular 'therapy' of (the patient's) desire. When broaching the question of the aims of desire, Lacan also knew that, at least since the Ancient Greeks, it had been consistently addressed within the context of philosophical reflections on ethics – a discipline which not only revolves around the challenge of identifying and defining robust criteria for differentiating between right and wrong, but also around in-depth examinations of the particular relationship (and the essential or contingent discrepancies) between human desire and various (socio-political) ideals of concrete outcomes and deliverables that are representative of the highest moral good. Considered in this light, it should not come as a surprise at all that Lacan titled his seminar *The Ethics of Psychoanalysis*, which invoked both a psychoanalytic interpretation of ethics and the formulation of an ethical system that is attuned to the highly specific circumstances of the psychoanalytic setting.

I do not know when exactly Lacan came to the conclusion that it would be a good idea to include a detailed critical analysis of Sophocles' *Antigone* in his seminar, yet the fact that he reserved a substantial portion of it to a discussion of ancient Greek tragedy was justified on two grounds. First, the goal of ancient Greek tragedy, which had been designated since Aristotle as catharsis (Aristotle, 1999, pp. 47–48) – a purification or cleansing of the psyche – featured explicitly in Breuer and Freud's *Studies on Hysteria* as the overall aim of their treatment paradigm, whereby they had defined it as the patient's process of releasing (through words or concrete actions) the disruptive affects that are attached to repressed unconscious representations (Breuer and Freud, 1955 [1895d], p. 8). After Freud abandoned the hypno-cathartic method of treatment in favour of an approach he termed psychoanalysis, which no longer relied on hypnotic techniques, he did not simultaneously relinquish catharsis as a suitable designation for the goal of the treatment, even though he would subsequently entertain alternative notions, such as 'working-through' (Freud, 1958 [1914g]). Second, in the final session of his seminar, Lacan offered another reason as to why ancient Greek tragedy deserves to feature in a research programme on the ethics of psychoanalysis:

> The ethics of analysis has nothing to do with speculation about prescriptions for, or the regulation of what I have called the service of the goods. Strictly speaking, the ethics of analysis implies the dimension that is expressed in what is called the tragic experience of life.
>
> (Lacan, 1992 [1986], p. 313, translation modified)[50]

I shall return to this second reason below, yet over and above the confluence of the goal of ancient Greek tragedy and the aim of psychoanalysis, Lacan thus averred that the study of ancient Greek tragedy could be highly instructive for practicing psychoanalysts, because the clinical psychoanalytic experience constitutes in itself a real-life confrontation with the tragedy of human existence. Innumerable ancient Greek tragedies have not survived the passing of time, yet Lacan would still have been spoilt for choice when it came to deciding which tragedy to focus on in his seminar. If he settled on Sophocles' *Antigone*, I believe it is not so much because it follows in the wake of *Oedipus Rex*, but because *Antigone*, perhaps more than any other tragedy, stages precisely the tragic impact of human desire.

When the time arrived for Lacan to commence his interpretation of *Antigone*, he would have also had to consider which methodology to employ – which interpretative techniques to use in order to distill the central contributions of *Antigone* and Antigone to the development of an ethics for psychoanalysis. In this respect, it is quite remarkable – although to the best of my knowledge no commentators on Lacan's reading of *Antigone* have ever highlighted it – that, when it came to analysing Sophocles' text, Lacan's conceptual toolkit was almost entirely empty. It is nothing short of astonishing, then, to observe that throughout his three (or four) lessons on *Antigone*, Lacan did not refer a single time to his famous triad of the Real, the Symbolic and the Imaginary, nor to any of the other concepts for which he had already gained a certain notoriety: jouissance, the fantasy, the signifying chain, the phallus and the *object a*. Likewise, with the exception of one cursory mention of the death drive (Lacan, 1992 [1986], p. 281), he did not bring out any of the classic Freudian notions that could have served a good interpretative purpose: the Oedipus complex, the superego, castration, penis envy, the pleasure principle and so forth. Even more noteworthy, perhaps, especially in light of an established practice within the field of applied psychoanalysis, or psychoanalytic interpretations of literature, is that Lacan completely shied away from attempting a certain diagnosis (and a concurrent pathologisation) of the characters in *Antigone*. At no given point did Lacan intimate, even in the vaguest of terms, that Antigone,

Creon or some of the other characters in the tragedy could be understood as literary exemplifications of hysteria, obsessional neurosis or psychosis. The only concept that is constantly present throughout Lacan's discussion of *Antigone* is desire. Yet whilst this notion was at least as important in Lacan's theory of psychoanalysis as the other terms mentioned above – and it should not be forgotten, here, that he had devoted an entire seminar to it in 1958–1959– desire is of course also the key issue around which the tragedy of *Antigone* unfolds. It would therefore be an exaggeration to claim that Lacan injected desire into *Antigone*, or that he reorganised the entire tragedy around (the ethics of) desire, because (the ethics of) desire is already the main theme of the play. It may not be coincidental that Lacan situated one of the most significant messages of *Antigone* in a verse in which the chorus glorifies the visibility of the young woman's desire, yet he would not have had to work hard to argue his point, because the word desire (ἵμερος) is already present, literally and distinctively, at the level of the text.

As I have attempted to demonstrate above, when interpreting *Antigone*, Lacan also generally avoided Lévi-Strauss's structuralist study of myth, with which he would have been deeply familiar, in favour of an implicit reliance on what I have called the 'Zadig-Morelli method', which Freud himself had singled out as the art-historical equivalent of psychoanalytic technique (Freud, 1958 [1914b], p. 222). In doing so, he followed the example of Heidegger's interpretation of *Antigone* in his *Introduction to Metaphysics* (Heidegger, 2000 [1953], pp. 156–176) and in his lecture course on Hölderlin's 'The Ister' (Heidegger, 1996 [1984], pp. 51–122), yet much as I would be surprised if Heidegger knew about Zadig and Morelli, I do not think that Lacan had in-depth knowledge of Heidegger's methods of reading in this particular instance. Most important, however, is that Lacan himself instructed his audience not to use conceptual tools as a magic talisman that would reveal the secrets of a text, but rather to trust the internal logic of the fictional space and follow its leads (Lacan, 1992 [1986], pp. 251–252). This is also why I preferred not to place this chapter under the title 'Lacan's Antigone', because I would feel very hard-pressed to concede that Lacan appropriated *Antigone* and/or Antigone. It is undoubtedly the case that he did not perform a purely inductive reading – as if this would even be possible – yet at the same time I do not think one could proffer the thesis that Lacan integrated or incorporated *Antigone* into a pre-fabricated or pre-established psychoanalytic framework. The Antigone that emerges out of Lacan's interpretation is distinctly unique and, as such, definitely Lacan's own Antigone and his Antigone alone, yet this does not imply that he went so far as to take ownership of Sophocles' intentions, the dramatic structure of the tragedy or the conflictual dialectics of desire that are being staged therein. Between May 25 and June 15, 1960, Lacan went on an intellectual journey 'with' *Antigone*, whereby he seemed more than happy to allow its eponymous heroine to take the reins.[51]

What did Lacan's interpretation of *Antigone* contribute, then, to the formulation of an ethics for psychoanalysis? Insofar as 'ethical system' refers to aims and objectives, how could the finality of psychoanalysis be (re-)conceptualised on the basis of what Sophocles' tragedy teaches us? In this context, I should first of all draw attention to one of the most tenacious (and arguably tragic) misreadings in the history of Lacanian thought.[52] Since the early 1980s – from the years before *Seminar VII* was even officially released in French – countless scholars of Lacanian theory and self-identified Lacanians have reduced the ethics of psychoanalysis to a single imperative: Do not give up on your desire![53] From Badiou to Žižek and Zupančič, and a pleiad of eager followers of Lacan in between, 'Do not give up on your desire!' has become the single most important ethical mantra to be derived from *Seminar VII*.[54] This precept, which has sometimes been rephrased as 'the ethics of the Real' (Zupančič, 2000), or 'the ethics of jouissance' (Zupančič, 2002), and for which Antigone would then be put forward as the principal literary prototype, has become so prominent and widespread as Lacan's most advanced formulation of a psychoanalytic ethics that the entire seminar on *The Ethics of Psychoanalysis* has occasionally been presented as driven by, or steered towards the explicit articulation of this one ethical maxim.[55]

The first problem with this interpretation of Lacan's *Seminar VII*, and Lacan's reading of *Antigone* within it, is that it cannot be substantiated on the basis of any kind of textual evidence. Not a single time during his entire lecture course did Lacan even come close to suggesting that 'Do not give up on your desire!' should become the ethical motto of psychoanalytic practice, and that the figure of Antigone could, in one form or another, then be hailed as its most sublime incarnation. Even though it is true that Antigone never gives up on her desire (to perform funerary rites on the dead body of her brother Polynices), this does not mean that she should therefore be elevated to the status of patron saint or fairy godmother of psychoanalytic ethics. The only time Lacan mentioned "*céder sur son désir*" (giving up on one's desire) in his seminar was in the final session. He never employed the expression with a negative – as in '*ne pas céder sur son désir*' (not giving up on one's desire) – and it never took the form of an imperative, let alone an ethical precept, even less an ethical axiom for psychoanalysis (Lacan, 1992 [1986], pp. 319–321).[56] As to 'giving up on one's desire', Lacan only proposed that, quite paradoxically, it may be the most fundamental thing (neurotic) human beings tend to feel guilty about, because the thought of 'having given up' on something routinely occurs alongside an impression of (self-)betrayal (Lacan, 1992 [1986], pp. 319–321).[57]

Needless to say, advocates of the adage 'Do not give up on your desire!' may argue that it was always already implicit in Lacan's discourse, or that, as a concise extrapolation of his words, it might still serve as a foundational principle for psychoanalytic practice. Unfortunately, this argument does not hold water and could only be formulated by someone who has never had any clinical psychoanalytic experience, or whose professional and/or personal interests are extremely far removed from what is at stake in the psychoanalytic treatment of patients. Were a psychoanalyst to operate with the ethical precept that patients should consistently, if not always explicitly, be brought to the point where they can accept that the source of their happiness is always to be found in 'not giving up on their desire', she or he would not only run the risk of aiding and abetting the patient to commit various (criminal) transgressions, but much more problematically he or she would also be acting upon the illusion that happiness coincides with the fulfilment (satisfaction or gratification) of desire. Were 'Do not give up on your desire!' to be framed in gold above the psychoanalytic couch, the patient would not only be spending money on learning how to exchange a life of suffering for that of a criminal, but the analyst would effectively be joining the reprehensible ranks of all those *faux*-experts who cunningly take advantage of someone's else's problems in order to enrich themselves through the sale of false hope and empty promises.[58]

What Antigone teaches Lacan, during the four weeks they go on a journey together, is that the realisation of one's desire does not by definition lead to happiness. Here is what Antigone tells Lacan after she has finally succeeded in going beyond ἄτη. Strange as it may seem, Dr Lacan, now that I have buried the body of Polynices, I am still not sure whether I have satisfied my desire to break the curse. For that uncertainty, which creates a great deal of mental turmoil, to go away, I shall have to wait until some kind of final judgement, yet when this moment comes, I shall no longer be alive to reap the fruits of my own act, should it indeed be decided that it was in accordance with my desire and that my desire was justified. Strange as it may seem, Dr Lacan, now that I have broken Creon's law and taken the opportunity presented to me in order to also break the curse that has brought so much misery upon my family, I still feel miserable, because I do not know whether the satisfaction of my desire, as I see it, will indeed have the desired effect. Strange as it may seem, Dr Lacan, now that I have ostensibly liberated my desire from any kind of constraint and I should have every reason to feel happy, I am not happy at all, because the price I have had to pay for my act seems extraordinarily high. It is not just that I have now been condemned to death, and that I shall be forced to take my own life in order to deprive Creon of the pleasure of knowing that I will suffer tremendously until I finally starve to death. It is rather that I am now no longer sure whether I was right in taking it upon myself to break the curse. In fact, I am no longer sure whether there really was a curse in the first place, because it may have just been my imagination. In any case, Dr Lacan, I cannot find the words to describe the source of my desire, as if my own being is not strong or resourceful enough to render it clear to myself. Strange as it may seem, I definitely do not know whether the realisation of my desire has resulted in something good, whether for myself, or for all those who shall come after me.

This is what Antigone tells Lacan during the time they spend together, but it is not what a psychoanalyst would expect to hear from a patient at the end of a psychoanalytic treatment. Much like Antigone, patients will always in some way be confronted with the fundamental tragedy of the human condition – the inevitability of death, the persistent elusiveness of (self-)knowledge, the desperate yet endless search for meaning – but unlike Antigone they are not expected to experience this tragedy as a result of the realisation of their desire, and even less to experience it as an irreversible *fait accompli*. In effect, contrary to what the aforementioned motto prescribes, one cannot not give up on one's desire, because being a (more or less) respectable, law-abiding citizen ineluctably requires compromise, and therefore a certain degree of (self-)betrayal. In order to ensure that patients do not, or no longer fall to pieces when they are confronted with the tragedy of human existence, the analyst may facilitate a process in which the relationships between desire and the law, the pleasure principle and the reality principle, are thoroughly examined and gradually taken towards an acceptable state of equilibrium. In the final instance, this will not only require patients to explore the fantasy that is sustaining their desire and all the illusory images of eternal bliss that might stem from its satisfaction. It will also require them to acknowledge and assume the tragic reality of the human condition, notably that the very 'fact of being' shall always remain insufficient to lead one's life successfully, properly and happily. It will require them to acknowledge the tragedy of intrinsic human vulnerability, in order to find the pathways to some form of (transient) goodness and (momentary) happiness. Here, the finality of the psychoanalytic treatment reconnects with the conclusions of Martha Nussbaum in her influential book *The Fragility of Goodness*: a well-lived life is predicated upon the acceptance that living well cannot be divorced from the impossibility of always being well (Nussbaum, 2001). In the final instance, this ethical dimension of the finality of the psychoanalytic treatment will require analysts themselves to adopt a certain desire. However, in order to formalise this 'desire of the analyst' (Lacan, 1992 [1986], p. 300) – as the non-negotiable foundation of the ethics of psychoanalysis – Lacan would need another ten years and quite a few additional psychoanalytic encounters with fictional and other heroines.

Notes

1   This chapter has benefited tremendously from the critical comments of Armand d'Angour, who kindly verified all my interpretations of the ancient Greek for general accuracy and philological consistency. Elissa Marder also read through the entire text and made various valuable criticisms.

2   Throughout this chapter, I shall refer to Sophocles' play as *Antigone* and to its eponymous heroine as Antigone.

3   Much like all the other seminars Lacan delivered between 1953 and 1963, *L'éthique de la psychanalyse* was presented as part of the psychoanalytic training programme of the *Société française de psychanalyse*. However, this did not exclude other people from attending. For instance, in the opening session of *Seminar VII* Lacan explicitly saluted the presence of the linguist Roman Jakobson (Lacan, 1992[1986], p. 12).

4   I should nonetheless emphasize, here, that I shall restrict myself to an explication of Lacan's commentary, and that the suggestions for further reading will be primarily confined to materials in which one or the other point in the text is explored in more detail. As such, I shall engage only tangentially with the secondary literature on Lacan's interpretation of *Antigone*, which is quite substantial, especially in the Anglophone world. Readers wishing to assemble a list of secondary sources should at least include Irigaray (1985[1974]), Kowsar (1990), Lee (1990, pp. 122–132), Lacoue-Labarthe (1991), Guyomard (1991, 1992), Loraux (1986, 1991), Jacobs (1996), Chanter (1998), Van Haute (1998), Butler (2000), de Sauverzac (2000, pp. 175–199), Rabaté (2001, pp. 69–84), Copjec (2002), Leonard (2003, 2005, pp. 101–130, 2006), Zupančič (2000, 2002, 2003), Sjöholm (2004, pp. 101–110, 2014), Weber (2004), Griffith (2005, 2010), Miller (2007), Hurst (2008, pp. 318–347), Shepherdson (2008), De Kesel (2009[2001], pp. 205–248, 2015, 2018), Marder (2009), Eagleton (2010), Jaramillo (2010), Morel (2010), Söderbäck (2010), Meltzer (2011), Naveau (2011), Neill (2011, pp. 211–235),

Clemens (2013, pp. 63–83), Freeland (2013), Honig (2013), Lauret (2014, pp. 80–86), Roudinesco (2014[2011], pp. 129–139), Themi (2014, pp. 41–63), Ruti (2015, pp. 99–118, 2017, pp. 46–56), Žižek (2016), Finkelde (2017), Harris (2017, pp. 125–162), Balaska (2018), Zafiropoulos (2019, pp. 85–113), Luepnitz (2020) and Zupančič (2023).

5 The only source materials in which *Antigone* received some psychoanalytic attention before Lacan explored the tragedy are Chandler (1913), van der Sterren (1948, pp. 109–126, 1952), Fromm (1959[1948]) and Kanzer (1950). Of these five studies, van der Sterren's 1948 monograph offers by far the most comprehensive reading of Sophocles' Theban trilogy –*Antigone, Oedipus the King* and *Oedipus at Colonus* – but his emphasis is still predominantly on Oedipus rather than Antigone. Freud himself had known Sophocles' Theban trilogy since his secondary school days, but he never ventured beyond the central intrigue of *Oedipus the King* (Rudnytsky, 1987, pp. 11–12, 318). Also, after he had been diagnosed with jawbone cancer in 1923, Freud tended to refer to his youngest daughter and closest companion Anna as his Antigone, thereby invoking Antigone's unconditional love for her incapacitated father during the last years of his life in *Oedipus at Colonus*. See Falzeder, Brabant, and Giampieri-Deutsch (2000, p. 352) and E. L. Freud (1970, p. 106). For a wide-ranging discussion of Anna Freud as the Antigone of psychoanalysis, see Stewart-Steinberg (2011, pp. 96–143).

6 For some reason, the English translator of *Séminaire VII* did not translate a sentence in the original text in which Lacan asserted that there is actually no field in ancient Greece where the horizon has remained closed to its underlying structure: "*d'ailleurs il n'y a pas chez les Grecs de champ où l'horizon soit resté fermé à la sous-structure*" (Lacan, 1986, p. 281).

7 For the historical confluence between the morally good and the beautiful, see for instance Plato (2007, p. 247[520c]). The number in square brackets, here, refers to the so-called Stephanus pagination of Plato's texts, which is reproduced in most editions of his work. In his *Critique of Judgement*, Kant reiterated that "the beautiful is the symbol of the morally good" (Kant, 2007[1790], p. 180). It would seem that Hegel was the first to propose a radical distinction between the good and the beautiful, yet the convergence of the two notions continued to flourish during the Romantic period and even informed Wittgenstein's 1921 *Tractatus*, albeit as a parenthetical remark (Wittgenstein, 1961[1921], p. 86). See, in this respect, Walker (2012). For a comprehensive critical study of the intersection between ethics and aesthetics, and its influence on European literary traditions, see Ellison (2001).

8 In his *Lectures on the History of Philosophy*, Hegel referred to Sophocles' heroine as "the heavenly Antigone, that noblest of figures that ever appeared on earth" (Hegel, 1955[1819–1830], p. 441), whereas in his *Aesthetics* he designated *Antigone* as "one of the most sublime and in every respect most excellent works of art of all time" (Hegel, 1975[1820–1829], p. 464). In the documents that have survived, Hegel mentioned *Antigone* for the very first time in a handwritten marginal note to a sentence from a 1796 manuscript that is generally known by its incipit *Jedes Volk . . .* (Hegel, 1989[1796], p. 368). We also know that during his adolescent years, Hegel translated various parts of *Antigone* in German, endeavouring to capture the original metre of the verses in an ongoing dialogue with Hölderlin, yet the text of these translations has not survived (Rosenkranz, 1844, p. 11). During the nineteenth century, Hegel was by no means alone in having recourse to superlatives when describing the tragedy (Steiner, 1984, p. 4) and Lacan himself intermittently echoed Hegel's judgement, although for quite different reasons.

9 The numbers refer to the verse numbering in the original text of the play, which has been reproduced in most English translations of *Antigone*, although the reader needs to be aware that some English versions, such as the translation by Fagles (Sophocles, 1984), have adopted a different numbering. Whereas Lacan primarily relied on the 1947 bilingual Greek-French edition by Pignarre and published by Garnier (Sophocles, 1947;

Lacan, 1992[1986], pp. 254, 270), I shall use the 1998 English translation by Lloyd-Jones (Sophocles, 1998), providing alternative renditions of the Greek when useful or required.

10 In *Seminar VII*, Lacan initially argued that it is *by means of* pity and fear that catharsis is accomplished (Lacan, 1992[1986], pp. 247–248), yet later on he posited that fear and pity need to be superseded in themselves for catharsis to happen (Lacan, 1992[1986], p. 323), reiterating this statement one year later, in *Seminar VIII*, on *Transference* (Lacan, 2015[2001], p. 279). The reader should note that in the English text of the latter seminar, Aristotle's words have been reproduced incorrectly.

11 For an insightful reflection upon the intersections of trauma, abreaction and catharsis in Breuer and Freud's work, see Starobinski (2003[1999], pp. 174–197).

12 Without providing a detailed overview of this historical extrapolation of catharsis into the medical domain, Lacan indicated that one can find traces of it in Molière's 1666 farce *Le médecin malgré lui* (*A Doctor in Spite of Himself*), in which the fake doctor Sganarelle explains to the father of a young girl who has lost her ability to speak that her disease could be alleviated by the purgation of her 'morbid humours' (Molière, 1959[1666], p. 186). More interestingly, Lacan also suggested that Freud could have come across the medical meaning of catharsis in the works of the eminent classicist Jacob Bernays, his wife's uncle, who had written a seminal essay in 1857 on Aristotle and ancient Greek tragedy, in which he had argued that catharsis should be interpreted primarily in a therapeutic sense (Bernays, 1857, 1880). Since he had only verified the historical significance of Jacob Bernays in the first volume of Jones' biography of Freud (Jones, 1953, p. 101), Lacan formulated his remarks very tentatively, yet it has now been persuasively demonstrated that Freud would definitely have been familiar with Bernays' work (Funke, 1996). Lacan also wondered why Bernays' essay had been published first in Breslau, yet we now know that in 1853 he had been appointed there as Professor of Classical Philology at the *Jüdisch-Theologische Seminar* (Bollack, 1998, p. 107). For a fascinating discussion of Bernays' ideas on catharsis, see Porter (2015).

13 For the argument that *Antigone* is less about Antigone and more about Creon, that is, that Creon rather than Antigone is the protagonist of the play, and the textual evidence upon which this argument rests, see for example Frey (1878), Kitto (1956, pp. 138–178), Calder (1971) and Groot (2015).

14 In the English version of the seminar, Porter has translated '*point de visée*' as 'line of sight', which completely misses the point and renders Lacan's argument incomprehensible (Lacan, 1992[1986], p. 247).

15 Porter has translated *éclat* as 'splendour' (Lacan, 1992[1986], p. 247), a term which has been adopted uncritically in many Anglophone studies of Lacan's seminar, such as Freeland (2013), yet Lacan is not underscoring the grandeur of Antigone's appearance, but the blinding light that radiates from her presence. *Éclat* should be rendered as brilliance or radiance.

16 For the principle of the 'second death' in *Juliette*, see Sade (1968[1797], pp. 769–772) and Nobus (2017, pp. 61–67). With regard to *émoi*, the English translation is again inaccurate and confusing, because the translator has opted to render the word as 'excitement' (Lacan, 1992[1986], p. 249). Precisely in order to prevent his audience from interpreting the term as some form of emotion, Lacan adduced its etymological roots, emphasising that *émoi* is neither an emotion nor an unequivocally positive, uplifting experience. It definitely has nothing to do with 'excitement', as the English translation suggests. In the absence of a clear English equivalent, one could have recourse to a circumlocution such as 'being beside oneself', which would come very close to what *émoi* conveys. If I have chosen the term 'turmoil', it is because this notion at least captures the strong connotations of 'mental instability' in *émoi*, but also because this is how Adrian R. Price

has rendered it in his translation of Lacan's *Seminar X*, in which it is included within the matrix of anxiety. See Lacan (2014[2004], pp. 12–13).

17 Here, the English translation, which reads "the point where the false metaphors of being (*l'étant*) can be distinguished from the position of Being (*l'être*) itself" (Lacan, 1992[1986], p. 248), is totally nonsensical, partly because Porter has failed to realise that there is a rather embarrassing transcription error in the original French text – '*métaphores fausses*' (false metaphors) should have been '*métamorphoses*' (metamorphoses) – and partly because he has completely ignored the Heideggerian terminology (*l'étant, das Seiende* vs *l'être, das Sein*) and thus also the conventional English translations of these concepts ('that which is' vs 'being'). In her recent essay on *Antigone*, Zupančič has sadly reproduced Porter's translation literally, thus also ignoring both the transcription error and Lacan's Heideggerian terminology (Zupančič, 2023, p. 55).

18 It would seem that Lacan only quoted the last two verses of this four-verse sentence, so that Antigone's lament is reduced to "with my mother and father in Hades below, I could never have another brother" (Lacan, 1992[1986], p. 255; Sophocles, 1998, p. 87).

19 In another, rather embarrassing transcription and translation error, the name of Hermann Hinrichs appears in the French edition of Lacan's seminar as "Irish" (Lacan, 1986, p. 297) and in the English translation as "a certain Irish" (Lacan, 1992[1986], p. 254).

20 For more detailed reflections on the nature and implications of the debate surrounding the authenticity of 909–912 and the entire passage of 904–920 in which the words feature, see Pischel (1893), Jebb (1900, pp. 258–260), Schadewaldt (1929, pp. 82–99), Agard (1937), Wycherley (1947), van der Sterren (1948, pp. 110–118), Kirkwood (1994[1958], pp. 88–89, 163–169), Kaufmann (1979[1968], pp. 219–225), Szlezák (1981), Murnaghan (1986), Sourvinou-Inwood (1989), Neuburg (1990), Foley (1995), Cropp (1997), Benardete (1999[1975], pp. 110–114) and Honig (2013, pp. 123–140).

21 Whereas Sophocles wrote κεκευθότοιν ('are concealed in') in verse 911, Aristotle reproduced the word as βεβηκότων ('have gone to'), probably because he quoted from memory rather than from a written source document. See Sophocles (1998, p. 86) and Aristotle (2020, p. 446).

22 At this point, the English translation is infuriatingly flawed, because when Lacan said to his listeners "*aucun [des termes que j'aurai poussés devant vous] ne pourra jamais, de mon fait, servir à quiconque de gri-gri intellectuel*", Porter made Lacan proclaim that "none of the terms will in the end enable anyone of you to turn into an intellectual cricket on my account" (Lacan, 1992[1986], p. 252). The word '*gri-gri*', which is more commonly written as '*gris-gris*', refers to a talisman, an amulet (i.e., an object endowed with magical powers). Unless Porter thought that the word '*gri-gri*' was an idiosyncratic onomatopoeia, it is a mystery to me how he arrived at the conclusion that it should be rendered as 'cricket'. And what on earth would it mean for someone to turn into an 'intellectual cricket'?!

23 Over and above the methodological confluence between Lacan's and Heidegger's interpretative strategies of *Antigone*, it is also remarkable how their conceptual developments converge upon an instance of 'the formidable', which Lacan situated in the sublimity of Antigone's 'unbearable brilliance' and Heidegger recognised in the uncanniness (δεινόν, terrible wonder) that the chorus invokes in verse 332 as the defining characteristic of all human beings (Heidegger, 1996[1984], pp. 63–64). In his commentary on *Antigone*, Lacan also referred on two separate occasions to the verses that had caught Heidegger's attention, going so far as quoting them in full the second time, yet without mentioning Heidegger's name. See Lacan (1992[1986], pp. 267, 274), where the verses have been misprinted. During his discussion of *Antigone*, Lacan equally referred to 'Logos', the essay by Heidegger he had translated into French, yet without mentioning Heidegger's

reading of the play (Heidegger, 1956[1951]; Lacan, 1992[1986], p. 276). For excellent critical analyses of Heidegger's views on *Antigone*, see Pearson Geiman (2001) and Fleming (2015).

24 The notes of the lectures in which Kojève commented on the sixth chapter of *The Phenomenology of Spirit* have not been retained in the heavily abridged English edition of Kojève's lecture course (Kojève, 1969[1947]).

25 For detailed analyses of Hegel's discussions of *Antigone* in the context of his overall conception of tragedy, see Jagentowicz Mills (1986), Donougho (1989), Berthold-Bond (1994), Chanter (1995, pp. 80–126), Conklin (1997), De Boer (2008), Burke (2013) and Vuillerod (2020). The most incisive commentary of Hegel's interpretation of *Antigone* is undoubtedly that performed by Derrida in the left column of *Glas* (Derrida, 2021[1974], pp. 164–214).

26 With regard to *Oedipus at Colonus*, Lacan substantiated his point with reference to the famous words μὴ φῦναι ('not to be born'), as sung by the chorus in a gripping reflection upon Oedipus's inescapable fate (Sophocles, 1998, p. 547), yet he wrongly designated them as the final words of Oedipus (Lacan, 1992[1986], pp. 250, 305, 313). Lacan commented on these words on numerous occasions. See Lacan (1988[1978], p. 233, 1993[1981], p. 244, 2006[1962], p. 657, 2015[2001], p. 301).

27 If Miller decided not to do so, it is clearly because the text of Lacan's words on June 15, 1960 was considered too short, which was in itself due to the fact that for that day Lacan had asked Pierre Kaufmann to give a lecture on beauty and the sublime in Kant's work. As Miller had done with the previous editions of Lacan's seminars, all major contributions by participants, such as this one, were consistently omitted from the transcription.

28 In effect, Antigone 'buries' Polynices twice. The first time, she is not caught by the men keeping watch over the dead body (Sophocles, 1998, p. 27) yet after Creon's guards have removed the dust that had been sprinkled over Polynices' body, Antigone performs her act again, and only then is she caught in the act (Sophocles, 1998, pp. 37–39).

29 When he first introduced ἄτη, Lacan claimed that it is also the root of the French word '*atroce*' (atrocious) (Lacan, 1992[1986], p. 263), yet this is factually incorrect, because the etymology of '*atroce*' and 'atrocious' is the Latin word '*atrox*' (sombre, cruel), which is itself derived from '*ater*' (black).

30 Of these four verses, the general meaning of 613–614 remains disputed, if only because the word πάμπολύ does not really make sense. The sentence after the colon is supposed to suggest 'great riches' or 'enormous wealth', yet this is not conveyed by the semantic spectrum of the Greek word. See Sophocles (1999, pp. 228–229). The point is arguably philological, yet it is not at all insignificant, here, because one could say that Lacan's interpretation of the phrase is as good as any other.

31 Both here, as well as in numerous other places in the French and the English editions of Lacan's seminar, the Greek contains a misspelling. Most, yet by no means all, of these errors have been listed in Bergounioux (2005, pp. 67–86).

32 Classicists have argued for decades whether ἁμαρτία is meant to indicate a 'tragic fault' or a 'tragic flaw', the first option suggesting an 'accidental mistake' and the second referring to a 'character defect'. See, for instance, Hyde (1963) and Golden (1978). Outside the *Poetics*, the word also appears five times in Aristotle's *Nicomachean Ethics* (Aristotle, 1934). For an excellent discussion of these mentions, see Van Braam (1912). In his seminar, Lacan opted to translate ἁμαρτία as 'mistake', 'blunder' or 'stupidity' (*bêtise*), whilst simultaneously disagreeing with Aristotle that this 'error' always typifies the tragic hero, because he felt that, at least in *Antigone*, it only defines the "counter- or secondary hero", that is, Creon (Lacan, 1992[1986], pp. 258–259, 277).

33 When reflecting upon Creon's excessive punishment, Lacan reminded his audience of how one of the libertines in Sade's *Juliette* also fantasises about the possibility of making his victims suffer forever, even after they have been tortured to death. In this context,

he again invoked the 'second death' in the system of Pope Pius VI, rather than the more directly relevant fantasy of everlasting torment in the discourse of the libertine Saint-Fond, although the two perspectives are evidently related. See Lacan (1992[1986], p. 260) and Sade (1968[1797], p. 369). See also Lacan (2006[1962], p. 655) and Nobus (2017, p. 61). However, rather than its being an unequivocal index of Creon's excessive cruelty towards his niece, there is an alternative reading of his decision to bury Antigone alive. By killing a relative, Creon would run the risk of attracting the wrath of the gods and calling down divine punishment upon Thebes and himself, so instead of 'actively' killing her, walling her up in a cave would be a specious solution to ensure that his hands remain clean and the community stays safe. See, for example, Sophocles (1998, p. 87), where Creon states: "We are guiltless where this girl is concerned." I am grateful to Armand d'Angour for drawing my attention to this passage and highlighting Creon's cunning strategy to avoid further divine retribution.

34 Much like the previous 'contamination', Lacan did not mention this one either, yet he did draw attention to the fact that in the discourses of the guards, the chorus and Creon himself, Antigone is consistently referred to in condescending terms as ἡ παῖς (literally, 'the child', but in this *context* 'the girl' or 'the young woman'). See, for example, verses 423 and 654 (Sophocles, 1998, pp. 40–41, 64–65; Lacan, 1992[1986], p. 250).

35 It goes without saying that, in considering the presence of pity and fear within the play and its characters, Lacan moved away from the conception of catharsis advanced by Aristotle, for whom the effect is situated exclusively in the audience.

36 I am fully aware that my interpretation, here, differs radically from that of De Kesel (2009[2001], pp. 205–248, 2015), who argues that Antigone's beauty resides in her saying 'No' to Creon. In my reading, Antigone's 'No' to Creon is as attractive as any socio-political uprising or rebellion – admirable, courageous and inspiring, but not particularly beautiful. Antigone's defiance of Creon may very well be ethical, then, but it is not exactly aesthetic. I think that the source of Antigone's beauty, which spills over into the sublime and the uncanny, does not lie in her 'No' to Creon at all, but rather in her 'Yes' to transcending the curse, which she only manages to explain as motivated by her unconditional love for her irreplaceable brother.

37 For a more detailed explanation of Socrates' point about the attendants of Ares, see Plato (2011, p. 156).

38 Guyomard (1992) has posited that Antigone's intense love for Polynices is in itself a continuation of the incestuous desire that has brought misfortune upon her family, yet there is no textual evidence in Sophocles' tragedy that Antigone's love for her brother is passionate, romantic or sexual, so the argument is rather loose and impossible to substantiate on the basis of an in-depth reading of the play. The only time Eros is invoked in Sophocles' tragedy is when the chorus sings about Haemon's vehement defence of his betrothed (781) (Sophocles, 1998, p. 77).

39 Over the years, a number of scholars have indeed argued, although not always as an extrapolation of Hegel's assertion, that Antigone's spurious logic is but an indication of her unconditional love for Polynices. See, for instance Bowra (1944, p. 95) and Knox (1979[1968], p. 180).

40 For a detailed discussion of the differences between ἐπιθυμία, ἵμερος, πόθος and other ancient Greek words for desire, see Plato (1998, p. 61[419e-420b]) and Sedley (2003).

41 Lacan claimed that *Sophocle, c'est l'humanisme* (*Sophocles is Humanism*) was redolent of "the name of one of the many works" he had consulted (Lacan, 1992[1986], p. 273). In all likelihood, the book Lacan had in mind here was the 1951 monograph on Sophocles by the American classicist Cedric Whitman. See Whitman (1951, pp. 92–93). Beyond the confines of Whitman's volume, it is worth noting that the idea according to which Sophocles' tragic representation embodies all the cardinal humanist values – in *Antigone* as well as Antigone – dates back to at least the sixteenth century. See, for example, the successful 1580 adaptation of the play by Robert Garnier (2000[1580]).

For a thorough discussion of αὐτόνομος in *Antigone*, which constitutes the first recorded instance of the word, see McNeill (2011).

42 Neither in *Seminar VII* nor elsewhere did Lacan develop this hypothesis further, and it remains difficult to justify, partly because Jocasta did act upon her incestuous desire for Oedipus, partly because the curse of the House of Labdakos did not come to an end with Jocasta's suicide.

43 When developing the point about Antigone's psycho-social isolation ἐκτὸς ἄτας, Lacan explicitly relied on the work of the influential German Hellenist Karl Reinhardt (Lacan, 1992[1986], p. 271; Reinhardt, 1979[1933]).

44 Porter has translated Lacan's '*à-bout-de-course*' as "a stance of the-race-is-run" (Lacan, 1992[1986], pp. 272, 279), yet this literal translation suggests that Antigone eventually becomes defeatist and fatalistic, which could not be further from the truth. Outside ἄτη, Antigone remains as defiant and courageous as she has always been. In the words of Simone Weil, who was often called Antigone by her parents and who regularly employed the moniker in the letters she wrote to them: Antigone is a typical Sophoclean heroine and therefore someone who obstinately "holds on and never lets [herself] be corrupted by misfortune" (Weil, 1998[1936], p. 19).

45 The word Antigone uses to describe herself in her final lament is δύσμορος (919). It literally means 'ill-fated', but Lloyd-Jones has also rendered it as 'unhappy' (Sophocles, 1998, p. 89).

46 The expression 'between-two-deaths' was only offered to Lacan *after* he had finished his commentary on *Antigone* and it remains unclear which of the seminar participants coined it. Miller's title 'Antigone between-two-deaths' for lesson 21 is therefore misleading, because it suggests that the term was already employed at that point in the seminar, whereas it was only produced afterwards, as is clear from lesson 24 (Lacan, 1992[1986], p. 320). The fact that Lacan liked the expression can be inferred from his essay 'Kant with Sade', in which he employed it with reference to the status of the victims in the fantasy of absolute destruction of Sade's libertine heroes (Lacan, 2006[1962], pp. 654–655), and from the opening session of *Seminar VIII*, in which he rather bizarrely situated it "in the adventure of *Oedipus Rex*" (Lacan, 2015[2001], p. 7).

47 In a remark following Pierre Kaufmann's presentation on June 15, 1960 (see note 27 above), Lacan also referred to Lévi-Strauss's inaugural lecture at the *Collège de France*, which took place on Tuesday, January 5, 1960.

48 The term 'mytheme' did not appear in the original English version of Lévi-Strauss's paper (Lévi-Strauss, 1955), but was added by him when he re-translated the text into French for the collection *Anthropologie Structurale*, which was published in July 1958 (Lévi-Strauss, 1958[1955], p. 233). As such, it also featured in the subsequent English translation of this book (Lévi-Strauss, 1963[1955], p. 211).

49 Lacan returned briefly to this mythical background of Antigone's death towards the end of lesson 22, where the influence of Lévi-Strauss's structural study of myth is again clearly noticeable (Lacan, 1992[1986], p. 299).

50 In a sense, Lacan had already suggested this idea in his second lesson on *Antigone*, in which he stated: "[T]he structure of the ethic of tragedy . . . is also that of psychoanalysis" (Lacan, 1992[1986], p. 258).

51 It is interesting to see, in this respect, that Lacan himself spent some time talking about the significance of the word 'with' in the tragedy itself. See Lacan (1992[1986], p. 265).

52 To the best of my knowledge, the only scholar who has exposed this misreading in all its logical inconsistencies and fallacious repercussions is De Kesel (2018).

53 I can state this date with confidence, because on January 26, 1983, Jacques-Alain Miller devoted an entire session of his seminar to this particular mis-interpretation, whereby he argued vehemently, yet evidently to no avail, against the promotion of 'Do not give up on your desire!' to the status of a Lacanian ethical axiom. See Miller (2018, pp. 193–204).

54 See, for instance, Badiou (2001[1998], p. 47), Žižek (1989, p. 3, 1994, p. 70), and Zupančič (2000, pp. 250–251).
55 In fairness to Žižek, I should nonetheless point out that he did not repeat the precept in the introduction to his own, rather well-crafted adaptation of *Antigone* (Žižek, 2016). For recent instances of the reduction of Lacan's ethics of psychoanalysis to the single precept that one should not give up on one's desire, see for example Ruti (2012, p. 71), Critchley (2019, p. 130) and Luepnitz (2020, p. 355).
56 Porter has translated the phrase "*céder sur son désir*" rather clumsily as "having given ground relative to one's desire" (Lacan, 1992[1986], pp. 319–321).
57 The reason why Lacan emphasised the paradoxical nature of his proposition is that guilt is conventionally attributed to the opposite of 'having given up on something'. Giving up on something implies that one does not do what one thinks one is supposed to do, yet guilt is much more commonly associated with having done what one thinks one is *not* supposed to do.
58 For a painfully sinister example of how 'Do not give up on your desire!' could easily be turned into a justification for criminal acts, I can refer the reader to the case of Yerodia Abdoulaye Ndombasi, a rather charming, jovial and altogether amicable man who was Lacan's personal butler for almost fifteen years – from the late 1960s until Lacan's death in 1981 – and who I had the pleasure of meeting in person during the early 1990s. During the mid-1990s, Yerodia (or 'Abdou' as he was commonly known) moved back to the Congo in order to serve as a minister in the government of Laurent-Désiré Kabila. In 1998, he could be heard on the Congolese radio encouraging the genocide of millions of Congolese Tutsis, an act for which the International War Crimes Tribunal in The Hague subsequently issued an arrest warrant. Abdou was never tried, but when asked about his motives, he did not hesitate to quote his master Jacques Lacan as having stated that one should never give up on one's desire . . . See, in this respect, Hendrickx (2001) and Nobus (2016).

References

Agard, W. R. (1937). Antigone 904–920. *Classical Philology*, 32(3): 263–265.
Aristotle (1934). *Nicomachean Ethics*. Trans. H. Rackham. Cambridge, MA and London: Harvard University Press.
Aristotle (1962). *The Politics*. Trans. J. A. Sinclair. Harmondsworth: Penguin Books.
Aristotle (1999). *Poetics*. Trans. S. Halliwell. Cambridge, MA and London: Harvard University Press.
Aristotle (2020). *Art of Rhetoric*. Rev. G. Striker. Trans. J. H. Freese. Cambridge, MA and London: Harvard University Press.
Badiou, A. (2001 [1998]). *Ethics: An Essay on the Understanding of Evil*. Trans. P. Hallward. London and New York, NY: Verso.
Balaska, M. (2018). Can There Be Happiness in Psychoanalysis? Creon and Antigone in Lacan's Seminar VII. *College Literature: A Journal of Critical Literary Studies*, 45(2): 308–329.
Benardete, S. (1999 [1975]). *Sacred Transgressions: A Reading of Sophocles' Antigone*. South Bend, IN: St. Augustine's Press.
Bergounioux, G. (2005). *Lacan débarbouillé*. Paris: Max Milo.
Bernays, J. (1857). Grundzüge der verlorenen Abhandlung des Aristoteles über Wirkung der Tragödie. *Abhandlungen der historisch-philosophischen Gesellschaft in Breslau*, 1: 35–122.
Bernays, J. (1880). *Zwei Abhandlungen über die Aristotelische Theorie des Dramas*. Berlin: Hertz.

Berthold-Bond, D. (1994). Hegel on Madness and Tragedy. *History of Philosophy Quarterly*, 11(1): 71–99.

Böckh, A. (1824). Über die Antigone des Sophokles. *Abhandlungen der historisch-philologischen Klasse der königlichen Akademie der Wissenschaften zu Berlin aus dem Jahre 1824*, 1: 41–88.

Böckh, A. (1828). Über die Antigone des Sophokles. *Abhandlungen der historisch-philologischen Klasse der königlichen Akademie der Wissenschaften zu Berlin aus dem Jahre 1828*, 1: 49–112.

Bollack, J. (1998). *Jacob Bernays: un homme entre deux mondes*. Villeneuve-d'Ascq: Presses Universitaires du Septentrion.

Bowra, C. M. (1944). *Sophoclean Tragedy*. Oxford: Clarendon Press.

Breuer, J. and Freud, S. (1955 [1895d]). Studies on Hysteria. In *The Standard Edition of the Complete Psychological Works of Sigmund Freud* (Vol. 2). Trans. J. Strachey. London: The Hogarth Press and the Institute of Psycho-Analysis.

Burke, V. I. (2013). The Substance of Ethical Recognition: Hegel's Antigone and the Irreplaceability of the Brother. *New German Critique*, 40(1): 1–27.

Butler, J. (2000). *Antigone's Claim: Kinship Between Life and Death*. New York, NY: Columbia University Press.

Calder, W. M. (1971). The Protagonist of Sophocles' "Antigone". *Arethusa*, 4(1): 49–52.

Chandler, A. R. (1913). Tragic Effect in Sophocles: Analyzed According to the Freudian Method. *The Monist*, 23(1): 59–89.

Chanter, T. (1995). *Ethics of Eros: Irigaray's Rewriting of the Philosophers*. New York, NY and London: Routledge.

Chanter, T. (1998). Tragic Dislocations: Antigone's Modern Theatrics. *Differences*, 10(1): 75–97.

Clemens, J. (2013). *Psychoanalysis Is an Antiphilosophy*. Edinburgh: Edinburgh University Press.

Conklin, W. (1997). Hegel, the Author and Authority in Sophocles' Antigone. In L. G. Rubin (Ed.), *Justice vs. Law in Greek Political Thought* (pp. 129–151). New York, NY and Oxford: Rowman & Littlefield.

Copjec, J. (2002). The Tomb of Perseverance: On Antigone. In *Imagine There's No Woman: Ethics and Sublimation* (pp. 12–47). Cambridge, MA and London: The MIT Press.

Critchley, S. (2019). *Tragedy, the Greeks and Us*. London: Profile Books.

Cropp, M. (1997). Antigone's Final Speech (Sophocles, Antigone 891–928). *Greece & Rome*, 44(2): 137–160.

De Boer, K. (2008). Hegel's Antigone and the Tragedy of Cultural Difference. *Mosaic: An Interdisciplinary Journal*, 41(3): 31–45.

De Kesel, M. (2009 [2001]). *Eros and Ethics: Reading Jacques Lacan's Seminar VII*. Trans. S. Jöttkandt. Albany, NY: State University of New York Press.

De Kesel, M. (2015). De ethiek van een mooi nee: Lacans interpretatie van Antigone. In M. De Kesel and B. Schomakers (Eds.), *De schoonheid van het nee: Essays over Antigone* (pp. 151–181). Amsterdam: Sjibbolet.

De Kesel, M. (2018). The Real of Ethics: On a Widespread Misconception. In B. W. Becker, J. P. Manoussakis, and D. M. Goodman (Eds.), *Unconscious Incarnations: Psychoanalytic and Philosophical Perspectives on the Body* (pp. 76–93). Abingdon and New York, NY: Routledge.

de Sauverzac, J.-F. (2000). *Le désir sans foi ni loi: Lecture de Lacan*. Paris: Aubier.

Derrida, J. (2021 [1974]). *Clang*. Trans. G. Bennington and D. Wills. Minneapolis, MN and London: University of Minnesota Press.

Donougho (1989). The Woman in White: On the Reception of Hegel's Antigone. *The Owl of Minerva*, 21(1): 65–89.

Eagleton, T. (2010). Lacan's Antigone. In S. E. Wilmer and A. Žukauskaitė (Eds.), *Interrogating Antigone in Postmodern Philosophy and Criticism* (pp. 101–109). Oxford: Oxford University Press.

Eckermann, J. P. (2022 [1823–1832]). *Conversations with Goethe*. Trans. A. Blunden. London: Penguin Books.

Ellison, D. (2001). *Ethics and Aesthetics in European Modernist Literature: From the Sublime to the Uncanny*. Cambridge: Cambridge University Press.

Falzeder, E., Brabant, E., and Giampieri-Deutsch, P. (Eds.) (2000). *The Correspondence of Sigmund Freud and Sándor Ferenczi: 1920–1933* (Vol. 3). Trans. P. T. Hoffer. Cambridge, MA and London: The Belknap Press of Harvard University Press.

Finkelde, D. (2017). *Excessive Subjectivity: Kant, Hegel, Lacan, and the Foundations of Ethics*. New York, NY: Columbia University Press.

Fleming, K. (2015). Heidegger's Antigone: Ethics and Politics. In J. Billings and M. Leonard (Eds.), *Tragedy and the Idea of Modernity* (pp. 178–193). Oxford: Oxford University Press.

Foley, H. P. (1995). Tragedy and Democratic Ideology: The Case of Sophocles' Antigone. In B. Goff (Ed.), *History, Tragedy, Theory: Dialogues on Athenian Drama* (pp. 131–150). Austin, TX: The University of Texas Press.

Freeland, C. (2013). *Antigone, in Her Unbearable Splendor: New Essays on Jacques Lacan's the Ethics of Psychoanalysis*. Albany, NY: State University of New York Press.

Freud, E. L. (Ed.) (1970). *The Letters of Sigmund Freud and Arnold Zweig*. New York, NY: Harcourt, Brace & World, Inc.

Freud, S. (1955 [1920g]). Beyond the Pleasure Principle. In *The Standard Edition of the Complete Psychological Works of Sigmund Freud* (Vol. 18, pp. 1–64). Trans. Ed. J. Strachey. London: The Hogarth Press and the Institute of Psycho-Analysis.

Freud, S. (1958 [1914b]). The Moses of Michelangelo. In *The Standard Edition of the Complete Psychological Works of Sigmund Freud* (Vol. 13, pp. 209–237). Trans. Ed. J. Strachey. London: The Hogarth Press and the Institute of Psycho-Analysis.

Freud, S. (1958 [1914g]). Remembering, Repeating and Working-Through (Further Recommendations on the Technique of Psycho-Analysis II). In *The Standard Edition of the Complete Psychological Works of Sigmund Freud* (Vol. 12, pp. 145–156). Trans. Ed. J. Strachey. London: The Hogarth Press and the Institute of Psycho-Analysis.

Freud, S. (1959 [1926d]). Inhibitions, Symptoms and Anxiety. In *The Standard Edition of the Complete Psychological Works of Sigmund Freud* (Vol. 20, pp. 75–174). Trans. Ed. J. Strachey. London: The Hogarth Press and the Institute of Psycho-Analysis.

Freud, S. (1961 [1924c]). The Economic Problem of Masochism. In *The Standard Edition of the Complete Psychological Works of Sigmund Freud* (Vol. 19, pp. 155–170). Trans. Ed. J. Strachey. London: The Hogarth Press and the Institute of Psycho-Analysis.

Freud, S. (1964 [1930a]). Civilization and Its Discontents. In *The Standard Edition of the Complete Psychological Works of Sigmund Freud* (Vol. 21, pp. 57–145). Trans. Ed. J. Strachey. London: The Hogarth Press and the Institute of Psycho-Analysis.

Freud, S. (1966 [1950a]). Project for a Scientific Psychology. In *The Standard Edition of the Complete Psychological Works of Sigmund Freud* (Vol. 1, pp. 281–397). Trans. Ed. J. Strachey. London: The Hogarth Press and the Institute of Psycho-Analysis.

Frey, K. (1878). Der Protagonist in der Antigone des Sophokles. *Neue Jahrbücher – Abteilung 1*, 117: 460–464.

Fromm, E. (1959 [1948]). The Oedipus Complex and the Oedipus Myth. In R. N. Anshen (Ed.), *The Family: Its Function and Destiny* (Revised edition, pp. 334–358). New York, NY: Harper & Brothers.

Funke, H. (1996). Bernays und die Aristotelische Poetik. In J. Glucker and A. Laks (Eds.), *Jacob Bernays. Un philologue juif* (pp. 59–75). Villeneuve-d'Ascq: Presses Universitaires du Septentrion.

Garnier, R. (2000 [1580]). *Antigone ou la piété: Tragédie humaniste*. Ed. J.-D. Beaudin. Paris: Honoré Champion.

Golden, L. (1978). Hamartia, Ate, and Oedipus. *The Classical World*, 72(1): 3–12.

Griffith, M. (2005). The Subject of Desire in Sophocles' Antigone. In V. Pedrick and S. M. Oberhelman (Eds.), *The Soul of Tragedy: Essays on Athenian Drama* (pp. 91–135). Chicago, IL and London: The University of Chicago Press.

Griffith, M. (2010). Psychoanalysing Antigone. In S. E. Wilmer and A. Žukauskaitė (Eds.), *Interrogating Antigone in Postmodern Philosophy and Criticism* (pp. 110–134). Oxford: Oxford University Press.

Groot, G. (2015). Anti-Antigone. In M. De Kesel and B. Schomakers (Eds.), *De schoonheid van het nee: Essays Over Antigone* (pp. 69–89). Amsterdam: Sjibbolet.

Guyomard, P. (1991). Sur l'éclat d'Antigone. In M. Cardot, Y. Duroux, P. Guyomard, P. Lacoue-Labarthe, and R. Major (Eds.), *Lacan avec les philosophes* (pp. 61–66). Paris: Albin Michel.

Guyomard, P. (1992). *La jouissance du tragique: Antigone, Lacan et le désir de l'analyste*. Paris: Aubier-Flammarion.

Harris, O. (2017). *Lacan's Return to Antiquity: Between Nature and the Gods*. London and New York, NY: Routledge.

Hegel, G. W. F. (1955 [1819–1830]). *Lectures on the History of Philosophy* (Vol. 1). Trans. E. S. Haldane. London: Routledge and Kegan Paul.

Hegel, G. W. F. (1975 [1820–1829]). *Aesthetics: Lectures on Fine Art* (Vol. 1). Trans. T. M. Knox. Oxford: Clarendon Press.

Hegel, G. W. F. (1989 [1796]). Jedes Volk . . . . In F. Nicolin and G. Schüler (Eds.), *Gesammelte Werke: Volume 1: Frühe Schriften* (pp. 359–378). Hamburg: Felix Meiner Verlag.

Hegel, G. W. F. (2018 [1807]). *The Phenomenology of Spirit*. Trans. T. Pinkard. Cambridge: Cambridge University Press.

Heidegger, M. (1956 [1951]). Logos. *La psychanalyse*, 1: 59–79. Trans. J. Lacan.

Heidegger, M. (1996 [1984]). *Hölderlin's Hymn "The Ister"*. Trans. W. McNeill and J. David. Bloomington, Indianapolis, IN and London: Indiana University Press.

Heidegger, M. (2000 [1953]). *Introduction to Metaphysics*. Trans. G. Fried and R. Polt. New Haven, CT and London: Yale University Press.

Hendrickx, W. (2001). Kuifje in Congo (1): Oog in oog met het monster. *Humo*, February 27, 42–47.

Herodotus (2014). *The Histories*. Trans. T. Holland. London: Penguin Books.

Hinrichs, H. F. W. (1827). *Das Wesen der antiken Tragödie in ästhetischen Vorlesungen*. Halle: Friedrich Ruff.

Honig, B. (2013). *Antigone, Interrupted*. Cambridge: Cambridge University Press.

Hurst, A. (2008). *Derrida vis-à-vis Lacan: Interweaving Deconstruction and Psychoanalysis*. New York, NY: Fordham University Press.

Huxley, T. H. (1894 [1880]). On the Method of Zadig. In *Science and Hebrew Tradition: Essays* (pp. 1–23). New York, NY: D. Appleton & Company.

Hyde, I. (1963). The Tragic Flaw: Is It a Tragic Error? *Modern Language Review*, 58(3): 321–325.

Irigaray, L. (1985 [1974]). The Eternal Irony of the Community. In *Speculum of the Other Woman* (pp. 214–226). Trans. G. G. Gill. Ithaca, NY and London: Cornell University Press.

Jacob, A. L. G. (1821). *Sophocleae Quaestiones. Praemittuntur Disputationes de Tragoediae Origine et de Tragicorum Graecorum cum Republica Necessitudine* (Volumen Primum). Varsaviae: Impensis Auctoris.

Jacobs, C. (1996). Dusting Antigone. *Modern Language Notes*, 111(5): 889–917.

Jagentowicz Mills, P. (1986). Hegel's Antigone. *The Owl of Minerva*, 17(2): 131–152.

Jaramillo, J. I. (2010). La Antígona de Lacan: Comentario al apartado 'La esencia de la tragedia' del Seminario 7, La ética del psicoanálisis. *Affectio Societatis*, 7(12): 1–15.

Jebb, R. C. (1900). Appendix. In *Sophocles: The Plays and Fragments: Part 3: The Antigone* (pp. 258–265). Trans. R. C. Jebb. Cambridge: Cambridge University Press.

Jones, E. (1953). *The Life and Work of Sigmund Freud: Volume 1: The Formative Years and the Great Discoveries (1856–1900)*. New York, NY: Basic Books.

Kant, I. (1997 [1788]). *Critique of Practical Reason*. Trans. M. Gregor. Cambridge: Cambridge University Press.

Kant, I. (1998 [1781]). *Critique of Pure Reason*. Trans. P. Guyer and A. W. Wood. Cambridge: Cambridge University Press.

Kant, I. (2007 [1790]). *Critique of Judgement*. Rev. N. Walker. Trans. J. Creed Meredith. Oxford: Oxford University Press.

Kanzer, M. (1950). The Oedipus Trilogy. *The Psychoanalytic Quarterly*, 19(4): 561–572.

Kaufmann, W. (1979 [1968]). *Tragedy and Philosophy*. Princeton, NJ and London: Princeton University Press.

Kirkwood, G. M. (1994 [1958]). *A Study of Sophoclean Drama* (New edition). Ithaca, NY: Cornell University Press.

Kitto, H. D. F. (1956). *Form and Meaning in Drama: A Study of Six Greek Plays and of Hamlet*. London: Methuen.

Knox, B. (1979 [1968]). Review: Sophokles, Antigone. In *Word and Action: Essays on the Ancient Theater* (pp. 165–182). Baltimore, MD and London: The Johns Hopkins University Press.

Knox, B. (1984). Antigone – Introduction. In *Sophocles, The Three Theban Plays: Antigone, Oedipus the King, Oedipus at Colonus* (pp. 35–53). Trans. R. Fagles. London: Penguin Books.

Kojève, A. (1969 [1947]). *Introduction to the Reading of Hegel: Lectures on the Phenomenology of Spirit*. Ed. A. Bloom. Trans. J. H. Nichols, Jr. Ithaca, NY and London: Cornell University Press.

Kojève, A. (2017 [1947]). *Introduction à la lecture de Hegel*. Ed. R. Queneau. Paris: Gallimard.

Kowsar, M. (1990). Lacan's Antigone: A Case Study in Psychoanalytical Ethics. *Theatre Journal*, 42(1): 94–103.

Lacan, J. (1986). *Le Séminaire. Livre VII: L'éthique de la psychanalyse (1959–1960)*. Ed. J.-A. Miller. Paris: Éditions du Seuil.

Lacan, J. (1988 [1978]). *The Seminar: Book II: The Ego in Freud's Theory and in the Technique of Psychoanalysis*. Ed. J.-A. Miller. Trans. S. Tomaselli. Cambridge: Cambridge University Press.

Lacan, J. (1992 [1986]). *The Seminar: Book VII: The Ethics of Psychoanalysis (1959–1960)*. Ed. J.-A. Miller. Trans. D. Porter. New York, NY and London: W. W. Norton & Company.

Lacan, J. (1993 [1981]). *The Seminar: Book III: The Psychoses*. Ed. J.-A. Miller. Trans. R. Grigg. New York, NY: W. W. Norton & Company.

Lacan, J. (2006 [1945]). Logical Time and the Assertion of Anticipated Certainty: A New Sophism. In *Ecrits* (pp. 161–175). Trans. B. Fink. New York, NY: W. W. Norton & Company.

Lacan, J. (2006 [1956]). Seminar on "The Purloined Letter". In *Ecrits* (pp. 6–48). Trans. B. Fink. New York, NY: W. W. Norton & Company.

Lacan, J. (2006 [1962]). Kant with Sade. In *Ecrits* (pp. 645–668). Trans. B. Fink. New York, NY: W. W. Norton & Company.

Lacan, J. (2014 [2004]). *The Seminar: Book X: Anxiety (1962–1963)*. Ed. J.-A. Miller. Trans. A. R. Price. Cambridge and Malden, MA: Polity Press.

Lacan, J. (2015 [2001]). *The Seminar: Book VIII: Transference (1960–1961)*. Ed. J.-A. Miller. Trans. B. Fink. Cambridge and Malden, MA: Polity Press.

Lacan, J. (2019 [2013]). *The Seminar: Book VI: Desire and Its Interpretation (1958–1959)*. Ed. J.-A. Miller. Trans. B. Fink. Cambridge and Medford, MA: Polity Press.

Lacoue-Labarthe, P. (1991). De l'éthique: à propos d'Antigone. In M. Cardot, Y. Duroux, P. Guyomard, P. Lacoue-Labarthe, and R. Major (Eds.), *Lacan avec les philosophes* (pp. 21–36). Paris: Albin Michel.

Lauret, M. (2014). *L'énigme de la pulsion de mort: Pour une éthique de la joie*. Paris: Presses Universitaires de France.

Lee, J. S. (1990). *Jacques Lacan*. Amherst, MA: The University of Massachusetts Press.

Leonard, M. (2003). Antigone, the Political and the Ethics of Psychoanalysis. *The Cambridge Classical Journal*, 49(1): 130–154.

Leonard, M. (2005). *Athens in Paris: Ancient Greece and the Political in Post-War French Thought*. Oxford: Oxford University Press.

Leonard, M. (2006). Lacan, Irigaray, and Beyond: Antigones and the Politics of Psychoanalysis. In V. Zajko and M. Leonard (Eds.), *Laughing with Medusa: Classical Myth and Feminist Thought* (pp. 121–139). Oxford: Oxford University Press.

Lévi-Strauss, C. (1955). The Structural Study of Myth. *The Journal of American Folklore*, 68(270): 428–444.

Lévi-Strauss, C. (1958 [1955]). La structure des mythes. In *Anthropologie structurale* (pp. 227–255). Paris: Plon.

Lévi-Strauss, C. (1963 [1955]). The Structural Study of Myth. In *Structural Anthropology* (pp. 206–231). Trans. C. Jacobson and B. Grundfest Schoepf. New York, NY: Basic Books.

Lévi-Strauss, C. and Eribon, D. (1991 [1988]). *Conversations with Claude Lévi-Strauss*. Chicago, IL and London: The University of Chicago Press.

Loraux, N. (1986). La main d'Antigone. *Mètis: Anthropologie des mondes grecs anciens*, 1(2): 165–196.

Loraux, N. (1991). Antigone sans théâtre. In M. Cardot, Y. Duroux, P. Guyomard, P. Lacoue-Labarthe, and R. Major (Eds.), *Lacan avec les philosophes* (pp. 42–49). Paris: Albin Michel.

Luepnitz, D. A. (2020). Antigone and the Unsayable: A Psychoanalytic Reading. *American Imago*, 77(2): 345–364.

Marder, E. (2009). The Sex of Death and the Maternal Crypt. *parallax*, 15(1): 5–20.

Marquis de Sade, D. A. F. (1968 [1797]). *Juliette*. Trans. A. Wainhouse. New York, NY: Grove Press.

McNeill, D. N. (2011). Antigone's Autonomy. *Inquiry*, 54(5): 411–441.

Meltzer, F. (2011). Theories of Desire: Antigone Again. *Critical Inquiry*, 37(2): 169–186.

Miller, J.-A. (2018). *Del síntoma al fantasma: Y retorno (1982–1983)*. Ed. S. E. Tendlarz. Trans. S. Baudini. Buenos Aires: Paidós.

Miller, P. A. (2007). Lacan's Antigone: The Sublime Object and the Ethics of Interpretation. *Phoenix*, 61(1/2): 1–14.

Molière (1959 [1666]). A Doctor in Spite of Himself. In *The Misanthrope and Other Plays* (pp. 165–199). Trans. J. Wood. Harmondsworth: Penguin Books.

Morel, G. (2010). D'un éclat féminin qui suscite la dispute: Lectures croisées d'Antigone de Sophocle par Jacques Lacan et Jean Bollack. In C. König and D. Thouard (Eds.), *La philologie au présent: Pour Jean Bollack* (pp. 185–199). Villeneuve-d'Ascq: Presses Universitaires du Septentrion.

Murnaghan, S. (1986). Antigone 904–920 and the Institution of Marriage. *American Journal of Philology*, 107(2): 192–207.

Naveau, L. (2011). Lacan avec Antigone. *La cause freudienne*, 79: 231–234.

Neill, C. (2011). *Lacanian Ethics and the Assumption of Subjectivity*. Basingstoke: Palgrave Macmillan.

Neuburg, M. (1990). How Like a Woman: Antigone's "Inconsistency". *Classical Quarterly*, 40(1): 54–76.

Nobus, D. (2000). *Jacques Lacan and the Freudian Practice of Psychoanalysis*. London and New York, NY: Brunner and Routledge.

Nobus, D. (2016). Psychoanalytic Violence: An Essay on Indifference in Ethical Matters. *Psychoanalytic Discourse*, 1(2): 1–20.

Nobus, D. (2017). *The Law of Desire: On Lacan's "Kant with Sade"*. Basingstoke: Palgrave Macmillan.

Nussbaum, M. C. (2001). *The Fragility of Goodness: Luck and Ethics in Tragedy and Philosophy* (Updated edition). Cambridge: Cambridge University Press.

Pearson Geiman, C. (2001). Heidegger's Antigones. In R. Polt and G. Fried (Eds.), *A Companion to Heidegger's Introduction to Metaphysics* (pp. 161–182). New Haven, CT and London: Yale University Press.

Pischel, R. (1893). Zu Sophokles Antigone 909–912. *Hermes*, 28(2): 465–468.

Plato (1998). *Cratylus*. Trans. C. D. C. Reeve. London: Hackett.

Plato (2005). *Phaedrus*. Trans. C. Rowe. London: Penguin Books.

Plato (2007). *The Republic*. Trans. D. Lee. London: Penguin Books.

Plato (2011). *Phaedrus*. Ed. H. Yunis. Cambridge: Cambridge University Press.

Porter, J. I. (2015). Jacob Bernays and the Catharsis of Modernity. In J. Billings and M. Leonard (Eds.), *Tragedy and the Idea of Modernity* (pp. 15–41). Oxford: Oxford University Press.

Rabaté, J.-M. (2001). *Jacques Lacan: Psychoanalysis and the Subject of Literature*. Basingstoke: Palgrave Macmillan.

Reinhardt, K. (1979 [1933]). *Sophocles*. Trans. H. Harvey and D. D. Harvey. London: Wiley-Blackwell.

Rosenkranz, K. (1844). *Georg Wilhelm Friedrich Hegel's Leben*. Berlin: Verlag von Duncker und Humblot.

Roudinesco, E. (2014 [2011]). *Lacan: In Spite of Everything*. Trans. G. Elliott. London and New York, NY: Verso.

Rudnytsky, P. L. (1987). *Freud and Oedipus*. New York, NY and Oxford: Columbia University Press.

Ruti, M. (2012). *The Singularity of Being: Lacan and the Immortal Within*. New York, NY: Fordham University Press.

Ruti, M. (2015). *Between Levinas and Lacan: Self, Other, Ethics*. London and New York, NY: Bloomsbury.

Ruti, M. (2017). *The Ethics of Opting Out: Queer Theory's Defiant Subjects*. New York, NY: Columbia University Press.

Schadewaldt, W. (1929). Aias und Antigone. *Neue Wege zur Antike*, 8: 61–117.

Sedley, D. (2003). *Plato's Cratylus*. Cambridge: Cambridge University Press.

Shepherdson, C. (2008). The Atrocity of Desire: Of Love and Beauty in Lacan's Antigone. In *Lacan and the Limits of Language* (pp. 50–80). New York, NY: Fordham University Press.

Sjöholm, C. (2004). *The Antigone Complex: Ethics and the Invention of Feminine Desire*. Stanford, CA: Stanford University Press.

Sjöholm, C. (2014). Bodies in Exile: From Tragedy to Performance Art. In T. Chanter and S. D. Kirkland (Eds.), *The Returns of Antigone: Interdisciplinary Essays* (pp. 281–295). Albany, NY: State University of New York Press.

Söderbäck, F. (Ed.) (2010). *Feminist Readings of Antigone*. Albany, NY: State University of New York Press.

Sophocles (1947). *Théâtre de Sophocle*. Trans. R. Pignarre. Paris: Garnier.

Sophocles (1984). Antigone. In *The Three Theban Plays: Antigone, Oedipus the King, Oedipus at Colonus*. Trans. R. Fagles. London: Penguin Books.

Sophocles (1998). *Antigone, Women of Trachis, Philoctetes, Oedipus at Colonus*. Trans. H. Lloyd-Jones. Cambridge, MA and London: Harvard University Press.

Sophocles (1999). *Antigone*. Ed. M. Griffith. Cambridge: Cambridge University Press.

Sourvinou-Inwood, C. (1989). Assumptions and the Creation of Meaning: Reading Sophocles' Antigone. *Journal of Hellenic Studies*, 109: 134–148.

Starobinski, J. (2003 [1999]). *Action and Reaction: The Life and Adventures of a Couple*. Trans. S. Hawkes. New York, NY: Zone Books.

Steiner, G. (1984). *Antigones: The Antigone Myth in Western Literature, Art and Thought*. Oxford: Clarendon Press.

Stewart-Steinberg, S. (2011). *Impious Fidelity: Anna Freud, Psychoanalysis, Politics*. Ithaca, NY and London: Cornell University Press.

Szlezák, T. A. (1981). Bemerkungen zur Diskussion um Sophokles, Antigone 904–920. *Rheinisches Museum*, 124: 108–142.

Themi, T. (2014). *Lacan's Ethics and Nietzsche's Critique of Platonism*. Albany, NY: State University of New York Press.

van Braam, P. (1912). Aristotle's use of Ἀμαρτία. *The Classical Quarterly*, 6(4): 266–272.

van der Sterren, H. A. (1948). *De lotgevallen van Koning Oedipus volgens de treurspelen van Sophocles: Een psychologische studie*. Amsterdam: Scheltema & Holkema.

van der Sterren, H. A. (1952). The "King Oedipus" of Sophocles. *The International Journal of Psycho-Analysis*, 33: 343–350.

Van Haute, P. (1998). Death and Sublimation in Lacan's Reading of Antigone. In S. Harasym (Ed.), *Levinas and Lacan: The Missed Encounter* (pp. 102–120). Albany, NY: State University of New York Press.

Voltaire (1964 [1747]). Zadig. In *Zadig and L'ingénu* (pp. 17–104). Trans. J. Butt. Harmondsworth: Penguin Books.

Vuillerod, J.-B. (2020). *Hegel féministe: Les aventures d'Antigone*. Paris: Vrin.

Walker, K. (2012). The Dialectic of Beauty and Agency. *Philosophy and Social Criticism*, 39(1): 79–98.

Weber, S. (2004). Antigone's Nomos. In *Theatricality as Medium* (pp. 121–140). New York, NY: Fordham University Press.

Weil, S. (1998 [1936]). Antigone. In *Intimations of Christianity Among the Ancient Greeks* (pp. 18–23). London and New York, NY: Routledge.

Whitman, C. H. (1951). *Sophocles: A Study of Heroic Humanism*. Cambridge, MA: Harvard University Press.

Wittgenstein, L. (1961 [1921]). *Tractatus Logico-Philosophicus*. Trans. D. F. Pears and B. F. McGuinness. London: Routledge and Kegan Paul.

Wycherley, R. E. (1947). Sophocles Antigone 904–920. *Classical Philology*, 42(1): 51–52.

Zafiropoulos, M. (2019). *Œdipe assassiné? Œdipe roi, Œdipe à Colone, Antigone ou L'inconscient des modernes: Les mythologiques de Lacan 2*. Toulouse: Erès.

Žižek, S. (1989). *The Sublime Object of Ideology*. London and New York, NY: Verso.

Žižek, S. (1994). *The Metastases of Enjoyment: Six Essays on Woman and Causality*. London and New York, NY: Verso.

Žižek, S. (2016). *Antigone*. London and New York, NY: Bloomsbury.

Zupančič, A. (2000). *Ethics of the Real: Kant, Lacan*. London and New York, NY: Verso.

Zupančič, A. (2002). *Esthétique du désir, éthique de la jouissance*. Lecques: Théétète.

Zupančič, A. (2003). Ethics and Tragedy in Lacan. In J.-M. Rabaté (Ed.), *The Cambridge Companion to Lacan* (pp. 173–190). Cambridge: Cambridge University Press.

Zupančič, A. (2023). *Let Them Rot: Antigone's Parallax*. New York, NY: Fordham University Press.

Chapter 7

The Price of Freedom

On Not Giving Ground Relative to Desire

Sarah Meehan O'Callaghan

Have you acted in conformity with the desire that is in you? This is the critical question Lacan posits in the fourth and final part of Seminar VII, *The Ethics of Psychoanalysis* (1959–1960), in which he situates psychoanalysis as a practice that should ultimately take the analysand, at the end of an analysis, into the painful reality of the human condition – *Hilflosigkeit* – a reality from which not even anguish can protect us. This is the tragic dimension of psychoanalysis. In this seminar, the literary genre of tragedy provides Lacan with the landscape to illustrate the notion of the act inherent to 'the paradoxes of desire', paradoxes pivoted upon his evocative provocation in session XIV that, "the only thing one can be guilty of is giving ground relative to one's desire" (Lacan, 1997, p. 321). The realisation of desire in psychoanalysis, therefore, is not simply a matter of speaking, with free association the means of achieving a certain 'freedom' from repression, but in the final analysis, we must also act.

In this chapter, I would like to interrogate the ethical question of the singular subject's relationship to desire, in two distinct but overlapping parts, with particular reference to the final section of Seminar VII, *The Tragic Dimension of Psychoanalysis*. Firstly, I will consider the ethical implications of desire as both singular (such as within an individual analysis) and secondly, as an act contained within a wider social or socio-economic context. In other words, I will consider the difficulties and ambiguities concerning not giving ground relative to desire when we as human beings exist not simply alone but always in a relationship to the other/Other. In particular, the social or socio-economic reality of the singular subject is pervaded with structural inequalities, many of which are simply contingent to a person's birth and involve chance rather than volition; the race we are born into, a country with particular religious beliefs, customs, attitudes and so forth. While desire is fundamental to the being of the Lacanian subject and thus is an essential existential component of a life, a phenomenal account of the lived conditions of desire as both social and cultural expands on this being. If we take desire to be also imbricated within the social fabric, and that the human subject has common basic needs, we can consider what the consequences may be, or what is at stake in taking a stand against the Other. How do we, as subjects of the unconscious but also as subjects of the state, do our 'public good' collectively while remaining ethical

DOI: 10.4324/9781003450795-7

in the singular psychoanalytic sense? At the level of Lacanian desire, there is a problematic concerning the relationship of the singular and the collective, which has led me to consider that the price of freedom or even that of unconscious desire is not equal across citizens. While in this statement, I align freedom and unconscious desire as bearing the burden of a price, these two concepts, as I will discuss subsequently, are not equivocal. According to Lacan, no matter what path we take toward the 'good', we will pay a price. Apart from the obvious reckoning with what constitutes the good here, which in essence is the crux of Seminar VII, I argue it is important to elaborate further on what we can say of this price.

Therefore, in response to Lacan's dictum of not giving ground to desire (or rather what has become a dictum), it is important to articulate why exactly it is difficult to not give ground, and the differential circumstances surrounding this position. This interrogative response will also consider the equivocations of Lacan's statement as it is written in Seminar VII and its potential misinterpretations and distortions as it is applied or indeed misapplied in psychoanalytic discourse. While referring to Lacan's exemplification of the tragic heroes of antiquity (Antigone and Philoctetes), I would also like to consider the ethical stance of not giving ground in a contemporary context with particular reference to the award-winning film, *I, Daniel Blake* (2016) directed by Ken Loach. *I, Daniel Blake,* with its eponymous protagonist, is an illustration of contemporary Lacanian heroism – a man who ultimately takes a stand against the bureaucratic social security system that may have cost him his life. Although not all subjects will experience such an either/or position concerning desire at the end of analysis (your desire or your life), a literary or filmic example of such a limit point serves to illustrate the contingent and phenomenal world within which desire is formulated and 'realised'. Before entering a deeper analysis of not giving ground, we must consider a problematic of Lacan's ethical dictum, that is – the slippery and non-localisable characteristic of desire per se in any given act. As a result of the excessive dimension of desire, reading for the desire of another or judging the ethics of a particular act, cannot be completely satisfactory when desire itself exceeds anything we can say about it. Therefore, the question of desire as a signifier and not as a signified should be articulated.

The Question of Desire

Desire is one of the most fundamental – if not the most fundamental – concepts in Lacanian theory and practice. It is the *sine qua non* of psychoanalysis, the clarion call of a Lacanian. And yet in practice, that is, within intersubjective discourse, desire as a term slips in and out of reach, often ostensibly pointing to something other than its insubstantial essence and landing discursively on the slippery slopes of volition, the 'want' of something. In other words, there is an unintentional intentionality often associated with the concept of desire and this is something I argue is problematic. Over the years, I have encountered certain slippages with statements concerning desire in Lacanian discourse, including my own, slippages that involve too much of an object orientation to desire. We must remember that desire cannot be reduced to questions or implications such as, what is your desire? Do you desire to do X or Y? If you really wanted X or Y to happen, it would happen – as these types of statements sound suspiciously like positive thinking discourse. I claim that there is often an underlying assumption regarding desire even within psychoanalysis which is that the truth of your desire shows in the trajectory of your acts; that we can even identify a truth of desire. While this is true in part, we must not be too reductive; there are always so many factors at play. Although the process of psychoanalysis involves coming into the truth of one's own desire, that is a truth that manifests not so much as a signified, or a concrete meaning, but as a remainder of the effects of speaking through the unconscious. That being said, what could we say definitively about desire, given that in its very nature, it is that which goes beyond what can be said within a statement; it is both within the enunciating and the enunciated. Indeed, in lesson XXII of Seminar VII, Lacan asks: "What is desire?" To which he responds:

> [R]ealizing one's desire is necessarily always raised from the point of view of an absolute condition. It is precisely to the extent that the demand always under- or overshoots itself that, because it articulates itself through the signifier, it always demands something else; that in every satisfaction of a need, it insists on some-thing else; that the satisfaction formulated spreads out and conforms to this gap; that desire is formed as something supporting this metonymy, namely, as some-thing the demand means beyond whatever it is able to formulate. And that is why the question of the realization of desire is necessarily formulated from the point of view of a Last Judgment.
>
> (Lacan, 1997, p. 294)

Crucially as Lacan articulates in this quote, desire is not to be aligned with mean-ing per se or with a particular signified, but rather it is something that supports the metonymy of demand and 'means' more than what can be formulated – as demand is formulated through the means of the signifier. We can conceive of desire here as the excessive remainder of demand, a stream or pulsion that supports the move-ment of the signifier and the shift from object to object in the dialectics of demand. If we read this statement literally, desire supports the metonymy of demand but is not the actual metonymy. Furthermore, to 'realise' our desire is not the same as living the ongoingness of desire in the process of metonymy, for Lacan states that this realisation of desire is tied to an end point, a "last judgement". This end point of desire or its realisation in a last judgement bears the logic of the signifier, as meaning is retroactive: it can only be fully deduced from a completed sentence. To realise our desire, therefore, from the perspective in this seminar, suggests a final-ity, a morbidity, an end point. Desire is not simply at the crux of life, but also, as Lacan puts it: "the function of desire must remain in a fundamental relationship to death" (ibid., p. 304).

This is also why the end of analysis as situated within this context is so important to the trajectory of subjective desire, if we take it that desire can only be realised at the end. Thus the end is an act in itself, where the final curtain falls on the scene of analysis, an end from which the analysand gains perspective on the pain of existence at the horizon of what may have been hoped for from the outset. As De Kesel (2009 [2001]) explains, to fully realise our desire is to come face-to-face with the nothingness at the heart of desire, the fact that satisfaction leaves us with dissatisfaction, that desire's object is to go on desiring:

> The "good" the analysand demands henceforth means a satisfaction of her desire. But since we are nothing other than our desire, since desire is our very being, our demand in fact aims at extinguishing desire, which is to say that it aims at our death.
>
> (De Kesel, 2009 [2001], p. 4)

If desire achieves its 'object', and this object is not a typical concrete object, but satisfaction based on the lack of the object (the object a), what becomes of the subject? In this sense, to realise desire is to come face-to-face with death, the death of the subject whose birth (as being) is more linguistic than biological. In Seminar V, *The Formations of the Unconscious* (2019), Lacan specifies why desire for the human subject cannot be simply aligned to the pursuit of an object. The fact that we enjoy our desire complicates any simple understanding of happiness as an outcome of acquisition.

> Man's relation to desire is not a pure and simple relationship of desire. In itself, it isn't a relationship with an object. If the relationship with an object were already established, there would be no problem for analysis. Men would, as we can assume for the majority of animals, go to their object. Man would not have this second relationship, as it were, to the fact that he is a desiring animal, which conditions everything that happens at the level we call perverse – namely, that he enjoys his desire.
>
> (Lacan, 2017, p. 294)

From this reasoning, and with desire having a perverse quality, not achieving what we want may also be 'enjoyable'. Enjoyment, in Lacanian terms, is also a form of suffering and realising our desire does not necessarily bring satisfaction – possibly quite the opposite. While in Seminar VII, Lacan aligns the realisation of desire with *Hilflosigkeit* – as an epiphany of tragedy, in Seminar VI, *Desire and Its Interpretation* (1958–1959), desire defends against the pain of existence, a pain that lies beneath the fundamental fantasy, "of existing when desire is no longer there" (2019, p. 63)[1]. In realising our desire, in other words, we may be left at the foothills of the pain of existence.[2] In Seminar VI, desire is what subtends the fundamental fantasy where the fragile o-object is veiled beneath the habitual activities of everyday life, until perhaps a crisis unfolds for the subject, such as grief or great loss.

As Lacan elaborated in Seminar VI, desire is that which causes a disturbance (in the form of enjoyment) in our being, and its relationship to the fundamental fantasy maintains a distance between the existential chasm of pain and our relative instability as subjects. The concept of desire as a perverse disturbance in being does not seem to tally with that which may provide a certainty of intention, regarding an object – that is, state what you want and then go for it, stand up for what you believe in, and so on. We are dealing with a much less concrete phenomenon than the want for an object.

Having laid out some of the paradoxes of desire, if we now consider again Lacan's statement, "the only thing one can be guilty of is giving ground relative to one's desire"; the equivocations of the statement are interesting, not least in the usual complicated expression of Lacan's formulations but also the ways in which it can be interpreted. Often, the paradoxes inherent to the proposition are lost and it is tempting to hear an injunction such as "never give up on your desire". We may even hear a subtle and associated injunction, "you are guilty if you give up on desire". The guilt Lacan speaks of here is not straightforward. It is not a form of moral retribution caused by committing a wrong act, but as Carol Owens (2012) cogently argues regarding the statement *"ne pas céder sur son désir"*, in terms of desire, guilt is a sign that one has betrayed oneself (p. 58). To further complicate things, we may ask, in Freudian terms, how many desires may we have at any given moment, desires which may be in conflict with each other? In other words, guilt is often the residue of unacknowledged or unacceptable wishes/desires (not unequivocal) arising in conflict with each other. The existence of ambivalence in relationships is a great example of this, love versus hate, one neither cancelling the other, but leading to potential conflict and guilt laden affects. Furthermore, guilt may not be the effect of a specific desire but even of the very pulsion of desire itself, depending on the superegoic constellations within which a subject may be situated. The very drive to authentic expression can be risky in a social context, as I am arguing in this chapter. Indeed, authenticity has been the subject of so many great philosophers – so no small feat for the human subject, it would seem. Often the consequences of betraying one's own desire lie in the form of symptoms, modes of acting out, inverted expressions of the desire that has gone unexpressed or unacknowledged. As we can briefly see then, Lacan's statement of not ceding to desire is equivocal and deeply complex. Of course, the way a statement is received subjectively is always inflected through the distortions of unconscious desire: we do not simply mean more than we say, but we hear more than what is said, including what we understand or assume to be not giving ground.

Not Giving Ground

In session XXIV, Lacan is clear that he is making a provocation, an experiment within the specific context of psychoanalysis; it "is in an experimental form that I advance the following propositions here. Let's formulate them as paradoxes. Let's see what they sound like to analysts' ears" (1997, p. 319).

To hear Lacan's statement as a prescription or a direct command of sorts is clearly not in keeping with the way it has been stated. If we do not take it as an injunction but as a provocation, the analytic emphasis should be placed on the effects of hearing the statement 'with our ears'. In other words, these propositions are not to be interpreted as related to the same principles as in those of neoliberal positivist reasoning. Lacan clearly distinguishes the psychoanalytic realm and the ethics of desire from the regulatory principles of the normative symbolic, including perspectives of reason and rationality. For example, one of the principles of economic thinking is that individuals are rational and act in their own best interests, the implication being that rationality is based on an implicit notion of the good – 'we know what's good for us'. Yet, Lacanian ethics is not concerned with this type of seeming rationality and economic good or in prescriptions for happiness. As Lacan says:

> The ethics of psychoanalysis has nothing to do with speculation about prescriptions for, or the regulation of, what I have called the service of goods. Properly speaking, that ethics implies the dimension that is expressed in what we call the tragic sense of life.
>
> (Lacan, 1997, p. 33)

Given the complexity of the concept of desire in Lacan's teaching, and the clear non-equivocation of unconscious desire to conscious intentionality or volition, we can wonder why it is easy to fall into the trap of aligning it so and segueing somewhat by default into a form of capitalist/acquisition discourse. To interpret not giving ground relative to desire as *simply* fighting for what you want, whether in a singular or collective sense, is too simplistic, and while there may be an element of truth in this, it is too much on the axis of the capitalist, neoliberal, positivity diatribe of contemporary times – and Lacan clearly does not want to align psychoanalytic discourse with this trajectory. The goal of analysis is not happiness, or the good as it might be deemed to be in a normative sense, that is, the achievement of the heterosexual genital relation or the acquisition of 'private goods'. Rather, the 'goal' of analysis, to use an ironic turn of phrase, is the collision of the subject with the structure of the good per se, as in the case of Antigone.

The classification of the good is often a result of convention (and societal trends) and is imbricated in the confluence of meanings inherent to the pursuit of pleasure and happiness. In other words, something may not be defined as good as such, but nonetheless orientates political and singular narratives of the paths we should pursue to achieve happiness. Therefore, we may perceive/assume something as good and not even realise it, yet our striving to achieve this particular aim or goal reveals something of a value judgement. To give a simple example, completing a course of study or achieving status in a particular field, while lauded as an achievement symbolically and socially, may not specifically be as good, depending on subjective implications (at a singular level), as it is conventionally assumed.

Lacan states that the good object of psychoanalysis is not the good inherent to the 'service of the goods', which he defines as "private goods, family goods, domestic goods, other goods that solicit us, the goods of our trade or our profession, the goods of the city, etc." (ibid., p. 303). Rather, the good, as a normative conventional category, is actually a barrier to realising our desire, as the relationship we have to the so-called good is mediated by the dialectic of the law and the signifier. In the above quote, Lacan appears to be taking a stance against the burgeoning capitalist discourse and the lure of the good as it is presented in the forms of typical goods. In the category of ethics, we are talking about a relationship at a basic level of the subject to an other or big Other. In psychoanalytic terms, this is an ethical orientation not based on personhood or individuality, as we potentially relate the ethical to other 'individual subjects', but an orientation of the unconscious to the very limits of pleasure and pain as they demarcate the bodily limits of the subject of the unconscious. According to De Kesel (2009 [2001]), this is an ethics that points to the real, a beyond of the symbolic, where the beyond is a place beyond the law.

> The term "ethical" no longer refers exclusively to everything that keeps desire within bounds, but also to what explicitly goes beyond or even quite simply against those bounds. This is the truly new thing psychoanalysis has to say about ethics. There is an "ought" that is situated beyond the moral "ought" of the superego, which can even go completely counter to it and yet still be regarded as ethical. This is to say that the ultimate orientation point of moral action lies – more radically than a classical ethics can claim – beyond the law.
>
> (De Kesel, 2009 [2001], p. 51)

If ethics is a field of study, or a subjective orientation that involves the presupposition of another of whom and towards whom we must consider our actions, for psychoanalysis, this Other is the Other of the Real – the very confrontation with our own jouissance as the enjoyment that pervades all paths of the good.

This is one of the reasons why it is hard to assess any act of desire as truly bearing witness to not giving ground to desire, for how are we to gauge the enjoyment of another hidden within every act of self-sacrifice or appearance of the good? And yet it is through the genre of tragedy and the figures of Antigone and Philoctetes that Lacan can find illustrations for his ethics of the Real. Most importantly, tragedy provides a spectacle of a story that has reached its ending, has culminated in a 'final judgement' and from which a path of desire through action can be traced: "Actions are inscribed in the space of tragedy" (Lacan, 1997, p. 313). In this aesthetic space, Lacan argues that a path of the hero is circumscribed through action, laid bare for the spectator, and this is a path potentially open to us all as ordinary subjects – "In each of us the path of the hero is traced, and it is precisely as an ordinary man that one follows it to the end" (ibid., p. 319).

Notwithstanding the ambiguities of reading for desire as a measure of Lacanian ethics (as a refusal of the normative good), we can at least designate not giving ground to desire as a stance that frees the subject, albeit momentarily from the mortification of the other's desire. Ironically, this freedom from the other's desire confronts the subject with the very limit of the symbolic order, and may come at the price of death or aphanisis, as Lacan elaborates with Antigone. While Lacan's argument is convincing, profound and aesthetically florid, his ethical heroes are unyielding to their position and idealistic. Why should a hero be so unrelatable? I argue we can consider the plight of the tragic hero and the idea of the limit from the perspective of need and the politics surrounding the administration of survival. This type of drama and the figure of the ordinary man turned hero – within a regime of neoliberalism – is exemplified in *I, Daniel Blake*.

The Ordinary Man

I, Daniel Blake (2016), directed by renowned filmmaker and social commentator Ken Loach, is a stark and brilliant film depicting a painful and unrelenting portrait of life on the margins of poverty in Britain, and the structures of bureaucratic impossibility and stigmatisation deeply ingrained within Britain's social welfare system. The film follows the lives of two people, in particular Daniel and Katie, who are struck down by circumstance due to ill health and single parenthood, respectively. Daniel Blake, the undoubted hero of the film, has recently had a heart attack and can no longer work. In order to survive, he needs to claim benefits (Employment Support Assistance), and under the state requirements, he is put through a horrific Kafkaesque circus of humiliation, suspicion and dehumanisation. Despite the reality of his physical condition, it is virtually impossible to claim benefits truthfully and avoid being pushed around by the bureaucratic Other. Indeed, Kafka's *The Trial* and its absurdist presentation of bureaucracy and punitive suspicion draws out the hidden and the obscene enjoyment of the law at work in governmental processes and agencies. The narratives of the government tacitly underline the concept of the good as being that which relates to growth, productivity and work at all costs, what Lacan might refer to as "the service of the goods". The working class, the underprivileged and the unfortunate are effectively on trial in the austerity-driven policies that have overshadowed Britain in the last ten to fifteen years. As Ken Loach has argued in interviews about the film, there is an increasingly cruel dimension to the policies aimed at those who are unemployed, with the punishment for not conforming to state sanctions and demands being that of hunger.

   This reality is represented in the film through the intransigence of the administrative automaton-like ciphers of the symbolic (i.e., the bureaucrats and job centre employees) with whom Daniel has to deal in attempting to claim his unemployment assistance. After encountering repeated frustrations and job centre assistants who sent him around in circles to fill out forms online when he is unable to use the internet and so forth, Daniel eventually comes to a breaking point and refuses to tolerate any more demands. As he leaves the job centre in anger, stating that he will not compromise on his dignity and self-respect any longer, he places himself in front of the exterior and public wall of the social services department. He writes in graffiti with a spray can in hand, "I Daniel Blake, demand my appeal date before I starve". In this moment of tragic proportions, we could say that Daniel[3] refuses to give ground relative to his desire to be recognised as a human being fairly and justly and steps outside of the demand of the Other into an authentic and brave stance of singularity. The tragic dimension of Daniel's act resides in the resulting deterioration of his health as a consequence of the lack of state support engendered by his stepping outside the system, and ultimately his death by a heart attack in the final scene of the film is quite possibly the final outcome of his stance. Although he stood up to the demand of the Other and is cast as a hero of the proletariat – we see how delighted the passers-by are with his act of putting graffiti on the job centre wall – this stance is implied to have cost him his life. In session XXIV of Seminar VII, Lacan is unequivocal that the definition of a hero (an ethical one regarding desire) is someone that has been betrayed with impunity (1997, p. 320), and that crucially the hero does not choose to return to the "service of the goods". He distinguishes the nuances of the ordinary man who after betrayal returns to the service of the goods versus one who refuses this position. Daniel Blake has been betrayed by the system and confronted with the injustice of the obscene jouissance of the bureaucratic Other, an Other whose demands that all subjects adhere to the law causes suffering and the potential eradication of singularity. We should be aware of one caveat however: in the final scene of the film, Daniel has received an appeal date for his hearing and is willing to receive state support again; this is the scene where he tragically dies. But perhaps acts of heroism can be affiliated with certain moments without permeating the whole narrative.

It is not so much an accurate interpretation of the object of Daniel's desire that is in focus here, but rather, how this spectacle, as in the examples that Lacan uses from theatre, is exalted to a true ethical moment of a beyond of the good, a moment (manifest as an image) that reveals the deadening hold of the repetitive dictates of the symbolic. Lacan's focus on tragedy in seminar VII is pitched on the axis of the imaginary (image of beauty) as a means of the transmission of the problematics of desire. It is through the paradigm of the beautiful that something is seen that is difficult to see. As Lacan says: "it being precisely the function of the beautiful to reveal to us the site of man's relationship to his own death, and to reveal it to us, only in a blinding flash" (Lacan, 1997, p. 295). We could say that this is part of the seduction of movies and literary cultural artefacts; they manage to escape censorship and reveal more than what they appear to reveal. *I, Daniel Blake* is not deemed to be an easy watch by the majority of people who have seen it and probably the fact that it may reveal something as beautiful would not be the first thing that comes to mind. Yet, I would argue, beauty can lie in the portrayal of a hidden reality, the catharsis of a truth revealed. The conundrum faced by Daniel Blake reveals the problematics of the subject's relationship to the state and the law and the inherent inequities often at play in this relationship. We are subjects of the unconscious but also citizens who have basic needs (for food, shelter, social interaction) and as a result, are all vulnerable to the potential obscenities of an unjust state ruled by "the service of the goods" and neoliberal doctrines of "growth, growth, growth" as was proclaimed by the recent (briefly positioned) Tory leader Liz Truss in a keynote address. The only so-called good inferred here is that of the economy and the assumption that an increase in the service of goods will benefit all. In other words, economic growth is the ideal good for all, a model which excludes the enjoyment of singular desire. Ken Loach's film refuses this ideal and, by so doing, creates a space for desire, an alternate point of identification and perspective.

The moment at which Daniel Blake refuses the demand of the bureaucratic Other and writes "I Daniel Blake" on the wall of the social services building is climactic and significant on many levels, not least linguistically. We cannot but be struck by the pertinence of the phrasing of Daniel's statement and the emphasis on the subject of the statement, I. Indeed, as Olga Cox Cameron points out in her study of Seminar VI *Desire and Its Interpretation* (1958–1959) and its Shakespearean elaborations on the tragedy of Hamlet, Lacan forges a very explicit link between the I as personal pronoun and its position as an analogue of the o-object. Cox Cameron explains:

> And before the end of this year's seminar, using a term he rarely employs, he will forge a very explicit link between the pronoun "I" and the o-object when he suggests that "on the plane of the unconscious" the o-object functions in such a way as to make it the analogue of this "I".
>
> (Cox Cameron, 2020, p. 18)

At the time of Seminar VI, the o-object is very much linked to the process of mourning and loss, and it is often through loss that we witness the profundity of what had been tacitly supporting us. The graveyard scene where Hamlet witnesses Laertes mourning Ophelia is the point at which Hamlet steps into his own desire for the previously repudiated Ophelia by stating "it is I Hamlet the Dane". This act marks a momentous shift in his position regarding the o-object (ibid., p. 77). His nomination of himself, in the place of her death, is directly related to the recognition of her loss, her elevation to the position of the lost object. It is only when Ophelia is dead and mourned by another that Hamlet realises his love for her; as such there is an end point, something final has occurred from which the realisation of his desire comes into view. In Ophelia's elevation to the position of the lost object, paradoxically a distance emerges between Hamlet and Ophelia, a distance from which he can act and nominate himself within that space of loss. For Daniel Blake, the moment at which he nominates himself, as when he writes the pronoun I as a means of refusal of his ill-treatment, marks a limit point of desire. Where the desire of the Other was a fantasmatic support of the o-object, that object whose shadow side is loss and pain, I will be. As Cox Cameron points out, Hamlet's realisation of his love for Ophelia re-establishes the fantasy surrounding the o-object rather than demolishing it (ibid., p. 77). And yet, the critical moment of nomination, also establishes a readiness to step outside of a protective fantasy, a moment of self-visibility and reclaiming of agency, as a response to what has been lost. In the graveyard scene, Hamlet has momentum; he re-establishes potency, not unlike Daniel's act of graffiti on the job centre wall.

If the realisation of desire, therefore, involves the loss associated with unveiling the o-object, then this is something we can only encounter at lived points of extremity. This raises the question: are these limit points and confrontations with the Real of the ethical position, moments that we can bring about through our desire, or do they happen as a consequence of contingent circumstance? In other words, are the moments where we are faced with the choice of not giving ground to desire a consequence of something that cannot be foreseen in advance? If so, this is a more anxiety provoking proposition, a question for which we can never really know the answer until we reach a limit. For Daniel Blake, this limit was brought about by contingency and the socio-economic system of his environment.

At the Limit

The climactic graffiti moment for Daniel Blake has been a last straw in a series of frustrations. Faced with the loss of his health, career, and having previously been an autonomous surviving subject, Daniel has had to succumb to the vulnerability[4] of being a subject citizen of the state inherent to the symbolic system. Without state support, he cannot survive, pay his bills or eat. The point at which he retaliates against the system is also built upon many previous losses and humiliations; it is as such a breaking point, a point from which he can't take any more frustration and from which he breaks free from the fantasy of the obedient citizen (collective position) to a more singular act of fair play. This breaking free of fantasy, however, is not without a cost, a destitution: Daniel ends up in poverty without benefits and his health suffers as a result. To call this a completely singular act would not be totally accurate as the actions of the Lacanian hero (ethical in desire not morality), although acting in aloneness – as in the isolation of the Sophoclean heroes – can bring change to the lives of others even if this is not intentional.[5] For example, Daniel's act of graffiti inspires other passers-by also impacted by the social welfare system, to join in the condemnation of the austerity measures and to give them the courage to retaliate and speak their minds.

One of the stark points the film depicts regarding desire, is that one can be ethical (fight for the good), achieve a certain freedom regarding desire and yet face dire consequences to this stance, one of which is ending up alone and encountering the loss associated with being an outsider. And yet, Lacan is clear that aloneness or solitude is not enough to account for the suffering of the tragic hero: "They are at a limit that is not accounted for by their solitude relative to others. There is something more; they are characters who find themselves right away in a limit zone, find themselves between life and death" (Lacan, 1997, p. 272). This limit zone between life and death is where Lacan places Antigone, whose refusal to obey the law of the state is not a refusal based on a standard or measurable good, but an act that elevates her to an image of beauty within an economy of desire and death. Of course, it is possible to argue that the experience of aloneness and solitude (or casting out from society) is a form of a limit zone between life and death, as the anxiety associated with this position can be simply unbearable. In *Escape from Freedom* (1941/1965), Erich Fromm argued that human beings are torn between two opposing experiences of freedom; 'freedom from' (a more negative form) and 'freedom to' (a more positive version). In the more negative form, we may experience a compulsion to 'escape from freedom' – a freedom, for example, induced by a deregulation of traditional mores, customs, restraints, toward authoritarian leaders – as the experience of singularity and the anxiety of aloneness can be overwhelming. The freedom we 'escape from' can be induced by a shift in the social order, where the expected unstable positions of identity are disturbed and set loose from traditional mores. For example, the historical development of capitalism created more choice of employment as opposed to the more set identities within a traditional feudal way of life. A more positive version of freedom, that of 'freedom to', can enliven us and is implicit in an experience of being authentically alive; it is closely related with spontaneity and the areas of love, work and creativity. If we are not beset by too much anxiety, or the need to conform out of fear of expulsion from the symbolic order, we are relatively free to choose the paths in the relevant significant areas of life. I say relatively as the socio-cultural/socio-political order can be so oppressive that modes of freedom may be too dangerous, regardless of the complexes inherent to the subject's fundamental fantasy and family of origin. Take the current situation in Iran, where today, as I write these words, a young man has just been hanged for his part in the recent protests against the regime. Or the example of migrant workers in Qatar, many of whom lost their lives in constructing the stadium for the 2022 World Cup. They may have been, technically speaking, free to choose to come to Qatar to risk their lives in such a venture, yet what kind of freedom was this choice? It is possibly more in the realm of 'freedom from' than 'freedom to'. Admittedly, the juxtaposition of freedom (in its usual connotations) and desire, in the Lacanian sense, is not an easy coupling, even though I am drawing inferences, particularly concerning the cost associated with both terms. In some ways, regarding the perverse enjoyment of desire, desire is not something we are free to do; we are more subject to it, or subjects of it – rather than being its master and there is potential freedom in realising this. That is, we may accept desire as disturbing and problematic rather than raising it to an ideal of a liberating freedom.

Fundamentally though, the path of freedom, through a reckoning with desire, demands a courageous stance. In many instances, either to a greater or lesser extent, we may risk alienation as a social symbolic death or even a literal, biological one. Of course, the risk of alienation is not the same as actually ending up alienated, but chance may always be a factor in the final analysis. Take the example of Marielle Franco, an outspoken lesbian politician in Brazil who was murdered in her car in 2018 during the election campaign of that year. There is camera footage of her poignantly saying in a political gathering, "I will not be silenced" as she spoke out about issues pertaining to women and sexuality. The climate in Brazil surrounding LGBT members of society is threatening, particularly within the political realm. Many members of the community fear for their lives. Who dares to take the gauntlet in such a climate? As I have already said, we need to be careful not to fully align these kinds of examples with the status of the Lacanian ethical hero, as if we could read for desire concretely. Alternatively, perhaps we could take issue with Lacan's reasonings on this matter and argue that the status of the hero does not have to be so uncompromising; can we not also experience pity and fear and still be heroic? It is clear in his elaborations of what constitutes a hero that Lacan seems to favour a concrete and staunch stance vis-à-vis the other, as he says of Philoctetes, who "isn't much of a man" (Lacan, 1997, p. 320):

> What makes Philoctetes a hero? Nothing more than the fact that he remains fiercely committed to his hate right to the end, when the deus ex machine appears like the curtain falling. This reveals to us not only that he has been betrayed and he is aware that he has been betrayed, but also that he has been betrayed with impunity.

So, it is because Philoctetes[6] is fiercely committed to his hate that Lacan is provided with an example of not giving ground relative to desire. Following betrayal and abandonment, Philoctetes does not return to the world of goods but is willing to sacrifice that return for his commitment to hate and misery. Philoctetes' heroic position is, therefore, a refusal of the social Other: 'I will not abandon my hate, I will not forgive you'. Is this what Lacan is saying is the radical ethical position of psychoanalysis? To be willing to go to the end[7] is to remain steadfast, unyielding, even if this is the antithesis of a Christian position of forgiveness, that is to forgive in order to free yourself of hate and resentment.

In some respects, the plight of Daniel Blake (an injured body with a loss of physical capacity) resembles that of Philoctetes. Within neoliberal culture, there is stigmatisation and casting out/abandonment, of those who cannot contribute to the system. The physically wounded individual is often in a Philoctetes cave, metaphorically speaking, as a result of stigmatisation and the internalisation of external values. Yet there is a certain paradox in the presentation of the figures of Antigone and Philoctetes by Lacan within the context of ethics, as figures of pure desire, as ideals of an ethical stance. Lacan does not want to provide, or is attempting not to provide us with a template of how to live, as in other ethical orientations, religions or philosophies such as Kant's categorical imperative. One simply needs to be an ordinary subject who pursues desire to the end, or an end, such as that of an analysis: "To have carried an analysis through to its end is no more nor less than to have encountered that limit in which the problematic of desire is raised" (Lacan, 1997, p. 300).

These tragic figures of antiquity provide Lacan with templates with which he can conceptualise the end of an analysis or the trajectory that the subject pursues along the axis of analysis. The end of analysis contains the path upon which the hero of Greek tragedy has already trodden upon, in that tragedy illustrates an encounter with the limits of desire and the end of analysis is that encounter. This limit that Lacan specifies is that of the question of the good around which desire circulates and to which he states, there is no sovereign good (ibid., p. 300). The analyst is aware of this and should not give in to the analysand's demand to provide an answer to the question of the good life. This should give us pause for thought. According to Lacan's instructions, an analyst should not underline as a goal of analysis what is constituted as (a) good in a normative sense, for example, a particular career, a relationship, children, and so on. The analyst should fundamentally give the only thing he/she has, which is their analyst's desire, in other words, their lack of being (*manque à être*). There is no consumerist, acquisitionist outcome for a Lacanian psychoanalysis. While this may be an ideal of psychoanalysis, I feel the reality on the ground is not so straightforward – particularly as a training analysis takes place within the trajectory of achieving a certain end, be it of becoming an analyst. The prospect of stepping outside the realm of the goods completely seems unlikely and even if we feel we have achieved this, the subtlety of the good and its seductive manifestations may still be operative. Indeed, one of the main points I have been making here is that the ground upon which we do not give ground is not equal across cultures and peoples. Apart from the practical realities of the ideal trajectory of analysis, perhaps Lacan's argument on the price that must be paid for both our desire and that of living the normative good life must be considered. We are caught in a difficult, if not impossible position; to conform to the normative good is to pay with our bodies, that of jouissance, to remain fast to our desire is to encounter the limit of death, the limit delineated by the signifier. As Lacan phrases this position:

> [T]he answer is, by virtue of the signifier in its most radical form. It is in the signifier and insofar as the subject articulates a signifying chain that he comes up against the fact that he may disappear from the chain of what he is.
>
> (ibid, p. 294)

We might ask, what does it mean to disappear from the signifying chain of what we are? Are we catapulted out from the chain of meaning where one signifier represents a subject for another signifier and to ex-ist outside the chain, in the Real, beyond the law that sutures us to the imaginary? This is what Lacan's previous statement appears to suggest and what Antigone has come up against in her refusal to capitulate to the law; for beyond the law of the state lies the law of the signifier. Those who transcend it, are in the hinterlands of the void. As beings born unto the signifier, and hence as beings who lack, we are forever in its debt.

A Price to Be Paid . . .

In Seminar VII, Lacan inscribes the notion of debt into the dialectic of language/ the signifier and the body. The price we pay for the metamorphosis of our desire is the pound of flesh we pay with our bodies, the operation that transforms the signifier into a metaphor. While in Christianity, the debt that must be paid for our sins is through a suffering or deficit in the afterlife, this accounting of good and bad actions is reformulated according to the principle of debt and the Other. Lacan states, "Sublimate as much as you like; you have to pay for it with something. And this something is called *jouissance*. I have to pay for that mystical operation with a pound of flesh" (ibid., p. 322).

With these Shakespearean echoes, Lacan argues that we pay with our bodies for the debt incurred through our position as subjects within the symbolic. To speak is to enter the collective pact: to encounter desire as that which mediates inter-subjectively as a paradox in which a desire that seems singular is born of the Other, a desire that may appear as consensus yet still contains a radical singularity – a singularity often represented by the symptom. Although Lacan speaks of the price that must be paid for desire, and defines this price as jouissance, there is more that should be said to articulate the suffering associated with jouissance and this excep-tional experience of the human condition. One of the questions I have been engag-ing with in this chapter is why is it so hard not to cede or give ground to desire? Clearly, according to Lacan's elaborations, in the context of the genre of tragedy, the answer lies in the path of the tragic hero, and this path is aligned with analysis; not simply with any analysis but one that has pursued the question of desire to the end whereupon we can make a judgement. The following statement by Lacan sums up the difficulty of analysis and why the end may be difficult to reach.

> As I believe I have shown here in the sphere I have outlined for you this year, the function of desire must remain in a fundamental relationship to death. The question I ask is this: shouldn't the true termination of an analysis – and by that I mean the kind that prepares you to become an analyst – in the end confront the one who undergoes it with the reality of the human condition? It is precisely this, that in connection with anguish, Freud designated as the level at which its signal is produced, namely, *Hilflosigkeit* or distress, the state in which man is in that relationship to himself which is his own death – in the sense I have taught you to isolate it this year – and can expect help from no one.
>
> At the end of a training analysis the subject should reach and should know the domain and the level of the experience of absolute disarray. It is a level at which anguish is already a protection, not so much *Abwarten* as *Erwartung*. Anguish develops by letting a danger appear, whereas there is no danger at the level of the final experience of *Hilflosigkeit*.
>
> (Lacan, 1997, pp. 303–304)

Lacan's emphatic portrayal of the end of analysis as an experience of absolute disarray, clearly does not conform with the demand for happiness and 'balance' so pertinent to the more populous notions of therapy and self-help so prevalent in our current times. A key component of the achievement of this end of analysis, or a limit point regarding desire, is the confrontation with ourselves as our own death – a confrontation with the Real no less, where the symbolic no longer functions to mediate danger with anxiety. This is what tragedy has allowed Lacan to illustrate regarding the elaborations of a final judgement of desire, an aesthetic space within which the resolution of an action/actions can be traced according to the path and limits of desire. However, literary tragedy is a story that has already been written, unlike that of the analysand at the end of analysis or the social protagonist fight-ing for change in more marginalised ways of life. Perhaps these lived experiences may bring elements of spontaneity and freedom, not determined in advance by the ethical benchmark of tragedy. Yet, can all these fights for social change and heroic self-sacrifices that may result be interpreted as a not giving ground, reaching the ethical limit point of desire? Not at all, and bearing in mind Lacan's prediction – "Only the martyrs know neither pity nor fear. Believe me, the day when the martyrs are victorious will be the day of universal conflagration" (p. 267) – but they certainly serve as benchmarks to consider the cost of resisting the desire of the Other.

Given the potential risks involved, it is clear that there are many times when we might choose consciously or unconsciously to avoid standing our ground out of the pressure of survival within the group formations of the social/cultural order. This also may be due to largely unconscious formations, and so when we feel we know what we want, we may not know that we do not really know what we want. In Erich Fromm's terminology, we could say that the experience of desire generates an anxiety of being alone, overwhelmed by the magnitude of the responsibility of freedom. Or in Lacanian terms, we could say that we do not want our subjective fantasies destroyed, the fantasies that shield us from the reality of the pain of the human condition.

The stance of not giving ground to desire can often entail making oneself visible; and this, depending on the circumstances surrounding the act, can have devastating consequences including losing one's life. To stand up to the Other often involves an act of heroism, a stepping into a potential sacrifice, giving up the monotonous homogeneity or the palliating reassurance of the Other into a more differential and uncertain reality. While at the end of analysis, the subject may find themselves alone at the brink of impotence regarding demand (the realisation that demand cannot satisfy desire), the ability to bear this position is not without a socio-cultural context. While it is better to avoid making reductive statements about marginal subjects who may find pain harder to bear, or be closer to breaking points, as resilience is also a function of enduring marginality and great pain, it is still important to consider that political factors can never be completely outside of an analysis. Lacan's development of the ethical position of psychoanalysis is the cultivation of a discourse that stands apart from the discourse of the common good, or that of science, the collective political et cetera. By contrast, in Erich Fromm's analysis of freedom, his vision for an ideal future that incorporates the more positive version of freedom, is a freedom to be spontaneous and authentically alive. In his view, part of the solution for toxic individualism is that of democracy, the decentring of power and the incorporation of the singular subject in the distribution of goods. Lacan does not provide political solutions to social problems; analysis addresses the symptom of the subject as, in part, a structural phenomenon of language in the enjoyment inherent to any relationship to the law, including the enjoyment of the law per se. In some cultures, the enjoyment inherent to the law and its accompanying political system becomes tyrannical. In fact, the system may become an administrator of perverse enjoyment, silencing and criminalising those who speak out against its injustices. We cannot ignore the extra difficulties pertinent to these scenarios and that the fight for the good oftentimes is the fight for basic freedoms: freedoms of speech, freedom to love without persecution, the freedom to be female as an equal. Indeed, the very capacity to be within the process of psychoanalysis is often the result of a certain socio-economic position, notwithstanding the analysts who work to a more socialist, accessible model. There is a price to exploring our desire, and it is not one that everyone can pay. Psychoanalysis is not beyond the service of the goods, therefore, although the ideal of a desire that points beyond the law may be. My main point here is to draw out the problematic of the ethics of desire as just that, a problematic, and to try and avoid imaginary reductionisms; this is in keeping with the accent Lacan has placed on the paradoxes of ethics.

In conclusion, we can consider whether outside the realm of tragedy, and even of psychoanalysis, the stance of not giving ground relative to our desire is an ideal or achievable position. It is important to reiterate that Lacan's proposition was experimental and not a prescription. Fundamentally, then, to take the statement too literally would be, precisely, to raise Lacan's dictum to the level of a good (an ideal), and therefore, as something that may take on a tyrannical superego injunction – never give up on your desire! In other words, we may internalise 'Lacanian ethics' as the good to which we should aspire, an outcome which may bring us happiness. If singularity is central in the realisation of our desire, only we can know whether we have given ground relative to our desire. This knowledge may be imparted to us through symptoms and associated guilt, not through concrete thoughts or speech. The observation of the conflict inherent to desire and its excessive dimension may, at least, point us in the direction of a limit, a reaching beyond which involves a stance of heroic proportions. However, this limit may not simply be that of the limit of the signifier, but also the limit we enjoy as socio-political subjects, and a limit to what we can endure as injustice. This is not to say that there are always tragic consequences for not giving ground to desire, as a singular subject within a collective order, but it is important to imagine the reasons behind the moments when this is difficult and its relative unequal distribution. If freedom comes at a price, then this is a price we must articulate theoretically and individually.

Notes

1 For further elaboration, see my book review in *Lacunae* (2021) of Olga Cox Cameron's *Studying Lacan's Seminar VI: Dream, Symptom, and the Collapse of Subjectivity*.
2 Perhaps the pain at the end of analysis may differ from the pain of existence Lacan is referring to here. A pain induced by great grief or loss where desire no longer functions.
3 Lacan stated in Seminar VI, *Desire and Its Interpretation*, regarding the Shakespearean character of Hamlet, that Hamlet is a poetic creation and not a real character. It is therefore hard if not impossible to provide a complete or accurate interpretation of a moment of seeming desire in a film, and this point opens onto a paradox of reading for unconscious desire in a literary or artistic work.
4 In an interview about *I, Daniel Blake* (2017, YouTube), Ken Loach explains that he deliberately chose a character such as Daniel Blake – ethical, hard-working and willing to follow the rules – so as to challenge the stereotype of the 'lazy benefits scrounger' so ingrained in British society. He states that the punishment for being unable to take part in the workforce and the hamster wheel of production is that of hunger. And this is a price the government are aware they are inflicting on vulnerable subjects – it is not done in ignorance.

5 Although an act may be characterised as singular in a psychoanalytic (ethical) sense, the more wide-reaching and social ramifications of this act cannot be known in advance by the agent of the act or even by an outside observer. The Sophoclean trilogy – *Oedipus, Antigone*, and *Oedipus the King* – is pervaded by transgenerational trauma and the consequences of the sins of the fathers. Although a mythical and literary figure, we cannot really isolate Antigone's staunch and 'beautiful' refusal of the law from the fact that her father Oedipus had been exiled after blinding himself upon realising his incestuous relation with his mother. Or that Antigone's act of suicide stands alone as singular without symbolic ramifications. For example, as Carol Owens (2012) argues, Lacan has made a 'blunder' of interpretation at this time regarding Antigone's 'idealised' act of not ceding to her desire in that he does not account for her self-destruction, her 'non-return'. According to Owens, Antigone's act of self-destruction should not lend itself to forming an ethical ideal for analysands. Owens states: "one thing we take as a given in the clinic, is that even though acts of self-destitution can have social effects through re-signification, it is not within the subject's governance to determine how. So in fact any symbolic divestiture can be variously interpreted" (p. 54). In this sense, then, does any singular act really stand alone? As human subjects, death always has to be accounted for, and that which once existed within the symbolic remains as a trace.

6 It must be said that Lacan's choice of Philoctetes as an exemplar of heroic ideals is interesting, particularly as Elaine Scarry (1985) points out in *The Body in Pain*, Philoctetes is one of the few pertinent literary examples of the body in pain. Pain is a mental or physical state that is generally defined in literature as being beyond the realm of representation. With the figure of Philoctetes, a body lame and in pain, Lacan is usurping the stereotype of the extraordinary hero, "one does not have to be heroic to be a hero".

7 At an online conference, *we must be willing to go to the end* (a symposium on the work of Slavoj Žižek) in August 2022, there was a fascinating tête-à-tête between Mari Ruti and Žižek on the subject of Lacanian ethics and concepts such as subjective destitution, the death drive and suicide. Ruti argued against what she felt to be a form of the death drive incorporated within the seemingly amoral stance of Lacanian theory on ethics (no right or wrong), advocating more for a stance of sublimation and not nihilistic destruction. Ruti also argued that certain acts should be condemned as simply wrong without any equivocation. Žižek vehemently disagreed that subjective destitution is equitable with the death drive, positing it more in the domain of freedom, or free from the usual compulsions inherent to the symbolic, and where the death drive is not operative. He used an example of someone who is no longer afraid to die but is not suicidal.

References

Cox Cameron, O. (2020). *Studying Lacan's Seminar VI: Dream, Symptom, and the Collapse of Subjectivity*. Ed. C. Owens. London: Routledge.

De Kesel, M. (2009 [2001]). *Eros and Ethics: Reading Jacques Lacan's Seminar VII*. Trans. S. Jöttkandt. Albany: State University of New York Press.

Fromm, E. (1941/1965). *Escape From Freedom*. Avon Books.

Lacan, J. (1997). *Seminar VII, The Ethics of Psychoanalysis, The Seminar of Jacques Lacan*. Ed. J.-A. Miller. Trans. D. Porter. London: W. W. Norton & Company.

Lacan, J. (2017). *Formations of the Unconscious, Book V: The Formations of the Unconscious*. Ed. J.-A. Miller. Trans. R. Grigg. Malden, MA and Cambridge: Polity Press.

Lacan, J. (2019). *Book VI, Desire and Its Interpretation: The Seminar of Jacques Lacan*. Ed. J.-A. Miller. Trans. B. Fink. Cambridge: Polity Press.

Loach, K. (2016). *I, Daniel Blake*. Writ. P. Laverty. Sixteen Films, Why Not Productions, Wild Bunch.

Loach, K. (2017). Q & A and Screening of "I Daniel Blake" at SOAS University of London. *YouTube*.

Meehan O'Callaghan, S. (2021). Book Review. Studying Lacan's Seminar VI: Dream, Symptom, and the Collapse of Subjectivity. *Lacunae*, (23): 136–150.

Owens, C. (2012). Paradoxes of Enjoyment, Paradoxes of Cruelty (on Not Giving Up on Desire . . .). *Lacunae*, 2(1): 50–61.

Ruti, M. (2022). The Limits of Lacanian Ethics: Or Why Going to the End Scares Me. We Should Be Willing to Go to the End: Symposium on Slavoj Žižek. *YouTube*, August 30/31. Study Groups on Psychoanalysis and Politics.

Scarry, E. (1985). *The Body in Pain*. Oxford: Oxford University Press.

Chapter 8

While Not Having the Last Word . . .

Calum Neill

By the time we arrive at the final session of July 6, 1960, Lacan has taken us through a dense, innovative, illuminating and perhaps not a little confounding engagement with ethics which directly and indirectly confronts salient aspects of the history of ethical thought, while also striking what might be understood as entirely new ground. Through the seminar we are constantly bounced between the two distinct, if mutually implicating, senses implied in the seminar's title. Insofar as Lacan is still primarily addressing analysts and trainee analysts, we should understand the title – *The Ethics of Psychoanalysis* – to indicate that his concern is ethics as it would pertain to the context of the clinic and the practice of psychoanalysis. This sense of the ethics of psychoanalysis already entails both a sense of what ought to be the ethical concern of practitioners of psychoanalysis and the overarching question of the point of psychoanalysis. Beyond this element of clinical instruction (as if Lacan were ever that straightforwardly didactic!), there is another sense in which we should understand the work of the preposition in the title. It is clear from Lacan's discourse that the ethics of psychoanalysis also, for him, concerns a new approach to ethics which is informed by and perhaps even grounded in the insights and theory of psychoanalysis. Psychoanalysis not only demands a new consideration of ethics due to the peculiarities of its practice but, bound up in this, it opens the way for a vital new consideration of ethics which at the same time emerges in response to a history of ethical thinking and steps away from this history to allow us to think again about one of the most contested fields in philosophy.

Lacan opens the final session by announcing that he will seek to conclude while only in part concluding. Ethics, for Lacan, does not readily admit conclusion, and this is part of the difficulty the field presents. Our thinking on or approaches to ethics cannot be fixed or offer anything like definitive answers, but neither can we refuse to engage, insofar as a refusal is itself a form of response. This is the aporia of ethics and Lacan seeks, then, to end with what he calls a "mixed grill" (1992, p. 311). His metaphor here already draws our attention to the fact that there is something to be consumed, but what is to be consumed is anything but straightforward. At this point in the session, Lacan ascribes the non-closure of ethics to the fact that ethics is always "excentric" (ibid.), which is to say that ethics necessarily

DOI: 10.4324/9781003450795-8

concerns something which is beyond our discourse, our understanding, beyond us, as we are before we encounter any such ethical moment. Ethics, that is, cannot be contained and, thus, no discourse on ethics which is really a discourse on ethics can be concluded. Ethics is not hermetic. It is not a tautology. The ethical, in order to be ethical, necessarily exceeds the *because I said so* of morality.

This takes us to the confusing claim often made of Lacan's ethics, that it is an ethics of the real. As he has taken great care and considerable time to elucidate in the seminar, through discussions of the poetry of courtly love, de Sade's prose and Sophocles' theatre, as well as engagements with philosophy, ethics ultimately always concerns an inscription or declaration. Ethics is, in this sense, always an ethics of the symbolic. But the preposition, once again, has to be thought through here. To say that Lacan's ethics is an ethics of the symbolic runs the risk of implying that it is contained within the symbolic, which is precisely the point he is warning against in his refusal to conclude. The symbolic cannot contain the ethical. It is perhaps this that lures people to the description of his ethics as an ethics of the real. But, really, Lacan's ethics is no more of the real than it is of the symbolic. An ethics which was truly of the real would be as impossible as it was nonsensical. There is, and can be, no ethics in the real, for the simple reason that ethics requires a judgement to be made.

An illustration is perhaps informative here.

On February 14, 2018, Nikolas Cruz entered his old school, Marjory Stoneman Douglas High School in Parkland, Florida, and roamed the corridors for a little over six minutes, ultimately shooting 34 people, killing 17 of them. With not inconsiderable competition, the shooting was the worst, in terms of fatalities, in the history of US school shootings. A little over a month later, a large rally took place to protest the lack of gun control in the US. X Gonzales (then Emma), who had been one of the school pupils present at the Stoneman Douglas shooting and, subsequently, one of the co-founders of the Never Again MSD gun control advocacy group, spoke at the rally. Gonzales named and evoked her schoolmates who had been murdered, pointing to the things they would never again do. And then she stopped. And remained silent. And remained silent. At first the silence emerged as a pause. The emotion weighed heavily. The audience waited in that silence, unsure when it would end, unsure what was taking place. In a logic anticipated in Lacan's 1945 paper *Logical Time,* the audience moves from a time of perception to a time of understanding. Gonzales remained silent for six minutes and 20 seconds, the duration of Cruz's shooting spree.

Of course, the full force of Gonzales's speech, or more importantly, her silence, only works once. For the time of perception or experience, when you are simply in the lived awkwardness of the non-speech, the symbolic framing of the event, the conventions of a large-scale rally, a rousing, heartfelt speech, are all suspended. We are plunged, momentarily, into the real of the event. As we emerge into the time of understanding, and the significance of the pause becomes clear, we, and the silence itself, are irrevocably recuperated to the symbolic and it takes on a particular meaning.

Lacan's theory of logical time, as we know, has three, not two, moments. As well as the time of perception and understanding, there is the time of concluding. It is this that lends the ethical dimension to Gonzales's silence. They have opened up a temporal space of experience which forces a confrontation, wherein each audience member is left to position themselves in response to the time of the killing. How we conclude, that is, is left to each of us. There is no *a priori* conclusion.

Gonzales's silence may be as close as we could imagine to an ethics of the real but, ultimately, the complex ethical dimension of her performance relies on a reinscription in the symbolic, and it is only from there that its effects can be adduced.

Action and the Desire Which Inhabits It

Lacan provides a late, but essential, definition, insisting that ethics consists in judgement. To be precise, in two judgements: a judgement in the action, and a judgement of the action. This, obviously, ties ethics to the notion of the act, which Lacan elsewhere distinguishes from what he calls "mere behaviour" (Lacan, 1977, p. 50). There must be, at least supposed, a judgement within the act itself and there must be a judgement of the act. Without these two moments, it makes no sense to describe what has transpired as ethical.

It is important to clarify that when Lacan emphasises that the judgement within the act must be at least supposed or implied, rather than strictly known, he is not engaging with a phenomenological point of the impossibility of accessing others' intentions. The act referred to here is the act of the subject themselves. The point is rather to re-emphasise the fact of the unconscious and the temporality of the decision. To claim absolute certitude over the motivations of one's own action is, of course, fanciful. Even when we think we know why we did what we did, such rationalisation necessarily takes place after the fact. The assumption of a judgement, and what that judgement might have consisted in, is necessarily retroactively posited from the point of having acted. We might imagine the act here as located in the chasm of the real. This would be to say that the act, in itself, is inaccessible, ungraspable. For an act to have been experienced, the chasm of the real must have been crossed and what would be taken to have been experienced inscribed in the symbolic. Recall that experience has its roots in *ex* (out of) and *per* (through). To experience is never to be in the moment. It is always, rather, to have come through and out the other side. Experience is always historical. It is always *to have experienced*.

Keeping open even the feasibility of an ethics emerging from psychoanalysis, whether in theory or practice, Lacan articulates this potential to the question of judgement. There might be said to be an ethics of psychoanalysis to the extent that psychoanalysis furnishes us with the means to provide a judgement. Such a judgement, clinically speaking, ought not to be understood as consisting in an uncovering of instinctual causes. This is not what psychoanalysis brings to the table. Rather, the promise of psychoanalysis, in the field of ethics, lies in its potential to help us explore the significance of the act in question. Again, the question is one of judgement but judgement here in the sense of a pronouncement on the act after the fact. This, for Lacan, is the core gambit of Freud's invention: that there is some sense that can be discerned in that which presents itself to be analysed. There is that which is taken to have been experienced and there is the judgement of that which is thus presented as having been experienced. The very separation (as though this were a simple process) of these two aspects is what is effective.

On one level, such an operation is not new or novel. Most generally it appears as an echo of the inscription on the Temple at Delphi: *Know thyself*. On the other, insofar as we understand Freud to have brought something new – the unconscious – into play, then it is of course distinct from any commensurate operation which preceded this moment in our intellectual history. Freud's invention changes how we relate to ourselves and thus necessarily changes how we consider the ethical.

The distinction between the effect of the psychoanalytic judgement and other seemingly similar judgements lies, for Lacan, in their supposed relation to the good. Herein lies, at least one aspect of, the ethical significance.

One way of approaching this is to assume a natural state of harmony or good which precedes experience. Lacan here appeals to the Confucian philosopher Mencius, who, more accurately, argued that people have the innate capacity for good insofar as they are endowed with the potential to be compassionate, righteous, law-abiding and wise. The fact that each of us is endowed with these potentials does not mean each of us becomes such. Circumstance and our own directions can lead us away from these capacities. Where Mencius places the emphasis on the good as our innate potential, Lacan turns the emphasis to the distance between such a supposed good and our lived experience. Such is this distance that it may lead to the Oedipal wish never to have been (*me phunai*), the fantasmatic erasure of the experience from which we have emerged (1992, p. 312).

Lacan has invited us to engage in a thought experiment; to consider ethics from the perspective of the Last Judgement. Such a perspective would, for Lacan, entail positing as the standard by which ethics might be considered, not simply action or intention, but the relationship between action and the desire which inhabits that action. Lacan's choice of words is pertinent here. He speaks of the action and the desire which inhabits it, rather than motivation, problematising or bracketing the common sense of action springing from volition. The action is inhabited by a desire, which may suggest the visibility of the action and the obscurity of the desire, while also confounding any straightforward notion of a chronological relation between the two.

Here Lacan is clear to distinguish the ethics of psychoanalysis from those conceptions of ethics which are concerned with what he calls "the service of goods" (1992, p. 313), where goods ought to be understood in both the moral sense and the more contemporary sense of provisions or merchandise. In eliding the two senses of goods, Lacan might be understood to be drawing our attention to the materiality and egocentrism of contemporary life, where what is good is stuff and what is good is good for me. The pluralisation of goods also suggests, when considered in the more strictly moral sense, the negotiation and compromise entailed in pluralism, where we like to assume, at least on a surface level, an open approach to moral questions which respects different cultural mores and perspectives. Lacan's ethics of psychoanalysis is intended to cut through this façade and address the question of ethics subjectively.

Lacan argues that ethics necessarily concerns action and that, moreover, any action needs to be understood within a context. What complicates this point is that, at least from a psychoanalytic perspective, the action in question, and the context in which it would appear, are both necessarily retroactively posited. Evoking classical Greek theatre, both in its tragic and comedic forms, Lacan appears to subtly present a sense of life as always fashioned as drama, which is to highlight both the constructed nature of the particular version of lived context in which any action must be taken to have occurred and to point to the conventions which tend to govern this construction.

In the case of life conceived as tragedy, Lacan perceives the relation between action and the desire that inhabits it as bound to the idea of death, but death here better understood as the aphanisis of the subject than the Heideggerian notion of being towards death. Drawing our attention to *Oedipus Rex* as the central tragedy of psychoanalysis, Lacan emphasises once again Oedipus's declaration *me phunai*, the expressed desire not to have been. The desire to not have been – *ce ne fus-je pour être*, as Lacan translates it in his next seminar (Lacan, 2001, p. 358) – is quite distinct from a wish to die. This emphasis on disappearance, Lacan argues, is evident too in comedy. The distinction between the two is that where in tragedy it is the subject who, eventually, disappears, in comedy, it is the phallus which disappears, leaving the subject to roll on. What both modes, and their combination in tragi-comedy, bring to light is the relationship of action to the desire that resides within it, even, or especially, if that action fails to ever adequate to the desire in question. The momentum here is captured in the question, which Lacan frames as having the force of a Last Judgement: "Have you acted in conformity with the desire that is in you?" (1992, p. 314). The core of this question then appears to lie in the relationship between action and desire. Lacan had earlier, as noted, specified that ethics consists in a judgement in the action and a judgement of the action. This question with the force of a Last Judgement appears to refer specifically to the latter. After the fact, would you judge that the act was equal to the desire that inhabited it?

It would seem, however, that in both the case of the tragic and the comic an affirmative answer here is strictly impossible. In the former, there would be no subject left to answer, while the latter is precisely sustained as comedic insofar as the answer is, *No, not yet*.

This, for Lacan, is what distinguishes the ethics of psychoanalysis from what he terms traditional ethics, the service of goods. Lacan has already explored this ethics of service of goods through the figure of Creon in Sophocles' *Antigone*. The ethics predicated on the service of goods is concerned with maintaining a certain status quo, of keeping things moving in a more or less ordered fashion. It is, says Lacan, the ethics of Aristotle's golden mean. What Creon allows us to appreciate is that this maintenance of order is not a neutral position which might be implied in the concept of the golden mean. Rather, the maintenance of order is always the maintenance of power. It is a morality of the master.

This, for Lacan, is not necessarily to be dismissive of order or power. They have their place. But it is important to distinguish this master morality from the ethics of psychoanalysis. The ethics of psychoanalysis is concerned, as we have seen, with desire. The maintenance of order is concerned with the suppression of desire: "As far as desires are concerned, come back later. Make them wait."

The Imperative of the Impossible

To speak of an ethics of desire might be understood to imply an ethics of self-interest. However, this is quite the opposite of what Lacan has in mind. For Lacan, the ethics of psychoanalysis leans on Kant in this regard and his demarcation of the ethical (or in Kant's language, the moral) from the pathological or sensible. With Kant, Lacan emphasises that the field of ethics has no concern with human interests.

Where traditional morality was concerned with what was possible, the ethics of psychoanalysis would be better framed as being concerned with the impossible. The imperative of such an ethics is, then, truly imperative. Such a perspective necessarily opens up a chasm, the space of the real in which the prescriptions of a morality are not already inscribed. Importantly, if the directives of an ethics are not already inscribed here, if this space of ethics is necessarily a space without pre-conceptions, then the desire that would be proper to it is not something that could be judged in advance. There is not good desire or bad desire. Rather it is desire beyond good and evil. This is the core point of Lacan's juxtaposition of Kant and Sade. Once you strip away the preconceptions, once you truly remove the interests which would motivate traditional ethics, interests which then evoke a *reductio ad infinitum*, there remains no means to distinguish the Kantian from the Sadist.

To locate the ethical in that which exceeds the pregiven is all well and good, insofar as it alludes to an ethics of openness, a certain untetheredness. But, really, this is not to say terribly much. On the one hand, we have ethics or morality tied down to and by traditional prescriptions which demarcate in advance what is and is not acceptable; on the other, we have a boundless freedom which emerges from the exposure of the groundlessness of the former. Everything is already determined or anything goes. Neither perspective really takes us very far.

Against this disappointing conclusion, Lacan excavates something more in Kant's ethics. In his conclusions to *The Critique of Practical Reason*, Kant famously states that there are "[t]wo things [which] fill the mind with ever new and increasing admiration and reverence . . . the starry sky above me and the moral law within me" (Kant, 1997, p. 133). The relevance of these two phenomena, for Kant, lies, at least in part, in their boundlessness and in their accessibility. The starry skies above speak to our externality, our being as *res extensa*, and connect us to an unending series of "worlds upon worlds", to an infinite "systems of systems" and, adding another dimension to this ceaseless ceaselessness, to a time unbound, open both in terms of its beginning and its end. In a similar manner, the moral law within situates us in world which is infinitely unfolding insofar as our understanding of and response to that world can know no end. A world, then, which is infinitely demanding.

Lacan questions the immediacy and obviousness of this appeal Kant makes. When we stare up into the night sky, he wonders, do we really connect with an infinity of worlds and systems within systems? Or do we not rather, as he pithily puts it, encounter a construction site? Lacan's point here is that our scientific progress has perhaps reduced the wonder which Kant assumes and has brought us to a more prosaic or limited understanding of our planet as being but one small, insignificant element of the universe. Alluding to Paley's famous analogy between the universe and a watch – the idea that the consistency and constancy of the laws of nature suggest that they can be understood as a coherent design, which in turn then suggests the necessity of a designer – Lacan asks what meaning would the presence of a designer add to our experience in the universe. His answer is that the idea of a designer, the idea of God, adds only the basis of thinking the subject qua subject, which is to say it adds the plane of signification; "In the beginning was the Word, and the Word was with God, and the Word was God" (John 1:1, King James Version). Where, for the philosophers, the existence of God is something which can never move beyond the realm of speculation and, for the religious, it is evidenced in revelation, for the psychoanalytically minded, the existence of God would require a signal and for the signal to be a signal it would need to already articulate to a system of significance. An emanation from far away is only an apparition, an occurrence, unless it articulates to what is said. That is to say, you can interpret celestial activity anyway you like, but it is all musing and fantasy unless it conforms to or confirms that which is already articulated.

The same point of interpretation can be adduced closer to home. Lacan makes reference to Jules Dassin's 1960 film, *Never on Sunday*, bringing the question back to ethics or morality. *Never on Sunday* concerns a clash of moral positions, in that the central male character, Homer, an American classicist, is affronted by the lifestyle of the central female character, Ilya. As an outsider to the modern Greece of the film, but convinced of his intimacy with the authentic Greece of the classical age, Homer feels empowered to not only judge Ilya's behaviour but, by extension, to judge the entire ethos of Greece and its supposed moral and cultural collapse. In juxtaposition to this supposed position of authority, Homer periodically engages in a pastiche of Greek crockery smashing, which serves to subtly undercut his lofty assumptions. Dassin, as director, humorously mocks Homer's displays by foregrounding the ringing of the till each time this happens. Whatever grand ideas Homer seeks to impose, the local barman has the last laugh as he profits nonetheless. Lacan's reading of this element of the film acknowledges the fact that, however completely Kant is able to cleanse the field of ethics of pathological motives, there is no escaping the accounting that pertains to ethics. The cash register rings. Without a judgement in and of the act, there is no sense in which what has transpired can be claimed as ethical. Of course, Kant's solution to this problem, which he clearly recognised, was to postpone the accounting, the judgement, to the afterlife. This, of course, solves nothing as the supposition of the judgement to come is necessarily fore-echoed in this life. This point can be illustrated through the first iteration of Lacan's well-known graph of desire (Lacan, 2006, p. 681). In order to be able to posit itself as subject, the subject must already have passed, retroactively, through the trajectory of the signification. This renders the subject impossible without language and impossibly split by language. This splitting is what constitutes the want of being that institutes desire.

In what he characterises as the post-revolutionary perspective, we, or at least some of us, have rejected or postponed desire and succumbed to the system of the service of goods. In the context of Seminar VII, that is in the summer of 1960, Lacan wants to emphasise that this subjection to the service of goods, in terms of its ethical structure, is the same for both the capitalist status quo and for the revolutionary left. This raises an important question for our current engagement with Lacan's social application of the question of ethics. Increasingly the idea of an oppositional left appears to have receded, while at the same time the notion of an end to capitalism is heralded, not in its revolutionary overthrow, but in its Oroborian self-defeat and its morphing into a neo-Feudalism. It is questionable how much traction such a perspective actually has, how accurate it would be to claim we are moving, or have moved, from a system predicated on exploitation to one predicated on extortion. Nonetheless, it may be helpful to consider the place of desire in such a move. If for Lacan, the revolutionary left are destined to unwittingly reproduce the same organisational structures as the capitalist state, insofar as their universalist aspirations do not actually affect the relationship between the individual and their desire, then what of a system in which the consumer is no longer required to work in order to consume but, rather, the former consumer itself becomes the product on which the system is fuelled?

Lacan's own argument is that modernity may have relegated the position of God to the basket of the obsolete, but the judgement which is essential to the structure of the Christian world view persists. Where the former, as Kant's argument requires, relies on a notion of an afterlife, in our secular times we have objective guilt. The picture may have changed, but the structure is just the same.

Call Yourself Alive?

It is here that Lacan proposes his famous dictum, that "from an analytical point of view, the only thing of which one can be guilty is of having given ground relative to one's desire" (1992, p. 319). Lacan's first comment on this proposition, which he says he wishes to present as an experimental paradox, is that whatever its status in relation to any ethical position, it is something which is supported by analytic experience. Which is then to say that this claim is not in fact, or not necessarily, an ethical claim at all. Lacan is rather proposing a description of what occurs. When one feels guilty, what one feels guilty about, and the extent then of one's guilt, is the extent to which one has reneged on one's desire.

People do compromise on their desire, and they do this for what they perceive to be good reasons. Having the best of intentions, however, does not stop one from feeling guilty. At the same time, one may perfectly well – as Peter Abelard, the twelfth-century theologian, argues – desire something and choose not to act on it. For Abelard, desire itself is not sinful, and neither is the act in itself. It is the intention that conjoins the two which is amenable to God's judgement. Lacan's pithy point is that while Abelard's arguments may solve the problem of judgement, or the problem of guilt in the juridical-moral sense, they don't appear to have solved the problem of guilt in the affective sense. We still feel guilty.

If intention and desire are separated and the latter is to be subordinate to the former, then this in no way resolves the force of the desire. Guilt and, to add to that, neurosis, will be the consequence. This is what makes this particularly and precisely the concern of psychoanalysis. Desire is that which propels us and when it is thwarted by "good intentions", it doesn't disappear. Just as the protagonist of Greek tragedy has their path marked out for them so, Lacan argues, do each of us. The difference is that while the path may be marked as a hero's journey, determined by structures which precede and exceed us, it is each of us, as mere people, who must tread that path.

As an example of such an ordinary man, Lacan presents Philoctetes, the titular hero of another Sophocles play. Philoctetes is a remarkable archer, and the inheritor and bearer of Heracles's esteemed bow. On route to Troy, Philoctetes is bitten by a sea viper and the wound begins to smell so bad that his erstwhile compatriots abandon him on the island of Lemnos. There he suffers alone for ten years until the Greeks, in need of the bow, which it has been told is necessary to win the war with Troy, return to retrieve it. Philoctetes, however, angered at his abandonment, refuses to help the Greeks, refuses even at the cost of saving himself. It is this commitment to his hatred that, for Lacan, elevates him to the status of hero. Crucial in the story, for Lacan, is the fact that Philoctetes was betrayed. The idea of giving ground relative to one's desire is, Lacan argues, always accompanied, in one way or another, by a betrayal. This betrayal may simply be the subject's betrayal of their own trajectory, which would be to say, the having given ground relative to their desire, or it may be that they have tolerated a betrayal by another, one who had committed to work with them. That is to say, either they themselves compromise on their desire or they accept the thwarting of their desire by the actions of another. Either way, we can say, their position involves a certain self-abnegation, one which entails, as Lacan puts it, "a contempt for the other and for oneself" (1992, p. 321). This for Lacan, is a Rubicon moment. The contempt entailed in so ceding on your desire is one which cannot be uninscribed. In this sense, the guilt that arises in response to such compromise and contempt functions as something like an ethical compass. It doesn't necessarily tell us what is right – there is no sovereign good to provide such an answer – but it helps one to know their own desire.

From this, Lacan formulates three propositions:

Firstly, as we have explored, the only thing of which one can be guilty is of having given ground relative to one's desire.
Secondly, that a hero may be defined as one who can be betrayed with impunity, insofar as the betrayal is a necessary part of their journey. Where the hero accepts the betrayal, then they are effectively betraying themselves. Where the hero does not accept the betrayal, they do so because they are acting in conformity with their desire.

The flip side of this would be the third proposition, that the ordinary man is one who is, let us say, successfully betrayed. Their betrayal succeeds in compromising their desire and putting them back on the well-worn track of the status quo, the service of goods. The fact, however, that the experience of facing and compromising on one's desire cannot be unwritten means that such an experience leaves the ordinary man forever after at a loss. The one who compromised on their own desire is neither choosing to pursue it nor free to ignore it. Rather they are effectively mired in guilt. Put simply, in facing your desire and the possibility of refusing it, you experience guilt. This feeling functions to alert you to your desire, to the truth of your desire. The hero is the one who pursues it. The ordinary person refuses it and chooses instead to harbour the guilt which follows, an experience of guilt which effectively tethers them to the *what might have been* in such a manner as to forever change the temper of quotidian life they have chosen instead.

What Lacan might be understood to be proposing here is what we might think of as living versus a half-life. The renunciation of the status quo of the service of goods may not bring happiness or ease, but it offers the possibility of being alive. The rejection of desire may in fact appear to be the choice that brings some ease, but it is then an ease rendered uneasy by the fact of having refused aliveness. Can you, as Nina Cassian puts it, "Call yourself alive?" Can you choose the desire that means "For the first time/you'll be aware of gravity/like a thorn in your heel, and your shoulder blades will ache for want of wings/ . . . and every memory you have – will begin/at Genesis"? (Cassian, 1988, p. 1). Or, in more familiar philosophical terms, with Nietzsche, it is to say, "Let looking away be my only negation! And, all in all and on the whole: some day I want to be a Yes-sayer!" (2001, p. 157).

What Lacan is proposing in summation is that the given notion of the good is precisely that which is given up in order to open the way to desire. This then is the case whether one pursues this desire or not. Desire here, Lacan clarifies, is not an adjunct to subjectivity. Neither is it something which can be limited, in a purely symbolic fashion, to the field of signification. As he succinctly puts it, desire is "what we are as well as what we are not" (1992, p. 321). Desire emerges in an act, and it is only in and through an act that one can truly relate to desire. As such, desire is not contained within the field of signification but is rather produced through the active engagement with the field of signification. As the subject is that which emerges (and fades) through the signification from one signifier to another, their emergence can be understood as the active mobilisation of this desire. The movement here is what Lacan calls sublimation.

Conventional definitions of sublimation tend to present it as concerning the displacement of energy from activities or objects with a biological or sexual interest onto objects or activities with less instinctual connections, or simply as the shift of libidinal energies onto socially acceptable or non-sexual pursuits. Such definitions tend then to emphasise the object or activity in question. There is a proper object of interest, usually of a sexual nature, and there is the more socially acceptable object of interest. Sublimation concerns the shift of interest from one to the other. The novelty Lacan brings to this is simply to emphasise the shifting between the objects. That is to say, where other psychoanalysts have tended to focus on the proper or primary and the secondary or socially acceptable object, Lacan focuses on the movement from one to the other. What is achieved in this refocusing is the realisation that there is no proper object and it is then this, the reconceptualization of an object as not *the* proper object, which ought to constitute the act of sublimation.

Lacan seeks to illustrate this reorientation pertaining to desire with the biblical reference to eating the book. The obvious point that Lacan might be seen to be making here is that we can easily choose to expend our time and energy on intellectual pursuits and ignore our hunger pangs. We can suspend an immediate inclination for something which appears less directly or obviously satisfying. However, when we re-emphasise the point about the change of aim over the change of object, Lacan's point seems to take us somewhere less obvious. Our engagement with culture is no more elevated than our devouring a sandwich to appease our hunger. The choice to shift from one to the other, however, when it entails a real choice, rather than an idle whim, is what allows us to encounter our desire.

Any such choice then necessarily entails a renunciation or, as Lacan says, it requires that we pay for it. Whether we choose to sacrifice desire or whether we choose to sacrifice the quotidian good, either way we pay. This payment then itself becomes part of the functioning of desire. The loss of (perceived) object which is an effect of sublimation is the payment that allows desire as lack to be maintained.

There is a cathartic dimension to this experience but, as the payment is made, no matter the choice, the catharsis too can be situated on both sides. Lacan illustrates this through appeal to the rituals of religion which simultaneously mark the sacrifice or suppression of desire and are elevated themselves to the focus of desire. The ritual becomes cathected with the sublimated force. Religion thus finds a means to maintain desire within the management of goods. The catharsis we encounter in ethics is of a different sort, where it is a matter of crossing the limits of not only fear but also pity, which is to say, surpassing the concern one might encounter for oneself but also for the other. Just as the temple at Delphi suggests, the crossing of these limits leads to a self-knowledge. This, Lacan insists, is the lesson of tragic theatre; it allows us to discern the limits of desire and better grasp our own limits. Theatre allows us to appreciate that pursuing one's desire doesn't entail a happy ending, but it also allows us to appreciate the value of prudence, which necessitates relinquishing our attachments. As such, Lacan's point might be understood to be that the lesson of tragedy is ethical not moral. That is to say, tragedy opens up a difficult space for the subject, one without definitive answers, rather than closing matters down in a prescriptive moralising.

What Is to Come

To where has this consideration of desire taken us? Lacan suggests he may have gone some way to establishing a science of desire. This should not be understood in the sense of the established human sciences, like psychology, which achieve little more than a support of the circulation of established goods. Neither should it be understood in the way we understand the physical sciences, those that Lacan a few years later described as engaged in a curious copulation with capitalism (2007, p. 110). Desire has, Lacan argues, been immobilised, tamed and betrayed by those who would claim to have something to say about ethics or right behaviour and has, as a consequence, been lost within or sublimated to the pursuit of knowledge. This pursuit of knowledge, decoupled from any true sense of the ethical, the sense of the ethical which Lacan argues we face when we confront, to the depths, our desire, this scientific pursuit of knowledge can lead to the worst but doesn't, in the course of this calamity, escape the confrontation with desire it sought to avoid. The science of desire can only be written as a giant question mark. This is the point. Whatever claims we might make for the nature of humanity or, on an ontogenetic level, an individual, in the realm of ethics, the only question which is really worth asking is, what will come? The ethical must, as noted above, always partake of two moments of judgement, the space between which entails the confrontation with desire.

This position can be seen in Žižek's comments on Covid vaccinations in his book *Surplus Enjoyment* when he suggests that the vaccine sceptical should be allowed to openly debate and doubt the efficacy or even the function of vaccines but they should, nonetheless, "obey regulations once the public authority imposes them" (2022, p. 26). Taking the case of the Slovenian response in the early days of the vaccination as an example, Žižek argues that the approach there was wrong-headed. The Slovenian government, according to Žižek, adopted a rather contra-dictory approach, publicly endorsing the idea of free choice while at the same time making vaccines effectively mandatory in order to access public services. People were free to choose whether or not to be vaccinated and, if they chose to be vaccinated, they were free to choose which vaccination they wished to have. The ramifications of choosing to remain unvaccinated were a seemingly self-imposed exclusion from, for example, public transport and buildings. This strategy allowed the government to achieve a high level of vaccination coverage, while being able to claim all along that people had made an individual choice. This free choice policy, argues Žižek, appeared to have misfired when a young student died from apparent post-vaccination complications. The student had opted for the Janssen vaccination, a vaccination it had been claimed offered full protection after a single dose. In the wake of this tragedy, the country experienced widespread anti-vaccination protests. Žižek's argument is that the government would have been better off enforcing a blanket vaccination programme. This, he claims, would have effectively depoliticised the issue.

While, clearly, Žižek's point aims at political efficacy, there is an implied ethical point. The liberal facilitation of open discussion, and thus multiple narratives, creates a practical impasse. A more authoritarian approach allows a decision to be made. What remains silent, or almost silent, in this argument is the question of whether that decision is the right decision. Following the argument of Lacan's seminar, it is clear that this ethical question is not so straightforward. The assumption that there is a discernible good resides with what Lacan has characterised as the traditional perspective, maintenance of the status quo. This is the servicing of goods which he exemplifies with Creon, but also with Alexander the Great and Hitler (1992, p. 315). In Žižek's example, we are quite literally concerned with the servicing of goods, both in the sense of protecting people's health and in the sense of servicing multibillion-dollar contracts and the profiteering of global pharmaceutical corporations. Žižek's conviction that the "right strategy" (2022, p. 301) would have been enforced vaccination assumes not only that such a strategy would have been politically expedient, but also that it would have produced the preferable outcome. The error in this thinking is precisely in this later assumption which ignores the unknown status of what is still a very new product. In such a case, as Lacan was already acknowledging fifty years before, science does not have the answers. Blind trust in the science is therefore only ever, at best, that. It is this unavailability of anything more solid which allows us to appreciate the force of Lacan's exploration of ethics. Just as in the clinic, where no answer is to be delivered from the other, so in the course of life, there is no discernible right way. There is the service of goods, but the ethical question is always whether to follow that path or not, so the proclaimed good of society, whatever the society, cannot by definition determine that ethical choice. The moment of acting, as opposed to merely behaving, requires a step beyond the confines of the already accepted, and the decision that emerges from this requires a new inscription, but one which will then necessarily open the way for further steps, further inscriptions, each of which will entail an encounter with desire, while never having the last word.

References

Cassian, N. (1988). *Call Yourself Alive?* London: Forest Books.
Dassin, J. (1960). *Never on Sunday*. Metro-Goldwyn-Mayer.
Kant, I. (1997). *The Critique of Practical Reason*. Cambridge: Cambridge University Press.
Lacan, J. (1977). *The Four Fundamental Concepts of Psychoanalysis*. Trans. A. Sheridan. London: Penguin Books.
Lacan, J. (1992). *The Seminar of Jacques Lacan: The Ethics of Psychoanalysis, 1959–1960*. London: Routledge.

Lacan, J. (2001). *Le Séminaire livre VIII: Le Transfert. Paris.* Seuil.
Lacan, J. (2006). *The Écrits: The First Complete Edition in English.* London: W. W. Norton & Company.
Lacan, J. (2007). *The Seminar of Jacques Lacan, Book XVII: The Other Side of Psychoanalysis.* London: W. W. Norton & Company.
Nietzsche, F. (2001). *The Gay Science.* Cambridge: Cambridge University Press.
Žižek, S. (2022). *Surplus-Enjoyment.* London: Bloomsbury.

Index

For Product Safety Concerns and Information please contact our EU
representative GPSR@taylorandfrancis.com
Taylor & Francis Verlag GmbH, Kaufingerstraße 24, 80331 München, Germany

www.ingramcontent.com/pod-product-compliance
Lightning Source LLC
Chambersburg PA
CBHW070329270326
41926CB00017B/3823

9 780367 420338